Remember Then

Women's memories of 1946-1969 and how to write your own

Janet Few

THE FAMILY HISTORY PARTNERSHIP

Published by
The Family History Partnership
57 Bury New Road, Ramsbottom
Bury, Lancashire BL0 0BZ

www.thefamilyhistorypartnership.com

First published 2016

ISBN: 978 1 906280 53 6

Printed and bound by
TJ International
Trecerus Industrial Estate
Padstow, Cornwall PL28 8RW

Dedication

This book is dedicated to my lovely ladies. Thank you all for embracing this project with such enthusiasm; I could not have done it without you. I started with a group of volunteers and ended up with eighty new friends.

Contents

The book and chapter titles are taken from the following songs, released during the period 1946-1969:

Remember Then - Written by Tony Powers and Beverly Ross, released by the Earls in 1962.

Homeward Bound - Written by Paul Simon, released by Simon and Garfunkel in 1966.

Rag Mop - Written by Johnnie Lee Wills and released by him with his band in 1950.

Dedicated Follower of Fashion - Written by Ray Davies, released by The Kinks in 1966.

Food Glorious Food - Written by Lionel Bart as part of the Broadway musical *Oliver* in 1960.

Rags to Riches - Written by Richard Adler and Jerry Ross, released by Tony Bennett in 1953.

School Days - Written and released by Chuck Berry in 1957.

I Feel Fine - Written by John Lennon, released by The Beatles in 1964.

The Young Ones - Written by Sid Tepper and Roy C Bennett, released for the film of the same name by Cliff Richard and the Shadows in 1961.

It's my Party - Written by Walter Gold, John Gluck Jr., Herb Weiner and Seymour Gottlieb, the most popular version was released by Lesley Gore in 1963.

The Times they are a-Changin' - Written and released by Bob Dylan in 1964.

Introduction

This book is what happens when you let eighty women spend a year and a half recording their memories of life in Britain throughout the pivotal period 1946-1969. This twenty four years was one of tremendous change in almost every area that they investigated. During this time, we moved from liberty bodices to mini skirts and from ration books to ready meals. We witnessed the emergence of youth culture, the comprehensive education system, conspicuous consumerism and a new wave of feminism; the Britain of 1969, was very different to that of 1946.

I had already written a book about the social history of the seventeenth century, *Coffers, Clysters, Comfrey and Coifs: the lives of our seventeenth century ancestors* (Family History Partnership 2012). As I was doing so, I regretted that I did not know more about the lives of the ordinary women of the time and that I could not ask them questions. I thought that now was the time to capture the turbulent years between 1946 and 1969, whilst there were still first-hand accounts to work with; thus the idea for this project was born.

The women who took part came from a variety of social, economic and geographical backgrounds. The project is about life in Britain but the volunteers are currently living as far apart as Greece, USA and Canada. Sisters took part, mothers and daughters joined in, as did groups of friends. Some ladies went to boarding schools, some to grammar schools and others to secondary moderns[1]. Some left school at fourteen, others have PhDs. Volunteers included only children, those with large extended families, those who grew up in care and those from one-parent families. The ladies were aged from fifty-nine to ninety-five, so some experienced this era as children, some as teenagers and others as married women with families. It was a great sadness that I was unable to recruit any volunteers who represented families that were newly arrived in Britain from the Commonwealth during this period; perhaps this is a reflection of the Britain of the time. I did however enlist those from Jewish and Catholic backgrounds, Anglicans, volunteers from various non-conformist groups and those who were brought up in households where there were no apparent religious beliefs.

Very little additional research has been done, the women's voices have been allowed to speak for themselves. Memories are just that and sometimes memory is fallible. Efforts have been made to check dates and facts but for the most part, the ladies' accounts have been taken at face value. What follows is made up of a selection of extracts from the contributions of my volunteers. The decision about what to include was made with the intention of reflecting the full range of participants' views. I was not just choosing comments that mirrored my own opinions, or that proved a point. Although I attempted to recruit volunteers from a range of backgrounds, of necessity, these ladies were those who were comfortable producing written text.[2] I was not setting out to conduct a piece of research whose methods would stand up to vigorous scrutiny from social scientists, yet I did not want to merely collect a series of unrepresentative anecdotes. The aim was not to write a comprehensive social history but to give a flavour of the period from the view-point of those who lived through it. Even reading the first names of my participants takes you back to the classrooms of the 1950s.

The ladies described their homes and neighbourhoods, clothes, housework and food, education and work, health and childrearing, leisure and celebrations, as well as tackling more emotive subjects, such as relationships and attitudes. Over a hundred illustrations and a comprehensive timeline of events evoke the essence of the era. This book is much more than just a collection of women's memories. At the end of each chapter is the brief that the volunteers were given when working on that topic. This can be applied to other time frames and will help the reader, male or female, to write reminiscences of their own.

I have tried to weave together the words of this disparate group of volunteers, using direct quotations from their reminiscences wherever possible, to reveal this period as seen through their eyes. The result is a many-faceted perspective of life at the time. The book allows those born after 1969 to gain an understanding of what life was like for earlier generations. If you lived through this era yourself, you will find yourself exclaiming, 'I remember that!' on every page.

Janet Few
Buckland Brewer, 2015

---

[1] See Chapter 6.

[2] In fact, at least three volunteers dictated their memories for typing by others.

CHAPTER 1

Homeward Bound:
homes and communities

Communities

Rose-coloured glasses suggest that, in the post-war period, we all lived in warm fuzzy communities where everyone supported each other. Certainly, 1950s' neighbourhoods tended to be self-contained and self-sufficient. Inhabitants worked, played, shopped, were educated and socialised within the home town or village, with only occasional trips to the nearest 'big town'. Many recalled the sense of mutual support that was associated with the close-knit communities of this time. "The neighbours who lived nearest to us were very friendly and there was a real support system there, with people helping out in all sorts of situations." "All our families lived locally and we knew our neighbours very well. People walked in and out of each other's houses without invitation and the doors were never locked."

For many, this sense of belonging was accompanied by a degree of reticence and formality. "We knew the names of every family on the street and would always stop to pass the time of day with them. Apart from a few other families with children of a similar age to me, we didn't always go in and out of each other's houses but if anyone was in trouble, they could always count on the neighbours to rally round and help." "We knew all our neighbours but my grandmother and mother always called people 'Mr and Mrs so and so' rather than by their first names and as children, we did the same, apart from close friends and neighbours who were known as 'Auntie' or 'Uncle'. When walking through Bideford with my mother the progress was very slow as she knew everyone and stopped to chat to them, much to our annoyance." "We weren't in and out of each other's houses all the time – there was some formality to it and good manners." "There was a, perhaps typical, English line which was not crossed, not getting 'too friendly' with the neighbours. We may have invited neighbours in to watch the Coronation on the rare television, or to use the telephone in an emergency but no-one mentioned any Saturday night rows."

Community spirit was not confined to villages but extended to suburbs and areas within towns. The division between those who felt part of their community and those who felt isolated from it, might be expected to reflect urban versus rural living, or the ubiquitous north-south divide. There was however no evidence of this. Instead, the difference seemed to come with housing type. Those who lived on council estates, in particular, wrote of a true sense of neighbourliness. This may be because many of these estates were newly built in the 1950s and 1960s and families all became newcomers together. Of course, a tight-knit community was wonderful for those who 'belonged'. It was however that very sense of belonging that naturally excluded not just those who lived elsewhere but incomers as well, who might find it difficult to integrate into a new locality.

Particularly for those living in rural areas, horizons could be quite restricted. "Looking back, I realise what a narrow and boring life we had. 'Parochial' I think is the best way to describe it. Our daily newspaper was *The Yorkshire Post* and weekly, *The Lincolnshire Times*. No one had the least bit of interest beyond this, other than the cricket (mostly Yorkshire). London was a lifetime away and any further afield was beyond imagination." In the 1950s, except in the most remote areas, all basic needs were provided for locally. "There was a bakery, a newsagent, a fish and chip shop, a hardware shop, a grocer, a Post Office and a hairdressers. We also had a few mobile shops visiting, a grocer, a greengrocer, a fish van came once a week and in between we had a man selling paraffin and the Kleeneze and Betterware salesmen with their suitcases full of brushes, polish and cleaning cloths." A variety of tradesmen were part and parcel of the local scene. "On this estate I remember the winkle seller coming to sell winkles and other shell fish on a Sunday, ringing his bell to announce his arrival. I had to go to his bike with a bowl and he would measure some out, which my mother and I had for tea with brown bread and butter. There were other deliveries on the estate because no one had a car. So we had the rag and bone man on his horse, the knife sharpener, the Corona[1] lorry, coal and milk – of course, bread, fish and meat." "In the early 1960s we had milk delivered in the orange and white, electric Unigate Dairy milk float. I think they also delivered other dairy products. Milk came in glass bottles with foil tops. Birds would often peck holes in the foil, particularly if you had the creamiest milk. The Corona man came with bottles of fizzy drink. Resourceful children would collect the Corona bottles and get the deposit money back on them. Coal was also delivered to the door, in a horse drawn cart. The ice cream man might drive past in the summer, with his distinctive chimes ringing out."

"The rag and bone man particularly sticks in my memory. He had a horse drawn cart and would shout out 'rag 'n' bone' for us to take out anything for recycling, not that that was a term in use then." He sold the donated items for his own benefit. "Round our way he gave sweets in exchange for rags. I got into trouble for swapping my school jumper for sweets! My mother reclaimed my jumper and gave him a piece of her mind, I had already eaten the sweets!!" Although goldfish seemed to be the most common 'payment' for donations, there were instances of rag and bone men giving pieces of china or even ducklings. "The rag and bone man was giving out ducklings in return for donations. We rescued one that was being badly treated by its new owner. We tried to look after it but it died in the airing cupboard."

Improved transport links began to erode the necessity for neighbourhoods to be self-sufficient. In addition, the coming of the eleven plus examination[2] meant that children who lived in the same area no longer necessarily went to the same school. Increased car-ownership made it practical to work, or access leisure opportunities, outside the immediate area. The reliance on the corner shop, a feature of many streets, diminished and gradually these closed as people were able to drive to the shops in larger towns. "Richmond was a big commuter dormitory town by then and it had a very transitory population, so it was not easy to make friends." "We were both working in the City, a bus ride away and didn't get to know any neighbours." People were less and less likely to remain in the town of their birth for the rest of their lives. As more young people went away to university or for training, their loyalty to their home town was weakened. The ease of obtaining employment, that was a feature of the 1960s, also meant that the concept of a 'job for life' was replaced by frequent changes of employer, often involving moving from place to place. By the 1960s, increasingly, people had lives outside the locality where their homes were and the total reliance on that community for employment, friendships, support and social activities was becoming a thing of the past. "There were no such things as street parties and nothing much in the way of a community feeling locally. Most people had moved there from somewhere else and 'kept themselves to themselves'."

For many, the community's institutions were an integral part of everyday life. Village Halls, libraries and parks were all well used. In larger settlements, the cinema formed another focus for residents. "The estate had at its heart a Community Centre, which housed a large dance hall with stage, a small meeting room, a small café, billiard hall and toilets. Behind it was a fishing lake (called The Pond) that was surrounded by tennis courts, two bowling greens and a play area with a sandpit and swings. Near the shops was a public library." "Just across the road from our house was the local Community Centre. This was really just one large room and served lots of functions. There were jumble sales, bingo and Saturday morning films for the children. It also held the annual flower show and the majorettes were based there. I can even remember the occasional wedding reception. The community really just organised itself and most activities were represented, including Brownies, Cubs and so on." "There were two parks, the little rec and the larger park where the library was. Parks used to have metal signs by the gates to tell you when they shut. Different times would be slotted in throughout the year, as closing time was usually dusk. You entered the rec through the gate and went up a long path before it opened out into a large piece of grass with flower beds and I think tennis courts. The big rec[3] was where the May Fair was held. There would be maypole dancing and if you were very lucky and very quick, you might manage to grab one of the streamers in order to have a turn."

This was an era when the locality was the children's playground. Although some families considered playing in the street to be 'common', playing outside unsupervised was the norm. Children might be warned about 'strange men' but they had the freedom to roam, unaccompanied by adults, often for hours at a time. "We played out all the time, only going home to eat. I don't remember anyone ever putting fear into us about strangers, probably because there weren't many around as people didn't travel around like we do today, so anyone new to the neighbourhood was soon spotted and had to be identified for curiosity's sake!" "Traffic and bogey men weren't really an issue". "After moving to our council flat we were on a small estate containing blocks of flats and houses. It was surrounded by fields and woods and there were trees and grass everywhere. There was very little traffic and we safely played outside all day. There were lots of children so large groups of us would play 'it' together. Either alone or with others we would roller skate around the pavements, ride our bikes on the path or road depending on the size of the bike wheels. I think if the wheel was over 20" it was meant to be on the path, over that you had to use the road. I had a 22" so it was road for me but we had done our cycling proficiency[4] at primary school. Going off and riding for an hour was quite normal and my mum was never concerned." "There was also a wood a little further afield, a long walk or shortish bus ride. All of the local children played there unsupervised. In fact we were sometimes given bus fare and sandwiches to take and stayed there all day making dens." "While I was still at primary school, at the weekend my friend and I used to meet 'down the fields' and just play all morning. We used to explore along by the river, discovering 'secret' glades and tiny islands. We did get very muddy sometimes. We weren't supervised, our parents had other things to do!" Boys might be given more freedom than girls. "I was not greatly restricted by my parents but was aware that my brother was always on a looser rein than myself."

Although serious 'gang warfare' was rare, children were territorial. "You played in the streets, mainly with the children who lived close by. There was a bit of a rivalry with children in other streets, who played with the other children in their street. You knew them from church or Sunday school but you tended to stick with your own group." "The Church Hill locality was known to us as 'Yon End' and we never went there to play, it was considered too rough. In my adult life I was told that we were known as 'Yon End' and they were not allowed to mix with us ruffians!" "We were very much influenced by Enid Blyton's 'Famous Five' and their independent explorations although, strangely, we never seemed to come across any exciting spies, smugglers or bank robbers for us to detect and capture (but we lived in hope!)."

Transport

In an era when communities were largely self-sufficient, there was far less need for car-ownership and for most of this period, many families relied on public transport for the infrequent occasions when a trip outside the immediate area was necessary. "From the start of my schooldays I walked to school, no-one arrived by car or in any form of transport. The only time we used the bus was to travel into Birmingham for one of my many hospital appointments, or to buy a winter coat." Immediately after the war, fuel rationing meant that horse-drawn transport was still in use and petrol-driven vehicles were scarce. "Cars were a rarity in the village; I remember my elder brother sitting on the roadside for hours waiting for a car to go past so that he could record the number plate in his book." "Our greengroceries were bought from a man who delivered them with a horse and cart. Coal supplies were also delivered in this way and big heavy horses pulling brewers' drays[5] could be seen in the city. Some milk deliveries in the nearby villages were made using horses and the milk travelled in big churns and was measured out in jugs. As petrol supplies eased and rationing of it ended,[6] more cars arrived and became more sophisticated (some even had heaters!) and the whole transport system grew at a furious rate."

Public transport was readily available, even in quite remote areas. "Since people, just after the war, rarely owned cars, the public transport system was excellent. Trains and buses were readily available and widely used." Buses were used regularly and some places had trams or trolley-buses. "Once we moved into town, then we had trolley-buses for transport. These were fairly silent and could be frustratingly slow, especially when traffic was busy at peak times. Every so often the poles came adrift above the bus which provided the power connection to the cables. The driver would have to get out of his cab and with another long pole kept on one side of the bus, try to reconnect his vehicle to the overhead cables."

Holidays might involve travel by coach or train; with steam engines running on some main-line passenger routes until 1968. Most trains consisted of compartments suitable for eight or ten passengers. These were often connected by a corridor, although some could only be accessed by the external doors, when the train was at a station. Carriages were first or third class, with a few designated as 'no-smoking' and occasionally ones for ladies only. "The trains were smoky, so windows were usually kept closed to avoid ash blowing in and the carriages had a distinctive train smell. Trains smelt of coal smoke and cigarettes. There was sometimes a restaurant car but we took a picnic and thermos, as did many other people. I always found myself getting lost in the pictures in the carriages. The advertisements for Blackpool, Felixstowe, Scarborough and other seaside resorts in that particular poster art form of the age. Girls in bathing hats throwing beach balls and children sitting on the sands. There was usually a mirror on the carriage wall for ladies to adjust their hats but I think I remember it had an opaque advertisement written across it for cigarettes or similar. I liked the netting luggage racks too and always wanted to climb up and sit in one, although in those days small children were expected to sit still and behave well and we usually did." Air travel was almost unheard of before the advent of the 'package tours' of the 1960s.

Even quite young children might travel alone. "My brother went on his own to school each day by train from the extraordinarily early age of about seven. I myself also remember being put on a train to travel on my own, at quite a young age, to visit some family friends in Kent. I was very anxious about how I would manage if I couldn't open the carriage door when I arrived (they had very stiff locks or had to be opened by lowering the window and opening from the outside) but my mother said very casually I could ask someone else to do it for me. The carriages were closed but there was usually one reserved for 'Ladies Only' if one felt nervous."

Many people relied on bikes to get to work or school; free school buses were usually only provided for those of secondary age who lived more than three miles from the school. "For many years my father cycled to his place of work. I recall the horrible damp smell of his black, oilskin cape when he had been riding in the rain." Motor bikes or scooters were a status symbol and became part of the youth culture[7] of the 1950s and 1960s. "It seems strange to think that my social life was dependent on buses and trains to get to clubs and pubs and parties but that was how it was unless you knew somebody with a car or a scooter; females didn't own such things in those days, it was a male domain." Motorbikes, with the addition of a sidecar, were also a popular form of family transport. "My father had a motorcycle and sidecar for a short time, when as a family we went to the seaside for picnics with my brother and me in the sidecar." "My father got a moped and later still, a Triumph motorbike with its lovely blue paintwork and finally a motorbike and sidecar, as he had a growing family to move about."

Car-ownership was for the well off, or those whose job necessitated it. "I think there were only three cars in the village belonging to the doctor, the undertaker and one well off gentleman, who took me to hospital as an emergency." Iconic cars of the period included the Morris Minor, the Austin 7, the Ford Popular, the Vauxhall Victor, the Hillman Minx, the Bubble car and the Morris Oxford. In 1962, Ford's newly launched Cortina, designed as a family car, cost £573,[8] nearly three-quarters of the average annual salary. "Young people did not often have cars of their own. When I was at university (1961-1964) I knew only one girl from a wealthy family who had her own car (a sports car) and this was considered very unusual." Three-wheeled Invacars were available for those with disabilities. Invariably blue, these little cars were an integral part of the street scene of the 1950s and 1960s.

There were various hazards associated with the transport of this time. The wearing of car seatbelts and motorbike crash helmets had not yet been made compulsory, drink driving was socially acceptable, smoking was permitted on the top deck of buses and protective gear for bicyclists was unheard of. "No one thought twice about packing half a dozen small children into the back of a Morris Minor van." "My cousin bought a second-hand Austin 7 during the latter part of the 1950s and used to cram four adults and three children into that car for outings".

This period also witnessed an number of innovations regarding transport of various kinds. Zebra crossings, double yellow lines, parking meters and motorways all arrived in our lives and the first hovercraft passenger services began. Sadly, there were losses too. London trolley buses ceased running and more significantly, in 1963, Beeching[9] initiated cutbacks that were to mean that the railway network was severely curtailed. "Motorways were built to accommodate the extra traffic, becoming especially necessary following the cut backs on the railways in the 1960s. At the same time, as road traffic accidents also increased; the booklet *The Official Highway Code* had to be updated to include the new roads and rules for driving on them."

The Homes we Lived in

"As young children, if we drew a house it was invariably a detached, two-storey, square box with a centre door, four-paned windows either side of the door, four-paned windows above those, an angled roof with a flat top, a chimney with smoke coming out of it, a front garden with a picket fence and a path to the door. In the London borough where we lived, there were no houses that even remotely fitted that description. They were exclusively terraced, with the front door to one side, tiny front plot containing a hedge and a few scrubby plants, straight path and no smoke from the chimneys, as this had been banned in 1956."

Unless they were students, it was unusual for young people to leave the family home until they married. Many homes were rented and newly-weds might begin married life in the home of one of their parents or in a room, or rooms, with shared facilities, within a larger house. "My first home consisted of three rooms in the top half of a house. We had a very small kitchen, one bedroom, where all four of us slept, a living/dining room and a shared bathroom. I can't remember using the bathroom much; I think we mainly washed or were washed in the kitchen. We were on the council housing list but apparently our accommodation was 'too good' for us to have any chance of ever getting a council house. There was no access to the garden."

The number of council homes available for renting increased during this period and was to come close to the level of privately rented properties. Being allocated council accommodation was usually seen as a chance to acquire improved living conditions. "All my young life my parents talked about 'the slum clearance' to come. This must have been planned for a long time and that was when the houses and streets where we lived would be demolished and we would be allocated a council house with a bathroom and a garden." "In 1950, Mum and Dad took possession of a two bedroom council or, as it was referred to locally, 'corporation', flat. It comprised two bedrooms, a bathroom and a kitchen/dining room/living room all in one." "If you could find somebody with a council property you wanted to move into and who wanted to move into yours, the council would agree to 'an exchange'."

For those who were at university or training college, there was a chance to gain independence and live in student accommodation, or to share with fellow students. "In 1961, I went to university and lived during term time in this old end-terrace house, which was part of a student hall of residence that comprised several houses, scattered up and down a few adjacent roads. I shared a small room with another student (whom I didn't get on with but we managed to tolerate each other for the first year). In my second year, I shared a large room in the attic with a good friend. Each of us had a bed, a wardrobe, a desk and a small bookshelf. There was a large kitchen where we could hand-wash our clothes (no washing machines available then), or make ourselves a drink. Meals were provided down the road in another house five or ten minutes' walk away." Some of this accommodation was far from luxurious. "It was in a pretty awful state. We had two rooms downstairs, two bedrooms upstairs and shared the bathroom with our landlady. We had to sleep in two double beds. They had very old, flock mattresses on weird bases made up of lots of small interwoven circles of wire. We had to add extra bits of wire from time to time to hold the base together." "I believe the places I lived in both in year two and year three would be condemned as unfit for habitation nowadays. Accommodation was hard to come by for students in Manchester, if you failed to get a place in student accommodation. One young lad, asked us what he should do as his landlady was a witch! He'd got home one evening to find her and a group of friends, dancing around the sitting room stark naked. We advised a visit to the Accommodation Officer, who found him a new place pretty quickly."

Purchasing a home was a big step but one which more and more people were taking. In post-war Britain, fewer than a third of householders were home-owners but by the end of the 1960s, this had risen to fifty percent. Mortgage rates varied but in 1960, were around six percent. "At that time, you were assessed for a mortgage solely on the husband's earnings (the wife would surely give up work to have babies) and were limited to a mortgage value of two and a half times his annual salary." "In 1955, my parents bought a two-bedroomed, semi-detached house for just over £600. This was on an estate where the houses had previously all been rented. Many houses were sold to sitting tenants but the elderly couple in our house did not want to buy and had refused to let the landlord put in electricity in case he put up their rent! As a result, it had no electricity, no hot water and no bathroom, just an outside toilet." Then, as now, prices varied with area. In 1954, a Victorian terraced house in Croydon cost £2050. In the same year, a £25 deposit secured a £2500 home in Walsall, on which the monthly mortgage repayments were £16 5s. The property was insured under a comprehensive policy for £3000. "In August 1962 we moved into our first house, which cost £2750. This was in Shropshire and was an extended country cottage with three bedrooms, a kitchen, sitting room, dining room and a bathroom, which was downstairs." "I married in June 1965 and earlier that year we viewed and bought our first home, it was a brand new, three-bedroomed, semi-detached house in a cul-de-sac, comprising of a through lounge/diner with French doors, a small but adequate kitchen and a separate larder, hallway and stairs leading to three bedrooms and bathroom which had a white suite, gardens of a reasonable size front and rear and a driveway with space for a garage; we paid £2400. It took most of our savings for the deposit and legal fees, we paid a 10% deposit and took out a 90% mortgage with the Halifax Building Society; the repayments were £12 5s 7d per calendar month."

The post-war housing shortage meant that some families were allocated 'prefabs'; prefabricated housing that was intended to be temporary. "After the devastation of intensive bombing during World War 2, large cities such as Liverpool were desperately short of housing. One of the solutions was to build prefabricated homes, which were always known as prefabs. I believe they were made in Scandinavia then eventually brought to the building site in 'flat pack' form, where they were erected on pre-prepared foundations and the electricity and plumbing were completed. My parents moved into a brand new prefab in 1947. Each prefab had a garden front and back and a corrugated iron shed, which was made from war surplus air raid shelters. Our shed was used to store coal. The prefabs were single storey with entrance hall, two bedrooms, a fitted kitchen, living room and bathroom. The 'back door' was actually at the side and led directly into the kitchen. This was fitted from new with a fridge, electric cooker and large water heater/boiler for washing. My Mum rarely used this due to the cost of heating the water. There was a single-drainer sink with cupboards below. There was also a floor to ceiling cupboard we used for food storage and another cupboard over the fridge." "It was not a very good idea to lean on the internal walls, which were so thin you could pretty well hear a conversation in any room from any other." "All the houses were built with airbricks in each room, these were soon covered with thick cardboard and tape in the winter months."

Utilities, Conveniences and Services

Some homes lacked basic utilities. "We did not have gas or electric and used an oil lamp in the living room, which was our main source of light. We took candles placed in candle sticks up to bed with us so we could see to get undressed and would blow the candle out once we got in bed. My father used to have to fill the oil lamp with oil and trim the wick; this would usually be done on a Sunday afternoon if he wasn't working." The electricity and less frequently gas, supply might be paid for via a pay-as-you-go meter. "Once a quarter the meter was emptied by a man from the Electricity Board. This was a big day because, as there was more in the meter than the cost of the electricity used, he left the balance, all in shillings. The news that the meter man was around spread like wildfire as everyone got a treat, including the children." "Our gas and electric were both on pay-as-you-go meters and had to be fed with 2s coins." "We had to go to the Gas Showrooms of the West Midlands Gas Board (WMGB) to pay for our coal and to the Electricity Showrooms of the Midlands Electricity Board to settle the electricity bill. Gas was paid for via a slot meter; my father had special rates because he worked for the WMGB."

Even when there was an electricity supply, it might have had its limitations. "It had electric lights and a rudimentary 5 amp system for power. It had been built with wall mounted gas lighting and the remaindered stubs from when this was cut off were visible in every room. Every other room was served by twin-pin round sockets. I also remember that if we wanted to have more than one appliance running at a time from the three pin socket, we had a Bakelite[10] adaptor and occasionally the system would be accidentally overloaded and someone would have to manually rewire the fuse in the bulky consumer unit in the hall. Before the flat was rewired, all the light switches were also Bakelite - round, with a small peg with a ball-shaped end as the switch. The contacts were not always terribly good and occasionally, the switch would make an ominous crackle as it was turned on or off, sometimes with the odd spark or two just for good measure. All the original wiring in the house ran in metal conduits which were surface-mounted, nothing was buried in the walls." "It was usually the man of the house who had to do the rounds at bedtime, ensuring that all plugs, apart from the fridge, were removed from their sockets. This nightly ritual also involved the shutting of windows, putting guards on any open fires and checking that external doors were locked and bolted."

Insurance was often paid, at regular intervals, to a representative who called at the door. "I have the contents policy document from the Motor Union Insurance Company Limited. I think one of my Mum's nephews was the representative, which is why she stuck with the same company for so long (but then you did then). The policy was first taken out on 24 October 1945, sum insured £300, annual premium 15s."

Heating might be rudimentary and was often confined to the downstairs rooms. The most common method of heating was by coal fire. "At that time, most people heated their homes with coal; in the winter months the fire would be 'banked up' at night in the hope it would keep the chill off and still be glowing in the morning, thus cutting out the relighting procedure, though the ashes would have to be emptied from the pan." "The house also had quite an extensive cellar where coal was stored and was delivered via a 'coal hole' in the pavement, which was covered with a cast iron cover which had to be blacked weekly." "The only heating was a coal fire in the lounge, a small gas fire in my parents' bedroom and a recalcitrant coal-fired black lead boiler in the kitchen, which heated the water. The dining room, the bathroom and my bedroom were always freezing." "The area became a 'smokeless zone' and we had to buy special fuel to burn which was more expensive than coal, I seem to recall the fuel was Coalite."

"There was never any heating upstairs. Both rooms had fireplaces in them where you could have an open fire. I only ever remember having a fire in the bedroom once and that was when my mum and I had flu and my dad had to stay off work to look after us. There was a very old metal electric fire where the element glowed red and had a grill over it and that was sometimes used to warm the bedroom before going to bed if it was very cold." "There were fireplaces in each of the four main rooms but the fire was normally reserved for the living room. We used to make spills[11] from cards, which were used to light cigarettes from the fire; both my parents were smokers at this time. I believe a gas fire had been installed in the tiled fireplace in the dining room. The bedroom fireplaces were blocked up to prevent draughts. Leaving the fire to go to bed in winter was always an effort, although we might have an electric fire on in the bedroom for an hour to try to make it warmer. These fan heaters were tiny and seldom up to the job. We also had a dark brown, tube shaped, electrical heater."

"Another ritual in the winter were the paraffin heaters, which were placed in the bathroom, dining room and hall. Dad would buy the pink paraffin on Friday nights and would then undertake the trimming of the wicks and refilling to get us through until the next week. The smell of these takes me straight back to my childhood. Over time, these were replaced with electric storage heaters and an electric radiant heater in the bathroom that cooked your head but not much else. We would dress in bed in the winter to try to keep some of the heat in us." "Heating was by paraffin stoves, smelly and dangerous but effective. Paraffin was easily available from general stores but if Mum was short of cash we just had to wear extra layers of woollies."

Central heating was rare until the 1960s, when it began to appear in middle class homes. Most central heating of this era ran on solid fuel (coal) boilers. Double glazing, usually in the form of metal-framed secondary glazing, began to be installed during this period but was still uncommon.

It was not unusual, particularly in rural areas, for homes to lack indoor sanitation, especially in the 1940s and early 1950s; in some cases there was no mains water. "We did not have electricity or mains water until about 1951; because we were at the edge of the village we were the last to have the facilities. We had a pump at the end of the back yard and would fill enamel pails with water to leave in the pantry." If there was a water supply, it might be cold water only. "There was a cold water tap but hot water was either obtained from the kettle for small quantities, such as washing up, our daily wash down or hair washing, or a gas copper (boiler) for washing clothes and for heating our bath water." "The Baby Burco replaced the copper for boiling water on summer bath nights, then later an immersion heater was installed, life became easier and bath nights became personal events." "There was also a gas-fired copper for washing clothes, a monstrous thing in blue enamel that mother dragged into the middle of the kitchen for wash days and attached to a gas tap with an orange rubber hose, there was always a whiff of gas when in use! It was lovely in the winter because it warmed everything up, horrible in the summer though, especially as it used to be used on bath nights to heat the water as the main fire would not be alight. This hot water was then carried upstairs in buckets and put into the bath."

"We didn't have an indoor toilet and the outdoor toilet was at the bottom of the garden. I don't remember having toilet rolls either, as my mother cut up newspapers into squares to hang up inside the toilet door. My father used to clean the toilet and empty the bucket, we had the moors at the back of the cottage and he used to dump all the rubbish in a pit on the moors which he would then cover over." "We had a tin bath that stood outside the back door and was brought into the scullery for bath nights (a Friday usually), it had to be filled with hot water from the kettle or saucepans and took ages to fill; we had no hot running water. My husband later built a bath into the scullery and built a table that fitted over it, so we used the table when the bath wasn't needed."

"My parents couldn't afford to build a bathroom on, so Dad put a bath in the kitchen. The bath was covered with formica-topped boards and doubled as a work/washing surface. We bathed once a week and had a separate plastic bowl for washing ourselves in. The drawback was that there was no access to the kitchen when bathing or washing! The outside toilet was at the back of the house. It had electricity but in the winter a small paraffin lamp was kept burning to stop the pipes freezing. To reach it you had to go out through the kitchen, which meant if someone was washing or bathing you had to go out the front door and round the side of the house!" "The scullery was where you washed as there was no bathroom." "There was no bathroom on our floor so we shared a bathroom and separate toilet with the middle floor flat. I don't remember how it was agreed which flat had the bathroom when but the toilet was available whenever one needed it, except when it was occupied of course! It had an old fashioned chain pull, a fancy mahogany seat and a floral toilet pan." In towns there was the opportunity to use public baths,[12] if the facilities were lacking at home.

Unless it was for business use, telephones were for the minority, with about ten percent of the population having a home phone in the 1950s. Even at the end of the 1960s only a third of homes were connected. For the rest, it was a trip to the telephone box, or to an obliging neighbour. "There were not many private lines in the early 1960s and we had a 'party line', which was shared. Before you made a call you lifted the receiver to see if any other party was using the line. If they were and your call was urgent you could ask them how long they would be and then replace the receiver. When they had finished their call you sometimes heard a little 'ping' on the telephone as they had put down the receiver. Before this we had used the telephone box on the estate which had a button 'A' and 'B' and took four old pennies." "We did have a phone, a brown Bakelite model with a small drawer in the base to house one's 'address book'. This sat on a small, dark wood table with a lower shelf used to house the phone books. London directories came in four volumes about an inch thick, A-D, E-K, L-Q, R-Z and there were no numerical prefixes, it was done by district, so a typical number in, say, Shepherd's Bush would be SHE 1111. In country areas the numbers were even fewer, so a call could be answered 'Truro 111', even for a city of that size."

Most communications were by letter, so phones were not seen as essential and even when installed, were used sparingly. "It was never taken casually; phoning people was a bit of an event and we had an armchair by the phone so that we could sit and do it properly." "When I came to the USA in 1963, I only called my mother once a year for Christmas. It used to cost $30 for three minutes in the 1960s." Letter writing to far flung family members was however a regular activity. "Letters would be collected and delivered by the General Post Office (GPO),[13] on foot, on bicycles or in their red vans, two or three times a day, including Sundays and the sender would expect their letter to arrive the following day." "We had to write Thank You letters for any gifts received. We knew the times of the letter collections (they were on the post box at the top of the road). It would often be my job to take Dad's letters to post and Dad would say things like, 'Go now and you'll catch the 4.30 collection'. As for letters delivered, there was a first post early in the morning and a second post which came around 11.00." The inter-war habit of sending postcards as a means of imparting important information was on the decline but holiday postcards were still sent in large numbers to family and friends.

"Writing paper and envelopes were often given as presents - packs of Basildon Bond and later, little notelets. I used a fountain pen, filled with blue or black or blue-black Quink.[14] We always had pink sheets of blotting paper handy too. Dad loved biros when they became part of daily life and always had loads." "My mother wrote to her mother every week and received one in return until grandmother died in 1970, this was done over a couple of nights prior to posting and if the return letter hadn't arrived three days later, mum would worry. I had a couple of pen friends that I wrote to regularly through school. Of course, this was the era of chain letters; those threatening overtones and promises of wealth, all of which never happened." It was relatively cheap to post a letter, 2½d for most of this period, rising to 3d in 1957 and 4d in 1965.[15] The system of first and second class post was introduced in 1968 and cost 5d and 4d respectively; from then onwards only first class letters were expected to be delivered the following day.

"As phone calls abroad were so rare, emergency communication was by telegram (see figure 14). Strips of paper with the message on were stuck to a sheet of paper and as these were charged by the word, they were necessarily brief. They were delivered in an envelope by a delivery man on a motor bike and if necessary, he could take a reply back with him. Telegrams were occasionally sent for congratulations for a special event, such as a wedding or significant birthday. They would also be used to pass on the news of a birth or a death in a family overseas. Telegrams were sometimes happy, sometimes sad, but always momentous."

Living Rooms

Particularly at the start of our period, many families kept one room, usually at the front of the house, as a 'parlour', which was reserved for special occasions. "The front room had a hook and eye latch on the door so that you didn't dash unthinkingly in. This room was hardly used and always seemed like the Holy of

Holies to me. There was an open fireplace which had a column of green and pink flowered tiles on either side. Aspidistras stood as guard to left and right. A large carpet square covered the floor and the three-piece suite was never seen without its dust covers. Peeping under them it looked brand new but was rarely sat upon. Other than this there were just two hard backed chairs and a tiny bookcase that held a set of children's encyclopaedias." "The parlour, with a three-piece suite of brown vinyl with darker brown velvety cushions, had a tiled fireplace and a coal fire. It was not used regularly, on special occasions mostly, Christmas, or if relatives came for the evening. We always had the Christmas tree in the parlour." In many terraced homes, using the main room as a rarely-used parlour, meant that 'living' might be confined to the kitchen, with a back scullery being used for the messiest jobs.

Furniture that was acquired when first setting up home was intended to last a lifetime. It was not until the advent of the 'throw-away society' of the 1960s that people started to replace furnishings in order to keep up with fashions, rather than because they were beyond repair. The collection of linen and other items that formed the bride-to-be's 'bottom drawer', together with wedding presents, were relied upon to give a couple a good start. Those wanting to purchase new furniture in the years after the war, when rationing was in force, had to buy the standard 'utility' brand. Until 1952, new furniture was only available for those who were newly married or who had lost their possessions due to bombing. Utility furniture was designed to make the most efficient use of scarce resources, such as timber. "The furniture in my small room bore the 'utility mark' which was issued by the Board of Trade to signify the approved construction at minimal cost."

"Chairs had linen chair-backs, or antimacassars as my Nana called them, usually cream-coloured and often embroidered, to protect the chair fabric from the Brylcreem used by many men on their hair in those days." "The dining room was really the living room, in that most daily activities took place there. Two easy chairs either side of the fireplace were where Mum and Dad sat in the evening. The radiogram was in the dining room. Sometimes Mum and Dad moved the furniture to the side, put on Victor Sylvester records and practised ballroom dancing up and down the hall and in the dining room."

"Furniture in the 1960s included a new, pink three-piece suite, covered in Dralon and a coffee table with spindly legs; I also remember a black wire magazine rack with coloured knobs on the bottom for feet and a sun-ray clock on the wall above the fireplace. There was a new dining table and sideboard at one end; also a cocktail cabinet with a pull-down shelf and a glass interior. Lots of exciting knick-knacks inside that, some of which I think came from my grandparents' hotel: wooden holders for plastic cocktail sticks, wooden drinks coasters with jokes on them (most of which I didn't understand) and a lovely yellow plastic Bambi figure, advertising Babycham. I also vaguely remember an elaborate piece of furniture that was supposed to be a 'home office' with lots of cupboards, drawers and secret compartments." "They bought a three-piece suite (three-seater sofa and two chairs) for the lounge in rust-coloured moquette. It was very itchy and each chair had a hand-embroidered chair back. They took out HP[16] agreements but were always careful and paid one off before taking out another." Iconic furniture manufacturers of the 1960s were Parker Knoll and G-Plan. The stylish living room boasted a standard lamp, a rubber plant, a hostess trolley, or even a bar constructed in a corner. "The fashion in the 1960s was for people to have a curved bar in their lounge and as I could not afford one I just had an area on my sideboard where I had a lamp and displayed my precious glasses I had received as a wedding present, an ice bucket made out of plastic and covered with luggage labels from all over the world as a design and a ruby red Globemaster Sparklets Soda Siphon."

Fitted carpets rarely featured until the 1960s. Carpet squares would be surrounded by linoleum ('lino'). Rugs were common and often home-made, housewives buying the necessary cut wool for rug making from shops such as Readicut. Net curtains were used to ensure privacy and curtains might be hung patterned side out for the benefit of the neighbours. Although, in general, fashions were slow to change, there was a revolution in furnishing styles in the 1960s. Floral soft furnishings gave way to abstract designs and what was once predominantly pink and blue now became orange and brown.

Living rooms of the 1950s began to acquire more non-essential accessories and the continental holidays of the 1960s brought souvenir ornaments into the home. "We had ornaments around the house, these were very often chalk-type ones won at the fair, or mementoes from holidays. They were usually small items that represented the place where we or a relative had been. They had the place name on them and some relevant picture or item of decoration." "The downstairs rooms were decorated with completely unrealistic plastic flowers, that were very popular at the time." "About this time my father found a new hobby, fish keeping and one corner of the lounge had two tanks, one above the other, in a wrought iron framework; the bottom one was cold water fish and the top exotics. I loved the angelfish and guppies with their long tails and tetras with their flashing colours. It meant we had the bubbling sound of the air filters all the time."

Archetypal accessories of the era included prints of Vladimir Tretchickoff's *Chinese Lady* and three ceramic flying ducks hung on the wall. Small ornaments were displayed on 'gay boxes', two interlocking squares that formed shelves. Ridgway's black and white 'Homemaker' china from Woolworth's was also popular. "My sister had made a trio of plaster of paris flying ducks from a kit she'd had as a gift and these were displayed on one wall. There was also a wooden knick-knack shelf made of interlocking slats of wood, which were all the rage in the fifties, on which were small Wade animals and other tiny souvenirs." "It was during these years that mugs became popular and the use of cups and saucers and formal tea services waned. Denby pottery became fashionable and fine china less so."

Means of entertainment began to arrive in 1950s' living rooms, although many retained their pianos, that had been a feature of inter-war middle class homes. By 1953, in time for the Coronation, a quarter of homes had acquired a television. This was to rise to sixty five percent of households by 1959 and ninety percent by 1964. Colloquially, the television might be known as 'the box', an abbreviation of the slang phrase 'goggle box'. "I remember going with my father to buy a new radiogram which was a large box-shaped piece of furniture which stood on the floor and contained a turntable and radio. The man in the shop gave me a 78rpm record of *Teddy Bears' Picnic*. The television arrived in 1953 for the Coronation and like many households, we had all the neighbours in to watch." "ITV was installed around 1959.[17] This involved an additional aerial and a gadget with a knob on it in the back of the set; this knob had to be moved to change channels." "I remember a television when I was four, it was on the kitchen sideboard then but I think that may have been when the sitting room was being redecorated, as it moved to the corner of that room ever after and sat on top of a 1930s' hostess trolley. The television was a black and white Ferranti, the screen was probably around twelve inches or less, polished wooden case with a fabric covered grille which contained the speakers, a knob to change channel (only two channels, BBC and ITV), one knob for volume, others for vertical hold and horizontal hold and you had to wait for the valves (visible if you looked in the back and replaceable) to warm up." "We had no remote controls in those days and the television took ages to warm up." "A Dansette record player appeared in early 1960s in two tone blue and cream with an autochanger which you could leave off so the same record played over and over again. This I did with a Desmond Decker record, until I was threatened with having it broken over my head!"

Kitchens

Kitchens might also be living rooms. "In the kitchen there was a black-leaded fireplace with a stove, a couple of easy chairs, a wall cupboard for crockery, a corner cupboard and the wireless on a small table as well as a wooden farmhouse-style table with dining chairs. Beyond the kitchen was the scullery with a shallow sink, a gas cooker and a copper for boiling the washing, plus a mangle." "We had a wood/coal fuelled Rayburn and a table and chairs, larder, sink and draining board, airing cupboard and marble slab for making pastry. We ate all our meals in the kitchen. Mum cooked almost everything in the Rayburn, which heated our water. My Dad bought a wireless for mum in the 1940s, which was kept on top of a cupboard, built by my father. We were bought a television by a relative in 1954. The TV was also kept in the kitchen, until about 1967, when it was moved into the sitting room." The scullery, the equivalent of today's utility room, was for messier jobs. "In the scullery there was a galvanised metal 'copper' for washing/boiling clothes. It was heated by a ring of gas jets under the boiler. There was a butler-type sink, for hand washing, with wooden draining board."

This was the era when labour-saving devices were finding their way into the nation's kitchens. "We didn't have a fridge for many years but early on we had an 'Osokool'; a polystyrene-covered box that was 'fed' with a cup of water every day and was supposed to keep things cool (see figure 17). In the summer, the daily fresh milk was also kept cool in the pantry and was stood in a bowl of cold water." "We had a cylindrical spin dryer with a rubber inner 'lid' that was supposed to stop clothes getting tangled in the works but wasn't always successful. This appliance would career over the floor as it spun the clothes violently. It had a spout near the bottom out of which came the water that had been dislodged. You had to put a washing-up bowl under the spout to catch the water. This required careful supervision as the cylinder could jerk round of its own accord, so that the spout was no longer over the bowl." "We eventually got a fridge around 1963. At some time we had a calor gas cooker which was used in the summer when there was no need for the Rayburn."

Formica was the material of choice for the stylish kitchen of the 1950s. Table-tops and units would be made from this material; powder blue, yellow and red were popular colours. Many kitchens still contained a walk-in larder or pantry. The concept of built-in units was still to come, although the free-standing, dresser-like kitchen unit, with a work surface, shelves and glass-doored cupboards was coveted. "My mum bought a 'Kitchenette'. It was a Formica dresser about six feet high and about four feet wide, with glass sliding-doored cupboards in the top and a leaf that dropped down so you could work on it." Furniture, particularly kitchen furniture, might be given a new lease of life by covering it with sticky-backed plastic, known by the brand names 'Fablon' or 'Contact'. This came in a variety of designs and was ideal for lining shelves and drawers. "The dresser had a top too high to really be considered a 'worktop', it housed the bread bin, cake tins and our massive old radio. The top was wood covered in 'Contact'.

Bathrooms

Indoor sanitation, of any kind, was something to be grateful for. "We still had an outside toilet but it was just across from the back door. We used scratchy Izal medicated toilet rolls. Although not ideal, this was an improvement to the squares of *Daily Herald* hung on a nail in the shared toilet." "Our downstairs toilet was in a built-on bit straight off the kitchen, called the scullery but we didn't have to go outside! Mind you, we did not have a wash basin plumbed in to the bathroom upstairs or to the downstairs toilet. The bathroom had a portable wash stand which had a metal basin that could be filled by bringing a kettle full of water up the stairs." Many households did have bathrooms but would be very unlikely to have more than one. En-suites were unheard of, although the household's one bathroom might be accessed through a bedroom. "My two brothers' shared bedroom was between the landing and the bathroom. So we all went through their room to get to the upstairs toilet." To have a second indoor toilet was unusual. "On the bottom dog-leg of the stairs was the downstairs cloakroom with its high-level cistern toilet. This was a real status symbol. We kept coats in it but rarely, if ever, used the toilet. I have no idea why not. Maybe mum didn't want to have two toilets to clean." "There was a very small bathroom with a separate toilet upstairs and also (my mother was very proud of this) a downstairs lavatory."

Many bathrooms were legacies of the Victorian or Edwardian era, with cumbersome, white sanitary-ware. Baths might be free-standing and made from cast iron, with roll tops and claw feet. Toilets had high-level cisterns with chains to pull. The 1950s saw the introduction of suites in pink, powder blue and sea green. More extreme colours, notably avocado, chocolate and maroon, did not become fashionable until the 1970s. Post-war suites tended to have smaller baths with side panels and low-level cisterns with lever flushes.

Bedrooms

Bedrooms were frequently shared. It was not unusual for a child to sleep in their parents' room until puberty, or to share a bed with a sibling. Divan beds began to replace bedsteads with head and foot boards and heavy oak furniture became unfashionable by the 1960s. Plain wooden furniture, suitable for painting at home, became popular. Kidney shaped dressing tables, with curtains concealing the drawers beneath and topped with three hinged mirrors, were desirable items. "I remember we bought a new single bed, a Slumberland and a white wardrobe and a fixture to match which had a half mirror and three drawers underneath. It cost £168 for the three items from Debenhams." Lloyd Loom basket chairs and ottomans were other typical acquisitions for 1950s' bedrooms.

Duvets only arrived in the UK in the late 1960s, so bedding was normally sheets, blankets and an eiderdown or bedspread. "The bedding was usually one white sheet, one or two blankets and in the winter, the outdoor coats were put on the bed as well." Like other household items of the time, bedding was expected to last and was repaired to extend its life. "Good housekeeping denoted that sheets would be 'turned in'; as the centre became worn, it would be cut down the middle and the outside became the new middle using flat seams. Doubles became singles and then became pillowcases and blouses. Our winter quilts were made from old materials cut into shapes with the centre being more old material to bulk them out. I remember coming home from school on a summer's day to find brown blankets on the washing line with 'US Army' emblazoned across the middle."

Sheets with candy stripes replaced plain white, then, in the 1960s, the company 'Brentford Nylons' popularised nylon sheets. These came in the colours of the sixties, orange and brown, as well as more traditional pastel colours. They were itchy and created problems with static electricity but were welcomed because they dried quickly and did not require ironing. "As a very small child I had a pink blanket that had been crocheted by my mum or granny. Later I had a pale blue, shop-bought blanket and a white one with pink, yellow and blue stripes on the edge. White sheets gave way to the ever popular candy stripes, narrow stripes in pastel colours: pink, purple, blue, green and yellow. Sheets were cotton in summer and winceyette[18] in winter. I also had a candlewick bedspread. Candlewick meant that the cover had tufts of threads, like candle wicks, pushed up through the material, either in rows or to form a swirly pattern." "On our bed we had white cotton sheets and pillow cases to begin with, replaced for a short time, by pale blue (electro-statically charged) Brentford Nylon sheets and pillow slips which were hot, sweaty and uncomfortable and gave off sparks, you could see in the dark! We changed over to blue 'non-iron' (a lie!) poly-cotton as soon as they became available. The sheets were topped with satin-edged, blue woollen blankets and a satin quilt. Duvets were gaining popularity and we replaced our blankets and quilt with one in about 1967, filled with goose down, with pale lemon and white striped seersucker covers."

Decorating and Maintenance

Until the 1960s, re-decorating was an infrequent and time-consuming activity that required a higher level of expertise than its twenty-first century equivalent. "Wallpaper came with a plain edge that had to be trimmed off at one side with scissors. This was a whole family job. My bedroom was decorated twice in the fourteen years I lived there." "For most of my early childhood, decorating was fairly restricted regarding choice; there were maybe twelve or sixteen paint colours in the shops. Gloss, emulsion, distemper and eggshell were the only finishes and you didn't get a colour chart to take home unless you borrowed it. All the chips in the colour chart were cardboard stuck-on samples of the actual paint itself, not printed. Emulsion paint was a thin liquid, prone to runs and drips, as was the oilbound and smelly gloss for doors and skirting boards and both had to be applied with care; the thixotropic gels of today had not yet been invented. Wallpaper was just that, printed paper and sometimes quite thin, so DIY was not easy unless someone in the family was skilled enough to get it up there without ruining it. With the exception of plain lining paper, all wallpaper had to be chosen from a pattern book and ordered up for delivery at least a week later, nothing came 'off the shelf'. The only heavyweight paper was Lincrusta, a thick sculpted paper treated with linseed, which had to be coated with an oilbound paint." Woodchip wallpaper, designed to be painted and useful for disguising uneven walls, gained in popularity in the 1950s. Polystyrene ceiling tiles were another innovation, which also helped to cover up a multitude of sins. The fire hazard associated with the latter was not regarded as an issue.

Like curtains and carpets, trends in wallpaper moved from the cottage garden floral patterns of 1950s to the orange and brown geometrical designs of 1960s. Fashion dictated that picture rails and dado rails were removed, along with Victorian fireplaces. Panelled doors and stair rails were hard-boarded over to create clean lines. "There was a fashion in the early sixties for blocking doors and stairs with hardboard. That was something my father could do as it didn't require much finesse! So all of the lovely doors and the stairs received the hardboard treatment and then my mother painted it all. Whilst he was at it, he made a bar to put in the hall. Now, my parents didn't drink but my mother had seen one and wanted one. It was curved and covered in white padded plastic that you stuck on. Then an edge was tacked on. It was quite ugly but took pride of place in the small hall with the recently acquired telephone on it."

For most families, decorating and household maintenance was the preserve of the man of the house. "I always assumed that changing a plug was something incredibly difficult: something which only a man with an engineering degree could do and later at university I was astonished when my room-mate showed me the very simple procedure. We used a nail-file to operate the screws and for years I put up with the pointy end digging into my palm until I discovered I could buy a screwdriver for 6d." "On no account could a wife approach the caretaker with any problem, she had to tell her husband and <u>he</u> would report it!" There were exceptions and gradually it became more acceptable for women to undertake these tasks.

Gardens

Once food rationing ceased, gardens gradually became decorative, rather than functional. This meant that there was now more room for swings and deck chairs, making gardens a space for leisure and not just a source of food. "The back garden was fairly small with an alleyway at the bottom, providing access and allowing us to put the dustbin[19] out each week. There was a crazy paving path down the length of the garden, a lawn, an apple tree, a shed at the end and flower beds round the edge. I remember cottage garden plants: red hot pokers, alyssum, London pride, forget-me-nots, nasturtiums, windflowers (Japanese anemones), honeysuckle, michaelmas daisies, lupins, rudbecia and antirrhinums." "There was a very small patch of lawn at the rear, a path which split the garden and there was a washing line which ran parallel, the rest was where Dad grew vegetables, fruit and potatoes, it seems that gardens were not as ornamental then but used more practically." "Behind the flower garden, Dad tended his vegetables and in that part of the garden, my Dad had made me a swing where I would sit and watch him weed and hoe."

Front gardens really only served to distance the house from the street. Their lack of purpose made them a luxury, so the larger the front garden the greater the boost to the owner's social status. "The front garden was a classic privet hedged affair, the same as all the others, I still hate privet hedge because of this blandness and the regimented look it gave everything. All the fathers out clipping away, to make sure it all looked the same."

Summary

The self-contained communities of post-war Britain were gradually being eroded, as better transport links and increased car-ownership broadened residents' horizons. This contributed to the demise of mutually supportive neighbourhood networks, where nonetheless privacy was respected. In towns especially, these were being replaced by environments where residents barely knew each other. This was exacerbated by 1960s' town planners' love of high-rise flats. This period saw basic utilities reaching almost every home, along with gadgets, luxury goods and labour-saving devices. The throw-away culture of the 1960s meant that household items were no longer expected to last a lifetime and fashion was replacing function when it came to choosing interior décor and furnishings. This all served to make the appearance of the 1960s home, very different from that of the 1940s.

The Brief

Describe your neighbourhood(s) and the communities in which you lived. What facilities did you have locally? Mention things like doctors, libraries, parks, shops and the countryside. Did you make use of these?

Did everyone know everyone else or did you live in isolation?

How near was the nearest 'big town'? How often did you visit it and for what purpose(s)?

Did you/your children play in the street, or unsupervised, in the locality?

Describe your homes during this period. Were they rooms, flats, terraces or detached?

Think about the number of rooms and how these were used. For example was the dining room used daily? Was the front room kept for best?

Were your homes owned or rented? Do you know how much you paid? Was the home just for the nuclear family or was it shared by a third generation or lodgers? Who shared bedrooms?

Who did the decorating/maintenance? Were there distinct gender divides in this respect? For example, would the women of the household have painted walls, put up shelves, rewired plugs, changed light bulbs? How often did you re-decorate or have new furniture?

Thinking of utilities, at what point did your home have things like electricity, indoor plumbing or a telephone? Include information about how much utilities cost.

Describe the furniture. What was the style? Was it bought new or second-hand? How much did it cost? When did the household acquire a radio, record player or television?

Include descriptions of soft furnishings such as carpets, rugs, curtains, cushions and bedding. What was home-made and by whom? How long were these expected to last?

Describe small items such as clocks and ornaments.

Write about travel and methods of transport. How often did you use public transport, what form(s) did this take and for what purposes was it used?

Did you own a car, if so what make? Was this bought new or second-hand? At what point in your life to did you acquire a car?

Write about the frequency of rail and air travel, for what purposes were these methods of transport used.

What methods of communication were used, for example letter and telephone and how frequently?

Chapter 1 footnotes

1   A popular brand of fizzy drink that was often delivered by a roundsman.
2   See Chapter 6.
3   'Rec' was an abbreviation for recreation ground.
4   Training in road safety for cyclists, followed by a practical test of proficiency.
5   Large wagons containing beer barrels.
6   Post-war rationing ended in 1950 but was reintroduced for five months in 1956-1957, following The Suez Crisis
7   See Chapter 8.
8   See Chapter 5 for an explanation of monetary values and pre-decimal currency that was in use until 1971.
9   Dr Richard Beeching's report led to 55% of stations (2363) and 5000 miles of railway track (30% of the total) being axed. The intention was to save money in the face of competition from increased road travel but in fact it brought the comprehensive railway network to an end and made rail travel impractical for those in neighbourhoods that lost their service.
10 Polyoxybenzylmethylenglycolanhydride, an early, rather brittle, form of plastic
11 Thin cardboard strips.
12 See Chaper 7.
13 The GPO was dissolved in 1969 and became The Post Office
14 A popular brand of bottled ink.

[15] 2½d was the cost of a standard letter, weighing up to 2oz. From 1957, the basic rate only covered letters up to 1oz and 4½d had to be paid for a 2oz letter. In 1965, the maximum weight for the lowest postage band was restored to 2oz.

[16] Hire Purchase payments by instalments.

[17] ITV first became available in 1955.

[18] A thick, brushed-cotton fabric, similar to flannel.

[19] Households purchased their own heavy, metal bins, which often had rubber lids. These were put out each week ready for emptying by the dustmen.

CHAPTER 2

Rag Mop: housework

Women's Work?

The belief that housework was 'women's work' was alive and well between 1946 and 1969. Whether or not the chores were allocated to adults or young people, there was a clear gender divide, with certain jobs being considered appropriate for the males of the family. "Dad had different tasks to do. He always did the 'manly' things such as shovelling a ton of coal into the cellar or mending shoes on a last." "My father did not involve himself in 'women's work'." "All these tasks were undertaken by my mother including whitewashing the ceilings. Mother also killed the pig every spring, cut it in pieces and then made sausages, pies and brawn. It was all women's work." "My brother was not expected to help at all. I remember asking my mother why he was not asked to help and her reply was, 'He's a boy.' End of story!"

There was general agreement that gardening, car cleaning, household maintenance and anything involving physical strength was acceptable for a man to undertake. "My father did everything to do with the car; he did the heavy work in the garden, including mowing the lawn; he did all the maintenance like replacing fuses and light bulbs and he did the decorating." "I don't remember Dad helping or even assisting Mum with any of the other chores. His job was to take care of the vegetable plot, the greenhouse and the rest of the garden and to maintain the car and the fabric of the house." Other tasks almost always fell to the females of the family. Often of course the man was working outside the home, whereas the woman was not. "My mother did nearly everything around the house. We had no running hot water so it was all hard going. My father did very little around the house or garden despite having a very well equipped shed. I'm not really sure why this was, except he worked a very long week and it was manual labour, so he must have been exhausted." Even when the woman of the house was working full time, respective roles as regards housework were similar. It was only amongst those who set up home in the mid-1960s that there was any sign of a more equitable division of labour. "I believed that, as long as I was contributing to our income, I was entitled to expect equal input from my husband to the household chores, so we used to have a 'blitz' on sweeping, dusting and cleaning on a Thursday evening. It was a revelation to my mother-in-law that her son could do housework as neither of her sons nor her husband had ever lifted a finger to help her, even though she had a job outside the home."

Most children were expected to do some household chores. "When my sister and I were old enough to start helping mum with the housework, we took turns, one cleaning the kitchen, bathroom and toilet and the other polishing the living room furniture, sweeping or vacuuming the living room, hall and bedrooms and making the beds. The one who cleaned the kitchen had to clean the cooker as well." "I can remember beating rugs on the washing line." "I had a very important job on Saturday. I polished the brass letter box and door knocker until they gleamed then swept the small front garden and the pavement in front of the house."

Paid Help

A few families employed servants, often to enable the wife to return to a career but this was unusual and limited to those of professional status. "My parents were introduced to Mrs Brown and Mrs Widger and they were to be a part of our lives for nearly twenty years. They scrubbed and washed everywhere before we moved in. There probably was a vacuum cleaner but everything else was done by hand. Mrs Brown only came for less frequent events but Mrs Widger came every day, arriving while we were having breakfast, starting on the washing up, then putting things away, making the beds and tidying and cleaning the rooms. Mrs Widger only began coming on a daily basis after my mother went back to full time teaching in 1958." "When I worked full time, we had a cleaner who came for two mornings each week and she was paid £3 per hour. She did all the cleaning and some ironing but refused to clean brass or to straighten the fringes on the rugs!" "My mother had a daily woman to baby-sit me and do the ironing and small cleaning jobs, then, when I was old enough to go to school, she'd get women in two or three times a week to do the hoovering and dusting. That's because she was working part-time as shorthand or audio typist, or as my Dad's book-keeper."

Sometimes these servants seemed to create more work than they accomplished. "We had to have the house almost immaculate before 'the char'[1] arrived and she was detailed to clean the bathrooms and lavatories, polish furniture, etc.. Half-way through her two hours my mother made tea and 'the char' drank hers in the kitchen while my mother sat in the lounge drinking hers." Live-in servants were almost unheard of. "I did have one friend in Putney who had a live-in nanny because her mother liked to play club tennis and their house had the space and I suppose they had the money."

For most, housework of all kinds was done by the family, with only such things as chimney sweeping or window cleaning being outsourced. "The first memories I have of cleaning were when the chimney sweep used to visit annually with his big brushes. He used to attach sheets around the fireplace and then feed the brush up the chimney, my brother and I used to have to go out into the road and shout when the big round brush came out of the top."

Routine

Housework was an all-consuming, full time job. In the years immediately following the war, many women spent ten or eleven hours a day cooking and cleaning.[2] Not only was the housewives' role more laborious in the post-war period than it is today but it was taken very seriously. For many families, the chores had a daily or weekly routine that was strictly adhered to. "As a young child, in 1946, I remember that house work was quite regimented. Monday - washday, Tuesday - ironing, Wednesday - downstairs cleaning, Thursday - upstairs cleaning, Friday - baking, Saturday - cooking and odd jobs e.g. mending, sewing etc., Sunday - day of rest." "Before she had to go back to work, in 1965 when my father died, mum cleaned every day, dusting and either hoovering or using the Bex Bissel carpet sweeper." "The beds were made, changed weekly, the bottom sheet washed and the top sheet put to the bottom, with a clean sheet on top and the pillow cases changed. The chamber pots were emptied into a bucket kept for the purpose and the potties were rinsed with a Dettol solution. Then downstairs was tidied, floors swept, mats shaken and surfaces dusted." "The stone doorsteps were cleaned with a pumice stone and door knobs polished with Brasso. The windows were cleaned with vinegar and screwed up brown paper." "Cleaning cloths were cut from garments/towels/sheets that were no longer serviceable." "As we had no vacuum cleaner, the carpets and rugs were often taken outside for a good beating. At that time I thought this was a fun job. Mother scrubbed the front step at least once a week and finished with donkey stone. The drain was always cleaned with San Izal." "We were lucky and had an inside toilet, which was cleaned regularly. Mum used to use a thick cloth and keep pressing it down in the toilet bowl until the water level had gone down then she would get something like Ajax to clean the bowl and put bleach down it to keep it clean."

"There was not much to do in the bedrooms, only sweep the floor and the mats and make the beds each day." "We had a dresser which was a two-door cupboard on the lower portion and shelves on the top. These would be dusted with a wet cloth or feather duster and every so often mum would remove all the china displayed on the shelves, wash it and return it. The table, which was in the best room, was dark wood and this was polished regularly along with the chairs and the piano. Our three-piece suite was made of leather, so that was polished as well." "Shine was a word that could be applied to many aspects of housework in my home. Furniture, especially our dark-wooden sideboard and dining table, had to be shone-up to within inches of its life and this meant polishing with a thick yellow duster and a tin of lavender-scented polish, invariably purchased from the Betterware man at the door and not forgetting a massive contribution of 'elbow-grease' of course! You had to be able to see your reflection in the table-top and this revered item was protected at meal times by a thick under-blanket with a pristine white tablecloth on top, then cork table mats for all dishes and plates. Banisters were similarly polished, as well as the fireside companion set and the doorstep of course and the brass letterbox and door numbers. The front drive was swept regularly with a wooden and bristle sweeping-brush, the dirt and dust being swept out of the gateway and into the gutter."

Spring Cleaning

The annual ritual of spring cleaning was undertaken by most families. Some of the tasks that this involved would be unimaginable to modern housewives. "Spring cleaning required that the rooms be emptied as far as possible and the carpets were taken outside and beaten. Sometimes they were sprinkled with cold tea leaves 'to absorb the dust' before beating." "Spring cleaning was also time to renew the mangle rollers and my job was to load them in a push chair and take them to the saw mills where the spindles would be put into nice new wooden rollers that no longer had a gap in the middle where the rollers had worn away."

Spring cleaning was not to be relished and often put a strain on the household. "One room would be tackled at a time, with all the furniture including wardrobes and other heavy items being moved and the whole room being thoroughly cleaned. Each room took about two days and was a time of trial for my mother and discomfort for the entire household." "Winter curtains and blankets were trundled round to the laundrette in the spring and then packed away with the ubiquitous mothballs to be resurrected in the autumn and fresh chintzy ones hung. The male members of the family (and any boyfriend who was unfortunate enough to call) were obliged to move wardrobes and large pieces of furniture, climb stepladders to clean light fittings and picture rails and hoist carpets (not fitted in those days) to be hung over the washing line and given a good beating with a sort of tennis racket made of cane." "This was a time for extra deep cleaning and taken very seriously, cupboards, wardrobes and drawers were turned out and shelves and drawers re-lined with paper, usually leftover wallpaper. Beds would be moved or sometimes taken apart so cleaning behind was made easier. Curtains were washed and ironed then rails cleaned before everything was put back. This was also a time when one or more of the rooms would be re-decorated or just the woodwork freshened up with new paint."

Labour-Saving Devices

Some households, notably those in rural areas, did not have electricity or hot mains water until some years after the war, making housework an arduous task. Most homes had open coal fires, which added to the dirt. "We lived in a house with no electricity, no hot water and my mother did all the cooking on the black-leaded stove. The coal fire was always lit and gas mantles were the only lighting." "Housework was much harder for my mother as the cottage we lived in did not have electricity and she did not have the luxury of modern labour-saving devices." "Rubbish was collected from big bins which were in the courtyard at the back of the flats and mum used to carry it down in the small bin which she kept in a cupboard in the living room which also had the kitchen sink in it with only a cold water tap."

The 1950s and 1960s saw many families gradually acquire items that made women's lives easier. The arrival of labour-saving devices meant that, by the early 1960s, the average number of hours per day spent on housework, including the preparation of meals, had fallen to eight. This was the era when the first fridge or vacuum cleaner often appeared in the home and devices to assist with the laundry were also within the scope of the budget of all but the poorest families. "Before we had a Hoover, we had a Ewbank carpet sweeper and after we moved, in 1960, to a house with a lot of wooden parquet flooring we had an electric polishing machine as well." "The fridge arrived in 1959, meaning that daily shopping was no longer necessary." "I had mum's old cylinder vacuum cleaner and my trusty broom and dustpan and brush as well as my Squeezy mop. Just before I had my first child I received a Frigidaire spin dryer for my twenty-first birthday. Dad also bought me a small tub, with a dolly and a wringer on the top." "Eventually mum was able to afford a small fridge so this was kept clean as well, usually cleaning it with bicarbonate of soda dissolved in water. In the kitchen mum had an electric kettle and an electric cooker."

These appliances represented a significant financial outlay, even for richer families. In the early 1950s, a fridge cost more than ten times the average weekly wage. In 1963, a Hoover vacuum cleaner retailed at £38 4s 10d. Notes from a diary of 1968 read, "The cooker is a Belling Compact Super Four (12 300 watts and serial No 0311289). The cost is £49 19s 6d. We shall be paying for it over three years at the rate of £4 8s every three months (to be added to our ordinary electricity bill). The total we will have paid eventually will be £57 16s." Unlike today however the expectation was that these devices would last, if not for a life time, then perhaps for twenty or thirty years.

Fires and Ranges

Although the trend for range cooking has seen a revival in the twenty-first century, in this period it was considered old fashioned. Modern gas and then electric ovens were coveted, not least because they were easier to clean. "My parents installed an Aga in the kitchen in the early fifties; it was expensive but it provided hot water, it was used for cooking and it kept the kitchen habitable. The kitchen floor was stone flags, there was nothing like a damp-course and the kitchen became very damp if left unheated. My father did all the work of fetching the fuel (anthracite) riddling the stove, emptying the hot ash and taking it out and adding the new fuel. It was heavy work, the anthracite had to be poured into a small hole in the middle of the hot plate; it was hard to lift the coal scuttle up sufficiently. The stove had to be brushed down and there were often spilled ashes to clear up."

"After Sunday lunch Mum laid newspaper on the floor and stripped out the oven, grill and cooker top for its weekly clean; it was a messy job but she couldn't rest until it had been done." "On Sundays the only domestic chores were cooking although once a month we had to stay in bed while Grandad black-leaded the grate." "I can remember my mother cleaning the large black range that we had in the living room. It was about six feet wide and three feet high. It had a hot plate on it. In the middle was where you built a fire with coals which had a grill in front of it and a little lid on the top, which you removed so you could put more coals in it, this was where you also put your kettle to boil on the removable lid. This provided the heat for the hotplates and ovens which were each side. The oven on the right hand side was wider than the one on the left. There was probably room for about three saucepans on this range but mum eventually bought an electric cooker, which was in the same room as this was a kitchen/living room. When she used the electric cooker we still had the range lit in the winter as this was the only source of heating in the room. At the back of the middle hotplate was a tube which went into the chimney so the smoke did not come into the room. The range was made of lead and it had to be cleaned regularly and was blacked with lead blacking which was a very dirty job to do but once done it looked good."

Open fires caused difficulties of their own; chimneys needed sweeping, grates cleaning and fires laying. When the 1960s brought, for many households, gas fires or even central heating, the workload was considerably lighter. "We had a coal fire in the living room and we had to rake out the old coals from the night before and make up the grate so that a new fire could be lit that night if needed." "The sound of the fire siren and sparks and smoke coming out of chimneys on the estate was not uncommon at the start of winter. It was sometimes caused by un-swept chimneys but more often caused by the use of the poor man's chimney sweep, that is a wad of burning newspaper shoved up the chimney to clear the soot, followed by the application of a tub of salt onto the fire in the hearth, to produce gasses to put out the chimney fire."

Floors and Windows

When it came to keeping floors clean, most of this period was a time of mopping lino, polishing tiles and sweeping carpets, frequently by hand. "My aunt bought us a linoleum-covered stair carpet which sat in the middle of each stair so this had to be cleaned with a wet cloth and the white paintwork either side washed as well. The floors in the dining room and lounge were covered with black Marley tiles and these were washed with the mop and then I would get on my hands and knees and rub a brand of polish called Elephant into them and then polish it off. This I would do by sitting on my bottom on a large duster and wriggling all over the floor."
"As a small child I would watch my mother clean the rooms, first picking up the mats and taking them outside in the yard to give them a beating with a brush and then removing any bits from the surface by brushing them with the hand brush."
"By this time, mum had a cylinder vacuum cleaner and sometimes used a carpet sweeper, for we still had mats in the hall and bedroom and a big carpet in the living

room." "Mum used to take turns with the neighbours to wash down the stairs in our block of flats and she used to clean along the front balcony landing. Our front step was painted red and every week mum used to clean it with red Cardinal Polish."

Although many households employed a window cleaner, the inside of the windows was the responsibility of the occupants. Particularly in an urban environment, keeping windows clean was a thankless task. "Most housewives cleaned the windows every week using a window leather and vinegar water. This was a very time consuming business and one's housekeeping skills were judged on whether the corners of these panes were truly clean and by the snowiness of the 'nets' that preserved privacy. This was not an easy task on the eastern edge of an industrial city before the clean air act came into being." "We had sash windows and the frames were made of wood which had to be washed down. Living in London there was a lot of dirt in the air which came from the amount of chimney smoke and the smoke from steam trains. Mum used to push the window up and sit on the window ledge facing into the room and then close the window over the top of her legs to hold herself there, then she would clean the windows with a wet cloth and then polish them with a chamois leather."

Laundry

Washing and more significantly drying, the family's laundry was not easy in a time before washing machines and spin dryers were widespread. For this reason, the laundry was one task where seeking outside help was common. Many families used launderettes, where they took the laundry and used the commercial machines themselves; some also mentioned using communal washhouses. Other families sent items, notably bedding, to a laundry to be done by others; even quite poor families might send sheets and collars. "All the bed linen was white and went to the laundry every week. The local laundry man called on a Wednesday. Mum had a laundry book, issued by the company, which she filled in in duplicate each week, one copy going with the laundry and one copy for her to keep and then she checked it back the next week."

Monday was the traditional day for doing the laundry. "Wash-day was always a Monday and Mum never varied from this, not even when she was retired and had an automatic washing machine." Accounts of wash-day and often it was an all-day activity, highlight just how onerous this task could be. "After she had got the fire alight we had to get water from the well and put into the boiler. She would wash the white shirts and sheets and other white items first and often use Reckitt's Blue to get the whites looking whiter. Before washing the shirts she would scrub the collars to get them clean using a scrubbing board and put soap on the collars and brush them. After the whites were done and hung on the line she would start washing the other items. I know she washed the woollens and nylon things separately in a plastic bowl and I think at times she used soap flakes. There was also a mangle in the wash house and I would often hold on to the end of the sheet for her so she could put them through the wringer. We had a bowl underneath the mangle to catch the water, which would be wrung out and then we used the water that was left to water the garden. We had a long clothes line and it would usually be full of sheets and pillow cases, which I would watch billowing in the breeze on a Monday morning. When the sheets were dry she would hang all the other clothes on the line and on a nice day it never took long to dry them."

Appliances, when they were available, frequently consisted of Baby Burcos to heat the water, single or 'twin' tubs[3] to do the washing and spin dryers. Most of these mechanised 'aids' required constant supervision, so saved labour rather than time. Mangles were still commonly used. "My mother had a single tub washing machine with a lift up mangle. When the mangle was in the upright position there was a metal lever to hold it which had to be banged with a hammer to get it in position. The machine was plugged into a socket and the tub filled with water through a hose and soap flakes and washing added. Washing took about four minutes and then the items were passed through the mangle and collected in a tray. The water was recycled back into the machine and afterwards emptied by a hose trailing through the back door. Rinsing was done by hand in a big white sink and Reckitt's Blue was added to give an extra whiteness. My mother also put things like detachable shirt collars into Robin starch. Washing was dried on a line with a clothes prop in the garden. We had an electric iron but no ironing board and my mother did the ironing on the kitchen table."

"Bad stains were treated to a good rub on a 'washboard' over a zinc tub before being added to the main wash. What I hated most was the stench of piles of cotton hankies being boiled in a big aluminium saucepan on top of the stove with added disinfectant and the slimy water being drained from them before using the wooden tongs to transfer them to the sink for rinsing, then adding them to the main wash. Tea towels were also boiled on top of the stove but not, thank goodness, with the hankies! As a young child I stood on a chair and turned the handle of our Acme mangle, while Mum fed the folded laundry through to wring out as much water as possible. Care had to be taken not to shatter any buttons, or fingers, in the mangle rollers!" "The laundry, always called 'the washing', was done on Mondays using a copper boiler, a dolly tub and a dolly peg. Our kitchen table cunningly disguised a mangle. 'Blue' bags were used to whiten the sheets and starch solution was made up for table cloths and shirts. Soap was often grated soap block and subsequently we had soap powders like Oxydol and Persil. Washing was dried outside on a long washing line but never on Sundays, or on a drying rack in the kitchen, hoisted to the ceiling. Other things were dried on a wooden clothes horse in front of the fire in the sitting room." "Some models of twin tub had a central agitator. When the water was hot enough, the powder was put in. As each load finished washing, I had to get them out of the washer and into the spinner using big wooden tongs. Then the soapy water was spun out of them back into the washer to be re-used.

Whilst the next load was washing the first load could be rinsed and spun. This was achieved by running cold water from the tap via a hosepipe into the spinner, this water was spun into the kitchen sink. Each load was rinsed two or three times. When all the clothes were done, there was a lever to be pulled up and then when the washer was turned on, the washer emptied via the hose into the sink."

"The washing was done in an electric tub, made by Servis, which had a dolly that rotated back and forth to make the clothes clean and it also had a small wringer on the top. For the large items such as sheets mum used to go to a big laundry, which was on the estate where there were large industrial washing machines and spin dryers, there were also sinks there for you to do hand washing with hot and cold water taps. In the winter, when it was hard to get the clothes dry and if she could afford it, mum sent the sheets and large items to a local laundry and dry cleaners which used to pick up and deliver. Eventually, mum bought a steam iron which made it much easier to iron as you did not have to use a wet piece of cloth between the iron and the clothes to get the wrinkles out. Dad's winter uniform he wore for work was made of a serge material and she used to steam it in front of the kettle and brush it to make it cleaner." "Heavier clothes, such as those made of woollen material, usually weren't washed. They were cleaned by brushing and if there was a stain, that would be cleaned with Dab-it-off, a dry cleaning solution in a bottle with a cloth pad on the top." Many families sent suits and coats to the dry-cleaners but this was likely to be an annual activity, even for suits worn on a regular basis.

Clean washing was very important, displayed as it was on the washing line under the scrutiny of the neighbours. "There was a fierce competitiveness amongst neighbours about whose washing was whitest, as I recall and advertisements for washing powders played along with this, 'Surf boils spotless, spotless white!' and 'New Tide, cleanest clean and snowy white!'" "Reckitt's Blue was used for white bedding and clothes, there was quite a stigma if washing was put out and seen to be grey rather than white; it was also a plus if washing was put out early in the morning." "I did not have a washing machine so most of my washing I did by hand or foot! The large Victorian bath was filled with hot water and the clothes were put into it to soak in soapy water, then after a while I would take off my shoes and stockings and walk up and down in the bath, agitating the clothes until the water was dirty. I then had to rinse them and wring them out by hand before I could hang them in the large communal garden. Not that they were very clean there because we had a main London train line at the bottom of the garden and sometimes there would be flecks of dirt on the clothes."

Even after mangling or spin drying, washing was still far too damp to wear. When the weather allowed, it would be hung outside on a washing line. Once the washing was pegged out, clothes lines were raised by the aid of a long pole with a hook on the top. "We had communal washing lines outside the flat, at least the posts were there, you had to provide your own line! My Mum used to put hers up and take it down each time, otherwise it would get filled by someone else! In the entrance to the flat there were two built-in drying cupboards. I never saw them used but I think they were coin operated and there were gas burners under the base." By the 1950s, rotary lines were available, allowing more washing to be dried in a smaller space. When the weather was bad the only option was to dry clothes indoors. Many households had a wooden dryer, usually consisting of four parallel lines, that could be let down from the ceiling on a pulley; alternatively, wooden clothes horses were used.

"After the washing was dried it was time for mum to do the ironing. This she did with a flat iron which was put on the range or electric stove if the range was not lit. She had two; so she could be heating one while she was using the other to iron. She had a thick cloth which went around the handle so she did not get burnt. She did not have an ironing board but ironed on the kitchen table, after removing the oilcloth and putting a thick ironing blanket and sheet on it. She had a large sleeve board that she used to do items which could not be ironed flat. After some time mum managed to get herself a Morphy Richards electric dry iron (we had not heard of steam irons). The flat did not have many electric plugs in the 1950s, as there were not many electrical devices to be had. Most people might have an iron, a radio and a cooker. If you were better off you might have some sort of food processor and a washtub with a wringer on top and if you were very lucky you might be able to afford a small television. So when mum had her electric iron it was plugged into the light socket, which meant that she could only do the ironing in the daytime." "I had an ironing board which was made out of wood and also a dry iron which rested on a piece of asbestos, when this wore out we bought another piece from the hardware shop and replaced it. No danger was attached to this in the mid-1960s." "Mum had cast iron irons heated on the stove; one heating while the other was being used. The heat of the iron was tested by spitting on it: if the spit jumped off as soon as it hit the iron, it was too hot! It was about right for cottons when it sizzled and disappeared straight away. It made life a lot easier when she acquired her first electric iron, though this had no thermostat."

Products

The cleaning products of the time were remembered with affection. Many of the brand names evoked memories and conjured up the essence of the era. "The cleaning products I recall were Ajax, Tide for washing clothes, 1001 for carpet cleaning and later on Mr Sheen, which I liked spraying around. Most of the cleaning products were 'Betterware' because of Uncle Bob next door, whose job it was to sell such things." "New cleaning products came onto the market by the score. Pledge furniture polish, Windowlene and Fairy Snow joined the Cardinal floor polish and Domestos in my cleaning cupboard." "I used Fairy Liquid for washing up (dearer but lasted much longer than cheaper brands), Stergene, a liquid detergent, was used for hand washing woollens and delicates." "The names I can recall are Daz, Vim and Mansion House polish. The cleaning lady also had to clean silver and brass and she used Brasso and Silvo, which turned the dusters black." "We used fewer cleaning products in the fifties; bleach, washing powder (Surf), Fairy soap in blocks, Brasso or Duraglit. My mother had an O-cedar mop (see figure 22) for wooden floors and it needed a special liquid, some form of oil probably. Gumption for cleaning the bath and washbasins, in tins. We used Airwick as an air-freshener in the lavatory, it was green liquid in a bottle and there was a wick which pulled out when the stopper was raised. By the sixties, aerosol sprays had arrived; they were only used when required."

"Much of the cleaning in the bathroom and kitchen involved the use of bleach and my mother's favourite brand was Lanry which was made locally in Lancaster. The bath and sink would be cleaned with either Vim or Ajax which were coarse powders; I seem to remember they were referred to as 'scourers'. If you used too much they left a residue which could feel quite gritty when you had your bath. A favourite for deep-cleaning kitchen cupboards was soda crystals, which seemed to cut through the grease and grime; these were also used for heavily stained washing."

"Later, when soap came off ration, my mother sometimes bought Lux flakes or Dreft for hand washing of woollens or delicate fabrics." "When detergents came in there was a lot of competition between brands such as Persil, Tide, Daz, Omo, Surf and Rinso, some made by the same manufacturer. They were easier to use than soap because they dissolved faster and included brighteners and other ingredients that made fabrics cleaner."

Other cleaning products included Stardrops, Handy Andy, Chemico, Flash and Mirro. Windowlene was a pinkish purple cream for cleaning windows that had a very distinctive smell. Once applied, it was left to dry and then the powdery residue was polished off with a clean cloth. Brillo Pads were used for scouring pans. Disinfectants were Jeyes Fluid, Domestos, Chlorox, Brobat, Parazone and Harpic.

All in all, keeping the house in a condition that would pass muster with the neighbours was time-consuming, dreary and monotonous but nonetheless it was seen as something that could not be avoided, at least by the females of the family.

The Brief

What was the daily and weekly housework routine? Comment on less frequent events like 'Spring Cleaning'.

Which home-making tasks were allocated to certain members of the family? Include cleaning, cooking, gardening, laundry, car cleaning and household maintenance. Cover the roles of women, men and children. Was there a distinction between boys and girls?

Mention work that was done by non-family members such as the use of servants, gardeners, window cleaners and laundry services.

What labour-saving devices did you have and when did you acquire them? How much did they cost?

What cleaning products were used?

Chapter 2 footnotes

[1] Daily cleaners, often hired to do the less pleasant tasks, used to be known as charwomen.

[2] In the twenty-first century, the average household (not housewife) spends three hours a day cooking and cleaning.

[3] One tub was used to wash and the other to rinse and spin.

CHAPTER 3

Dedicated Follower of Fashion: clothes

Clothing the Family

Until the late 1960s clothes were primarily home-made, if not by the women of the household then by a local dressmaker. Regardless of social class, it seems that garments of this era were minimal in quantity, washed only when visibly dirty and thrown away only when beyond any sort of repair. Adults' clothes would be 'made over' for children and out-grown clothing was passed on to smaller relatives or neighbours. Many ladies reported the 'one on, one in the wash and one in the drawer', principle. Why could you possibly want more than three of anything? When a new best dress was acquired, the old one was relegated to everyday wear. For children, the annual new 'best' outfit might be purchased to coincide with a special occasion, such as the Sunday School treat.

Outgrown knitted garments were unravelled and the wool was reused, either for other clothes or as part of multicoloured knitted or crocheted blankets. The unravelling itself was a therapeutic process, especially if the person winding the resulting crinkly wool couldn't keep up with the pace of whoever was pulling the garment apart, with a satisfying ripping sound. Some makes of new wool came in skeins, as opposed to balls; this too had to be wound. A willing, or not so willing, child would stand, hands outstretched some eighteen inches apart, with the skein round them to hold the wool, whilst it was turned into a ball by an older relative. If the required amount of wool for a new garment was beyond the current budget, balls could be 'put back' by the shop and purchased gradually, when finances allowed.

Sewing was a skill that all women were expected to possess. Many had hand sewing machines and the occasional mechanical knitting machine was mentioned. Clothes were made from tracing-paper patterns, sold by firms such as McCalls, Simplicity, Vogue and Butterick (see figure 36). Tailored clothes, coats and suits required a different level of skill and were less likely to be made at home. These items represented a significant financial outlay, even for professional families and might be saved for for months or even years. By the 1960s, clothing was often purchased via a catalogue such as those run by Littlewoods, Grattons, Marshall Ward or Empire Stores. At this time, weekly payments for catalogue items were given to the visiting 'tallyman', rather than being sent in by cheque, as later became the norm. Those lacking the ability to make their own clothes and the money to purchase them, resorted to buying second-hand from jumble sales[1] or the rag and bone man. The alternative was to rely on hand-me-downs.

"The language of clothes was different. Dresses, especially summer dresses, were 'frocks', casual trousers were 'slacks' or 'flannels', women's suits were 'costumes' and sweaters were 'woollies' because they were mostly wool. Jeans had not yet become ubiquitous." Although film stars did have some influence on fashion, in the 1950s, it was the royal family who were the 'celebrities' of the day. The royal children's fascination with tartan sparked a wave of kilt wearing girls, whereas adult women copied the hats and coats worn by the Queen. There was much less pressure to keep up with the latest trends, which, in any case, did not change so quickly then as they do now. Even those who perceived the need to be 'fashionable' were frequently constrained by the lack of financial wherewithal to continually renew their wardrobe. In what was, for most, a pre-television era, anyone living outside a large town found that they were not aware of the latest fashions and these took a long while to be adopted.

It was more important to be respectable than fashionable, although as the 1960s dawned, with its more radical fashions, what adults deemed respectable was diametrically opposed to what teenagers found desirable. By then, pop stars were beginning to have their own effect on the clothing market. "The concept of acceptable was to me not something that was universal but particular to my mother. Her yardstick was whether something fell into the category of 'common', which covered everything from women of loose virtue to girls who lived on the village council estate." "During these years there was a preoccupation with appearing common, pierced ears in my family were regarded as common, too much make-up was common and bouffant hairstyles were also common, as were dyed hair and short skirts. Painted nails, shock horror!"

Women's Clothing

Women who grew up before the second world war tended to stick with the styles of their young adulthood throughout their lives. Thus, in the 1960s, older women often had darker coloured clothes with longer skirts and thick stockings, which rarely stayed up well. Their cotton dresses tended to have tiny floral prints. In order to be respectable, those who had reached maturity by the 1940s continued to wear hats and gloves when they went out. The generation who were born in the mid-1920s seemed to be the first whose fashions continued to adapt to take account of the less extreme changes of later decades.

Fashion underwent several drastic transformations between 1946 and 1969. "In 1947 Christian Dior's 'New Look' arrived and skirts were lengthened to below mid-calf and generously flared below a tightly defined waist. Under the make do and mend[2] system it became acceptable for one or two contrasting strips of material to be inserted at knee level into skirts that were now too short to be deemed fashionable".

War-time rationing of clothing was still in force until March 1949. In 1945, when the clothing allowance was twenty four coupons per adult per year, a dress required eleven coupons, women's shoes seven and a man's suit was a minimum of twenty six coupons. If special work clothes, such as overalls, were required then extra coupons were issued. "I recall the embarrassment when the Headmaster measured the feet of anyone with adult-sized feet to obtain extra clothing coupons. I won!! Later in the year we could claim Wellington boots through school because we lived over 1½ miles away. I do not know if these were free or had to be paid for later." "Clothing coupons limited what could be bought and 'make do and mend' was a phrase in common use and even figured in newspaper advice columns. Skirts of adults' worn out dresses were converted into children's dresses and blouses; friends and neighbours sometimes contributed their coupons to acquire wedding dresses (or fabric) for local girls. Some wedding dresses were made of rescued parachute silk (see figure 29)." Curtain material was not rationed so, with a bit of ingenuity, could be used for clothing.

When there was no longer the necessity to use as little material as possible, fashions swung the other way and in the 1950s, full skirts were the order of the day. "Rock and Roll and the American college look was all the rage. Very full skirts were supported by full net underskirts, which were often stiffened by sugar solution and these were worn with ankle socks and a very tight sweater, providing one had the attributes to fill said sweater. This was assisted by circle stitched bras which had very pointed cups! A small triangular scarf was worn tied at the neck. Flat 'preppy' shoes completed the look." "At this time skirts were full, even if they were the lower half of a dress and the fullness was enhanced by wearing net petticoats; stretchy elastic belts were also in. In the summer we had what would be the forerunner of today's tee-shirt. Jumpers were quite large and called 'sloppy joes'. I also remember dirndl skirts which although full, were not as exaggerated as the other styles."

"We wore voluminous skirts over net petticoats and later hooped ones, which were a bit hazardous. If you sat on the hoops at the back, it tended to shoot up the front and show the world your underwear. You soon learned not to go upstairs on the bus as you descended the stairs like a parachute." "Sometimes petticoats with hoops were shorter than the skirts giving a 'lampshade' effect. These were banned at our school as the plastic kept coming out! I kept my stiff petticoat up with elastic braces." A diary entry from 1957 reads, "Mummy bought me lovely yellow dress with white spots, pair of red sandals and pair of blue beach shoes. v. nice. I feel at moments that if I could have piles of lovely petticoats all stiff, with yards of lace and frills of net and some sheer nylon 12 denier, I could be ecstatically happy. If ever I get any money, I shall buy loads and loads of nylon (thin) and petticoats (full) as I yearn for them." These much desired petticoats would be stiffened using a variety of methods, including Robin starch and hair lacquer, as well as the above mentioned sugar-water.

"The fifties were a time of formality and conformity in dress. There were conventions as to what was appropriate to wear on which occasion. Sometimes these conventions were specific, as in party invitations which stated a dress code: 'black tie' or 'lounge suits'. Sometimes they were more oblique, as in, 'What would the neighbours say if you go out wearing THAT?' Most people seemed anxious to conform and those who did not were regarded as suspiciously eccentric. There was a firm gender divide. Women on the whole did not wear trousers, men did not carry bags, apart from briefcases."

"In the early 1960s, my mother wore cotton dresses in summer with hand-knitted cardigans or occasionally a jacket. Short socks would be worn under sandals. I remember my mother and grandmother knitting identical woollen suits from a speckly wool. Women and girls had knitted 'twin-sets', a cardigan worn over a matching short sleeved, round necked jumper, fastened with a button at the shoulder. These would normally be made at home." Crimplene was a fabric of the 1960s, popular because it dried quickly and did not crease. It was primarily adopted by older women although both trousers and dresses were available. "Cotton aprons were worn. For older women, these were the inter-war, cover-all, wrap round style 'pinnies'. For women of my mother's generation, these were replaced by aprons that tied round the waist and did not cover the upper half of the body. These aprons were decorative as much as practical and might have frills round the edge. Perhaps increasing numbers of labour-saving devices made housework a less messy process and all embracing overalls were no longer necessary."

In the early 1960s, the fashion was for pencil skirts with kick pleats and cardigans that buttoned at back. The middle of the decade brought the iconic mini-dress styles, with which the fashion designer Mary Quant is associated. Skirt lengths for young women became shorter and shorter, much to the horror of their elders. Trousers were considered quite daring, particularly by older women and even in the 1960s, some fathers, husbands and employers disapproved of the fashion. "I had a Civil Service colleague who was sent home for wearing a trouser suit to work in the 1960s." They became acceptable for holiday wear first and initially were worn primarily by the younger generation. "Paula came home from town wearing a new trouser suit she'd made.... Wore my camel skirt, brown jumper, suede coat, brown shoes", reads a mid-1960s diary.

Jumpers were usually hand knitted. A diary from 1965 states, "Searched through my pile of knitting patterns for something to knit but couldn't fancy anything….. Chose pattern from my collection. Red, with grey (charcoal) fairisle at bottom, going to do polo neck. Went home for money, then 5.15pm we went to Harris's to buy 2ozs charcoal wool….Mum bought me a gorg. pair of brown gloves – actually plastic front and material (stretchy) back – but look quite expensive really. Also a vesty-top – M & S[3] turquoise bri-nylon, fably cosy. She bought herself a light grey M & S twinset and Heather a M & S pink cardi. with grey diamond pattern at bottom."

The 1960s saw the arrival of the 'boutique', with clothing aimed specifically at the younger generation. "I particularly remember Dorothy Perkins as they still had what we saw as an old-fashioned image, with wooden cabinets with glass-topped counters through which you could see lots of drawers underneath, containing all manner of underwear and other items of clothing. I can't remember when but a changeover soon happened and the cabinets were dispensed with and replaced with racks of clothes on hangers that you could take and try on in the communal changing rooms and have a giggle with your friends. I think C & A was one of the early shops where we could buy 'trendy' clothes and then Peter Robinson, which had a Top Shop section and Etam and Lewis Separates and Richards' Shops" In general, these shops aimed to sell cheaper items that were not designed to last. "Gradually, there were signs of moving towards today's concept of 'throwaway fashion' and acquiring a new wardrobe every season." In the 1960s, a dress from C & A might cost between 19s 11d and 29s 11d; heralding the advent of cheap, mass-produced and probably imported clothing. In contrast, a decade earlier, clothes were intended to survive for many years and were consequently better quality and thus more expensive. Prices paid in 1956 included dresses costing between £4 6s 9d and £5 3s 5d and blouses for £1 or £1 10s.

Men's Clothing

Compared to the frequent changes in female fashions, there was much less variation in clothing for men. When men were discharged from the army at the end of the war they received a 'demob' suit to replace their uniforms. "My father was a tailor. He had worked at Hector Powe's before the war and when he was demobbed, began making bespoke suits for gentleman just out of the army who only had mis-shapen demob suits. He didn't have a shop at first, he would measure them and fit them in hotels in Central London. He was more the sales guy and cutter. He would get others to make up the suits from his patterns and measurements, sending these to rag trade outlets in the East End. By the early 1960s, Burton's were making suits ready to wear, off the peg. My Dad did expensive bespoke and made to measure but the market began to collapse so he had to sell by 1965. Suits were three-piece in those days. The trousers were very baggy; he insisted on making suits for my three brothers as teenagers and by the early 1960s they always complained they were too baggy." Along with Burton's, John Collier and Hepworth's were notable tailoring chains.

"My father always wore trousers and a shirt (short sleeved in the summer) with a jacket or occasionally a sleeveless jumper. Ties were worn except on holiday. Even on the beach, unless actually swimming, he wore socks, sandals and a jacket, never shorts." "The life spans of 'sports' jackets (i.e. jackets that were not part of a suit) were lengthened when they wore thin at the elbows by adding a leather patch. Sometimes cuffs would be reinforced with leather strips as well. Boys wore short trousers at least until they went to secondary school at eleven, otherwise their clothes were the same as their father's." For adult men, shorts were worn on holiday if at all. Post-rationing trouser styles for older men often had 'turn-ups' at the hems. 'Drainpipe' trousers had very narrow, tapering legs and were worn by young men, who were copying the styles of pop icons like The Beatles.

"He used to wear shirts with separate collars, which were attached with collar studs, one at the back and one at the front. They must have been really uncomfortable. The collars were changed more often than the shirt, giving the impression of always wearing a clean shirt. I believe paper collars were available but I don't remember my Dad wearing them." "He wore collars from The Collar Box on his collarless shirts; they were collected every week for laundering and delivered back in their brown square boxes." Shirts were almost invariably white or with an unobtrusive stripe or check. In the late 1960s, the younger generation adopted highly pattered floral or 'psychedelic' shirts, jeans and velvet jackets.

Men would wear hand-knitted, v-necked jumpers or cardigans for casual wear. Sleeveless jumpers often came in fair-isle patterns. By the 1960s, these were known as tank-tops and might be worn by woman as well. Arran jumpers were also popular.

Teenagers

Certain styles of clothing became associated with particular groups that emerged as part of the youth culture of the 1950s and 1960s. "There were Teddy boys, with drape jackets, velvet collars and 'brothel creeper' suede shoes, with thick crepe soles. They were the best jivers and at a time when skirts were full, they tended to fly up and reveal knickers, so one had to be careful to wear the very best when out on a Saturday night. Shoes were sneakers or pumps, good for jiving too." "Teenage boys then wore suits for going out in, with bootlace ties. When my brother left school at fifteen he worked in Sainsbury's and he remembers, as a teenager, buying an Italian suit, bespoke by a tailor in Tonbridge and it cost 40 guineas, more than a month's wages. Apparently my dad was less than pleased." "'Beatnik' hair came in in the 1960s for teenagers. Scooter-riding 'Mods' wore shoe string ties, collarless jackets and 'Parkas' with sharp-toed 'winkle-picker' shoes. Rockers wore motorbike leathers, even if they didn't own a motor bike!"

"Late 1960s' teenaged fashions diverged according to whether you were a skinhead, a hippy or a greaser. I went for 'hippy' clothes, long floral skirts, tie-dyed tee-shirts and flared jeans, often decorated with embroidery. Straighter jeans could be converted into ones of more acceptable width by unpicking the leg seams at the bottom and letting in triangular-shaped pieces of material to create 'bell-bottoms'. There were wide floral ties for men known as 'kipper ties'. Girls might have 'kipper tie dresses' with the attached tie of a contrasting colour to the dress."

"There was a fundamental change in social behaviour especially with regards to fashion. Previously, fashion was dictated by the haute couture designers (Dior, Norman Hartnell, etc.) and the hoi polloi had to make do with inferior copies from local dressmakers or their own home-sewing attempts. Also, teenagers didn't really have their own fashions but jumped from children's styles into the same clothes their mothers were wearing. But suddenly, around the middle of the sixties, there was an explosion of young designers and shops aimed at young people: Biba, Mary Quant, Carnaby Street, etc.. In a time of full employment, young people had the money to spend on clothes and in a time of significant social changes there was a spirit of youthful confidence and exuberance, a kicking over of the traces left by the stuffy older generation. So skirts suddenly shot up and girls strutted about showing their thighs. We grew our hair long and wore psychedelic-patterned tent dresses and floaty scarves and lots of eye make-up. The boys also grew their hair and experimented with brighter colours influenced, no doubt, by the predominant pop groups of the day, who had now abandoned the identical suits worn at the start of the decade in favour of more casual or even shocking outfits. Our mothers continued to wear 'costumes', twin-sets and calf-length dresses while our fathers carried on wearing dark suits, jackets, ties, blazers and grey flannels."

Children's Clothes

Children of course grow, meaning that the adult principle of making clothing last until it wore out could not be applied. Children's clothing therefore was usually handed down or bought too big and made to last. Hems would be taken up to a suitable length on purchase and then gradually let down, usually leaving an indelible line that might be disguised with rick-rack braiding. Pieces of different material might be added on to the bottom of hems, legs and sleeves to extend the life of garments. In general, children's and young people's clothing were chosen by their parents until such time as they earned money of their own. It was the later 1960s before teenagers were likely to be given the opportunity of choosing for themselves.

Nappies were towelling squares, which were either purpose bought or created by cutting up old towels. "Large cotton pants covered my nappy, presumably with rubber pants in between. Nappies at this time were terry-towelling squares, worn with a muslin square inside and fastened with a nappy pin; a safety pin that had an additional outer clasp to stop it coming undone." "As a baby I wore hand-made, thick cotton, embroidered nightdresses and knitted cardigans. These would be protected by voluminous, home-made, cotton bibs when I was being fed." All-in-one stretch 'baby-gros' date from the very end of the 1960s.

Once toddlerhood was reached there was some differentiation between boys' and girls' clothing. Very small boys wore shoulder to crotch 'romper suits'. These were frequently smocked, as young girls' dresses might be and they buttoned together between the legs. Girls often had pleated skirts, held up by shoulder straps. This meant that the buttons could gradually be moved down to lengthen the straps as the child grew. Kilts were very popular. Some were attached to thin, petticoat-like tops, designed to be hidden under jumpers. Dresses for school-aged girls often had 'Peter Pan'[4] collars, puffed sleeves and matching knickers. There might be ties at the waist that were sewn into the side seams, forming half a belt, to pull the dress tight at the waist. There does not seem to have been much distinction between summer and winter; if it was cold an extra jumper went on.

"Another memory that stands out in relation to clothes was Whit Week (now Spring Bank Holiday). You had new clothes for Whit Sunday and went around the neighbourhood (mainly relatives and friends) to parade your new clothes and were given money. I don't know how I remember this but when I was nine years old I collected 19s 6d, a fortune. When I was about five and my sister nine I had a beautiful pale blue double breasted coat and my sister a 'costume' in the same woollen material. My sister's had a pleated skirt and a box jacket. We had matching blue shoes and handbags and the obligatory ribbons in our hair. If you were taking part in the Whit Walks or 'walking the scholars' (a parade of members of churches and Sunday Schools) you were dressed like a bridesmaid in a floor length white dress with a head-dress like a tiara in white and carried flowers."

It would be rare for girls to have more than one party dress at a time and if growth allowed, this would be made to last several years. Capped sleeved, short, buttonless 'boleros', often knitted in itchy angora wool, were a common accompaniment to a party dress. "My first party dress was a wonderful creation, white with, I think, embroidered flowers. The pièce de résistance was the petticoat. My mother had fashioned this from many layers of different coloured net, each slightly shorter than the last. There was an ongoing competition for having the most layers of petticoat and I don't recall being beaten."

"By the time I could walk I was usually in cotton dungarees with dresses on special occasions. Dresses had puffed sleeves and perhaps smocking across the front. By the mid-1960s I was wearing stretchy trousers with a sewn-in seam at the front and 'stirrups' under the feet. At this time tee-shirts began to appear as part of the wardrobe. Their fore-runner were aertex shirts, similar to today's polo shirts. Jeans as a fashion item came in about 1967." Many ladies recalled the battle they had to be allowed to wear jeans.

Underwear and Nightwear

The striking thing about underwear, particularly at the beginning of our period, was that there was so much of it. The need for both modesty and warmth in pre-centrally heated homes, combined to require women and girls to wear multiple layers of all embracing garments under their outer clothing. "Women always wore petticoats or 'slips' under their skirts. These could be full length or waist slips. By the 1960s, they were made from nylon and caused huge problems with static as they reacted with nylon stockings. Most of my generation (born in the mid-1950s) abandoned petticoat wearing before we reached teenage, although older women continued to wear slips." A nylon waist slip might cost £1 7s 6d. "As skirts got shorter, it was often necessary to roll the underskirt over at the waist, to avoid the embarrassment of 'having your slip showing', which at my school was a euphemism for being pregnant." 'Charlie's showing', was a hint that one was displaying a petticoat.

"Corsets made of pink fabric and reinforced by whalebone strips, were worn by our mothers' generation (see figure 33). They were fastened by a full length series of strong metal clips into hooks and had full length laces down the centre back which could be tightened (or loosened!) as required. If it could be afforded, they could be made to measure by the Spirella company whose ladies could visit by appointment to take measurements." "Roll-ons were a broad elasticised tube that was rolled on over the legs to the stomach where they performed the dual function of holding in excess fat and holding up stockings using the attached suspenders." In 1953, one of these wide pieces of elastic, stretching from the waist to the top of the leg, cost 25s.

"There were also liberty bodices. These were made of thick, fleecy-backed knitted cotton with strengthening tape down some of the seams. They were sleeveless and buttoned up with curious rubbery buttons. For older girls, I believe they had suspenders attached, so you could use them to keep your stockings up." "Liberty bodices were always cream with a round neck, shaped into the waist, a fleecy lining and three rubber buttons. There were no fastenings and it became a struggle to take off when you were growing out of it. This went over your vest and over that was a full underslip. No wonder I wanted it all off in the spring. Everybody seems to have worn vests, my mum had vest, corset and underslips." "The long lisle stockings were held up by suspenders fastened to rubber buttons on reinforced cotton liberty bodices. As one grew taller it sometimes became necessary to stoop forward to walk when they had reached their stretch limit! If the suspender rubber button had to be replaced, a sixpence or farthing could be substituted."

In the 1950s, it would be very unusual to go without stockings or socks, even with sandals. 'American Tan' was a well remembered shade of stockings. At first, rationing meant that women continued the war-time practice of staining their legs with coffee and drawing lines down the back of their legs to represent stocking seams. As stockings cost between 6s 6d and 11s a pair, stockings and tights, like socks, were not discarded when they had holes in. Ladders in nylons could be temporarily halted by the application of nail varnish or soap. These would later be mended and socks would be darned using a wooden mushroom inside the sock. Some drycleaners offered the mending of nylons as a sideline.

"Socks were usually short until I was at secondary school by which time long socks were fashionable and only the despised would be seen in short socks. Boys' long grey socks were often held up by elastic garters with little green tabs of material hanging down under the turned down top of the sock. These may have been part of cub scout uniform but they were certainly worn at other times too. At primary school we wore thick woollen tights in winter. When I was in the top year of the junior school (1966) my mum acquired some hideously thick stockings and

I daringly wore these instead. Using a red and white suspender belt, I pulled the stockings up really tightly so that the tops of the stockings almost reached my knickers. I think I was the first girl in the school to have stockings, even though they looked like tights! Very shortly afterwards nylon tights, initially called 'panti-hose', came in." 1s 9d has been quoted as a price for the early 'panti-hose' of the end of the 1960s. "At first, these had different coloured 'knicker' parts and there was a debate as to whether one should count these as knickers or wear actual knickers as well."

In the 1950s, camiknickers and French knickers were popular but older ladies wore bloomer knickers sometimes referred to as 'directoire' (see figure 35). Pants came up to the waist until the mid-1960s, when bikini knickers came in. "For children, underwear was more functional than pretty, navy blue or bottle green knickers for school and white aertex for weekends, vests were always worn, woollen in winter along with a liberty bodice and cotton aertex in the summer, I seem to remember a brand 'Chilprufe'." "I always had clean pants and socks every day but vests lasted a week and school dresses and blouses several days. I remember being amazed that a friend not only had a clean vest every day but that she took it off at night; this seemed the height of decadence. Pants however were removed at bedtime. These pants were white, or occasionally pink and by the mid-sixties, nylon had replaced a heavy, jersey-like, knitted cotton. My first brightly patterned pants, by then termed 'knickers', were purchased in about 1968." The brand names 'Cherub' and Woolworth's own 'Ladybird' label were quoted frequently. Many girls got their first 'Rosebud' bra from Woolworth's.

Before the advent of nylon in the 1960s, women's nightwear was a long, voluminous garment that was usually home-made. Cotton nighties in summer gave way to those made from a thick brushed cotton, known as 'winceyette' in winter. "I had two pairs of 'baby-doll' pyjamas when I was about nine, of which I was very proud. These consisted of cotton knickers and a smock style top with puffed sleeves." Men wore cotton pyjamas, often striped or with a paisley pattern. "When Brentford Nylons appeared on the scene we were all invited to wear nightclothes that would dry in a flash, didn't need ironing but were *so* uncomfortable to sleep in, especially if the sheets and pillowcases were also nylon; little sparks kept appearing like electrical shocks!"

"Most of the time, dressing gowns hung on the bedroom door and it was only if we were ill (very, very rare) or after a bath that the dressing gown was seen and that was only to go from the bathroom to the bedroom. To wear a dressing gown around the house would have been slovenly in the extreme." "I had a home-made, purple, candlewick dressing gown that I loved and wore for years." Woollen, home-made dressing gowns, were superseded, in the 1960s, by shop bought ones made from quilted nylon.

Underwear for men usually included 'Y-front' underpants and a string vest, a rather strange and seemingly pointless garment that resembled a cotton fishing net.

In winter, thicker singlets and long johns were worn. Combinations, still worn by older men in the 1950s, were an all-in-one undergarment with long legs made from thin wool with a flap at the front for access. Men's socks were often hand knitted. "My mother-in-law knitted my father-in-law's socks. When she got to the heel she would add a harder wearing thread to the wool to reinforce the part that got the most wear."

Men had large white hankies, often with blue initials embroidered in the corner. Sometimes these were worn as headgear on the beach. A knot would be tied in each corner of the hankie in order to make it head-shaped. "There were no tissues when I was a child, so we had cotton hankies. Those for children had pictures, such as nursery rhyme characters, on. I had a days of the week set of seven, depicting the 'Monday's Child is Fair of Face' rhyme."

Swimwear

"In the late 1950s and early 1960s, both women and girls had ruched swimming costumes made from cotton that was divided into small puffy squares with elastic (see figures 25 and 30). Presumably it was thought that one's shape was better disguised in this way." Many reported the embarrassment of the knitted swimming costume that inevitably sagged when it was wet. Some boys were still wearing all-in-one, over the shoulder costumes in the 1950s and these too might be woollen. School swimming meant the black 'regulation' swimsuit, with its cross-shaped straps between the shoulder blades and its accompanying thick, white rubber swimming hat. For leisure, swimming hats were more decorative and might be covered with rubber flowers, popularised by the American company Jantzen. Until the more liberated 1960s, modesty was everything. Changing before and after swimming usually took place behind the safety of a towelling 'tent', a large towel that was sewn into a tube and gathered at the neck with elastic. "Two-piece swimwear, in the form of a bikini, was introduced in 1946 but took a long while to become generally acceptable. Initially they were far more substantial than the modern bikini. The bottom halves came up to the waist and might resemble short shorts, rather than knickers. In the 1960s, before the briefer bikinis became more generally acceptable, the tops were bra shaped. Most women wore one piece swimming costumes, often with foam 'cups' for the bust and modesty skirts."

Footwear

In company with other fashions, footwear underwent many changes between 1946 and 1969. Older women might retain their pre-war, laced or buttoned, ankle length boots with small heels but younger women strived to keep up with the latest style. In the 1950s, flat ballet 'pumps' accompanied the wide skirts, or trainer-like 'sneakers' might be worn with tight trousers that finished just below the knee. Stiletto heels were popular and 'winkle-pickers', shoes with sharply pointed toes, were the choice of men of fashion. In the early 1960s the Beatles made small 'Cuban heel' boots, also known as 'Beatle boots', popular. Kitten heels and patent shoes were fashionable in the early 1960s. Later in that decade came platform-soled shoes and tight, knee high 'go-go boots' or 'kinky boots'.

Shoes were an expensive item in the post-war period and even those from wealthier backgrounds did not have wardrobes full of shoes. Shoes would be mended rather than discarded; some families were still doing this at home. Metal toe and heel pieces, known as 'segs' or 'Blakeys', would be added to the soles of shoes to make them last longer. Prices quoted in 1956 were 39s 11d for women's shoes, or as much as £3 4s 3d for a pair in patent leather. This was a week's wages for the family concerned. Other diary entries of the period mention 54s for a pair of shoes and in 1967, £1 17s 6d for a pair of size 5 sandals. The ritual of measuring children's feet in order to ensure that the shoes were suitable and had 'room to grow' was mentioned by many but this was a luxury that some could not afford. The cost of shoes meant that the ever growing feet of children caused real difficulties for poorer families. A solution, the wearing of plimsolls for everyday rather than just for sport, was a mark of poverty and sadly for this reason, was regarded as 'common'. Shoe shop chains included Freeman Hardy and Willis, Saxone, Trueform, Timpson's, Barratt's, Dolcis and Clark's. Clark's and Start-rite were the two main manufacturers of children's shoes and many girls had Clark's 'sun-lo' sandals in varying sizes.

"Shoes were leather and in a narrow range of styles. At any one time we might have one pair of shoes, one pair of sandals and perhaps a pair of wellington boots and a pair of slippers. On the beach we wore plastic shoes, with buckles that went rusty in sea water. These were revitalised in the late 1990s as 'jelly-shoes'. I was twelve before I had any kind of heeled shoes. In the late 1960s fashion boots and platform soled shoes made an appearance. We also started to wear white lace-up plimsolls, often customised with felt pen, the forerunner of modern trainers. Dr Scholl wooden-soled sandals and clogs with leather uppers also become popular."

"In winter, for school, it was lace-ups and in summer Finn Sandals ('Finn shoes are fine shoes that kiddies love to wear', was the advert); red or blue leather with a T-bar strap. I can remember going, to Saxone in Piccadilly, Manchester to be fitted for shoes and a big treat was to go on the x-ray machine where you could see your feet inside the shoes to make sure they fit and had growing room."

"The most popular ladies' slippers had bri-nylon fur round the tops. Slipperettes were often given as Christmas presents. These very soft-soled slippers had elastic round the top and arrived folded in half. I guess the idea was that they could be easily carried and put on when visiting friends. We were not obsessive about 'slippers indoors' at home but one of my friend's mothers always made us take our shoes off at the front door."

Outerwear

Until the very end of our period, coats were a costly article of clothing and would be expected to last many years. Coats, particularly those for children, might be hand-made, perhaps by a local dressmaker or tailor. As the shortages of war-time receded, coats became fuller and capes were popular. Women's wide coats of the early 1960s were closer fitting by the later 1960s and 'duster coats' became fashionable. These were thin, often short-sleeved and worn to compliment a narrow 'sheath dress'; they were designed to be ornamental more than functional. Belted 'trench coats' were popular as a shower proof coat. Fur coats were a status symbol and there was no stigma attached to wearing real fur. "My grandmother had a black fox fur necklet, complete with head and feet."

"When it rained we would wear plastic macs; one of the brand names was 'Pac-a-Mac'. These were heavy-duty plastic in a small range of colours and had a fairly short life span but did fold up into a small bundle. They were the forerunner of the kagool. We also had rain hats, much thinner, folding polythene hoods that tied under the chin with strings, only females wore these although both sexes wore plastic macs." "In the late 1960s, youth culture dictated the type of coat young people wore. Male hippies wore army surplus 'greatcoats'. Velvet jackets and embroidered denim jackets were wore by both sexes of hippy, as were afghan coats. These were embroidered sheepskin, with the fur worn inside. Skinheads wore parkas and greasers wore leather jackets." Duffle coats were another popular fashion of the 1960s, particularly amongst the younger generation. In 1967, one was purchased for an eleven year old for £5 17s 11d. The previous year, a charcoal grey greatcoat had cost £7 14s 6d.

For much of our period, hat wearing was obligatory. The style of a man's hat was dictated by his social standing. The professional 'white collar' classes, might wear a bowler hat. Working class men wore cloth caps, anyone in between wore a trilby. School boys wore caps that were more close fitting that those of older men. These were made from six or eight roughly triangular sections of cloth, often with a button in the centre where the segments joined. The peak would be heavily stiffened. Small boys might wear knitted balaclavas in winter. "Women wore headscarves or hats even to go shopping and would not have entered a church without a head-covering. Men, on the other hand, removed their hats as they stepped into a church or any other building and tipped their hat (a slight raising and forward tipping movement) on meeting a female acquaintance." Women's hats of the 1950s were often close fitting, made of felt and secured by hat pins. Post-war teenagers had largely abandoned hat wearing, although hats saw a revival as a fashion item, firstly the large, PVC caps of the 'Twiggy'[5] era, followed by the wide brimmed, floppy hats of the hippies, made from material or straw.

Small children of the 1950s, both boys and girls, often had velvet collared, woollen coats (see figure 26), that were copies of those worn by the royal children. "The first store bought coat I can remember was from Lewis's in Manchester. I was about nine, it was double breasted with reveres and a blue velvet collar and cost £4 10s." "Once I reached school age coats were usually purchased. Before then I had the obligatory home-made woollen coat with a velvet colour. Later I wore an anorak, known as a 'windcheater' (but pronounced 'windsheeter')." "As a toddler I had a fur fabric muff. This was a cylinder of material with a string attached so that it could be hung round the neck. The idea was that muffs kept our hands warm and it was probably easier than trying to get tiny fingers into gloves, although I wore mittens as well. The inadvisability of children who were still unsteady on their feet having no hands to save themselves when they fell over seemed to escape the designers of this item. Adults also had muffs, in their case without strings and probably made from real fur. Small children's gloves were attached to a long string and threaded through the sleeves of their coats so they did not lose them; no one suggested that they might garrotte themselves on the string." "For small children, summer sun bonnets gave way to knitted winter 'pixie' hats. These were basically two squares sewn together along two sides and fastened under the chin." Long knitted scarves would be crossed over children's chests and tied at the back, either under or over the coat.

Uniforms[6]

Several ladies mentioned professional uniforms; uniforms that were not always practical. "Once I started my nursing training in 1967 we had to wear thick, black, ribbed stockings with suspender belts. When making beds we had to flip over the plastic draw sheets on them and the static electricity created used to combine with the radiators behind us and our metal suspenders and give us electric shocks up the backs of our legs!" "As nurses we had four green dresses with three pleats around the hem. The regulation length was fifteen inches from the floor, no more, no less. The bodice was lined with white cotton, the buttons detachable and we had very stiff white starched collars fastened at the front and the back. We had short sleeves with stiff muslin cuffs, which really itched. We had twelve aprons each, which were attached at the bib and back with safety pins and a stiff buckrum belt in a colour to denote which year you were. The cap was a large square of stiff white linen, which had to be fashioned with folds, pleats and safety pins to make a butterfly cap. This defeated me completely but an adept colleague made them for me for at least a half of my Preliminary Training School. We wore black stockings, mine being held up with a very uncomfortable pink suspender belt from Ambrose Wilson and black lace-up shoes. The whole outfit looked lovely but was very uncomfortable."

A lady working for Pan Am airline wrote, "We had two suits with box shaped jackets and straight skirts that came to just below the knee. We wore this suit with a white fitted blouse with cap sleeves and single pointed lapels. We also had wrap around, three quarter length, pale blue cabin smocks with capped and cuffed, dolman sleeves. We wore a blue, pill box hat and little white gloves. We were also allowed a white scarf over our hats if the wind was howling and of course, we wore high heeled black shoes except during the cabin service when black flats were allowed. Stiletto heals were banned as we were told they could puncture the cabin floor! We each had a black leather, bucket, shoulder bag and a small square blue carry-on bag with the Pan Am emblem on it. I was very proud of my uniform."

Hairstyles

Like other aspects of fashion, changes in hairstyle were largely the prerogative of the young; older women frequently stuck to the styles of their young adulthood. In the early 1950s, many women wore their hair longer and put it up in a 'French pleat' or 'chignon'. For younger women, high pony tails accompanied the wide skirts of the time. False pony tails could be purchased but they came in a very narrow range of colours and did not stand up to any kind of scrutiny. 'Beehives' and 'bouffants' were styles that required plenty of volume and necessitated copious backcombing. As the 1960s dawned, hair was more often worn down, often at shoulder length, with the ends turned out in 'flick-ups'. The mid-sixties popularised very short, boyish 'pixie cuts' and by the end of the decade young girls were wearing their hair long, straight and loose.

Pre-school girls often had chin length hair tied up on one side with a ribbon. Curls were still fashionable and some girls of the 1940s and 1950s had their hair wound in rags at night, as was common in their mother's day. As girls got older, plaits, pony tails or bunches were the usual styles. "I always wanted to have plaits (also known as pigtails) and preferred bunches to a pony tail. Elastic bands were used. Sometimes these were tightened by dividing the pony tail or bunch and pulling upwards. This meant that my fine hair broke off at the level of the elastic band. We also had stretchy, nylon Alice bands to hold our hair back." "Hair was supposed to be tied back at school. By secondary school (1967) ribbons were a thing of the past. We had 'bobbles', two plastic beads on a figure-of-eight shaped piece of elastic. These were wound round the hair and one bead was pushed over the other to hold it in place, or large slides would secure a low pony tail." It wasn't until the mid-1960s that it was acceptable for girls to have hair short enough to show their ears. Young boys, on the other hand, were always expected to have very short hair.

Adult women, whose hair was not naturally curly, often had a perm[7] two or three times a year and then hair would be shampooed and set. "When she washed it at home mum would curl her very straight hair with plastic covered wire rollers, which had bristles through the centre; these were secured with plastic pins." Metal clasps, known as 'Dinkie curlers' might be used, particularly if one was trying to create a 'Marcel wave'. This was a style, reminiscent of a ploughed field, which was popularised in the 1920s but was still adopted in the post-war period, especially by ladies who had been young women when it first became fashionable. Older women in particular might go out in public with their hair in rollers, perhaps covered by a headscarf, although this was considered by some as 'common'. Hairnets were also worn, both by day and night, to keep 'sets' in place. Home hair dryers were often made of Bakelite; very superior models might have hoses leading to plastic hoods that would be put on over the curled hair. "Hair spray or lacquer, as it was called then, did not come in spray cans. I used to buy an empty manual spray plastic bottle in Woolworth's and alongside it I purchased a soft plastic tube which contained the hair lacquer and put this in the bottle to use. It really was just like a hard lacquer and kept your hair stiff." Until young women began bleaching their hair with peroxide in the 1960s, colouring hair was rare and was almost unheard of for men throughout this period. "No one we knew obviously dyed their hair, although my ballet teacher had a variety of pink and purple rinses."

Youth culture had its effect on the hairstyles of the young. Extremes of hairstyle, which often aped those of film or pop stars, were seen by many of the older generation as heralding moral disintegration. For young men, the rock and roll quiff was followed by the 'long' hair of bands like the Beatles. By the late 1960s, youths' hair might well reach shoulder length or beyond. "With the coming of Rock and Roll, Bill Haley kiss curls were the fashion, set in the old sugar water if we couldn't afford setting lotion and re-stuck into place on the forehead during the day with fingers wet with spit!." "My brother had a DA. I think that meant duck's arse! The hair was swept back each side and met at the back in a little quiffy thing which looked like a duck's tail. I remember him having a big quiff at the front, like Cliff Richard or Billy Fury. My brother also remembers going to London to have his hair done, he insists it was not in a barber's but a hairdresser's. I think this would have been before unisex hair salons. The hairdresser, male, did the DA and it was waxed so stiffly that my brother slept sitting up for a week so that he wouldn't mess it up!" Brylcreem was very popular for styling men's hair. Facial hair for older men rarely went beyond a neat toothbrush moustache. Until the late 1960s, younger men were invariably clean shaven. Beards and moustaches came in with the 'hippy' look and were usually accompanied by long hair.

Make-up

Subtle make-up was generally considered acceptable, even in the early part of our period. Foundation, lipstick and powder from a compact were commonly used. Rouge and mascara were gradually added to the list of what was normal. Mascara came in a solid block and this was wetted, often by spitting on it, so the mascara could be transferred to a small brush and applied. 'Panstick', a stick foundation produced by the Max Factor company under the slogan 'As used by the Stars', was popular. Woolworth's was a source of cheaper ranges of make-up and Boot's No. 17 range, aimed at teenagers, had just put in an appearance by 1969. Rimmel's 'Beauty-on-a-Budget' items retailed at 1s 3d. Prices recorded in diaries of the mid-1960s included Miner's mascara 2s 9d, Rimmel's pearly lip glow 2s 9d and Miner's long lash mascara at 4s 6d. Cleansing regimes were basic and mostly consisted of washing with soap and water or applying thick, greasy Pond's cold cream to remove make-up. Other ways of removing make-up were to use a white liquid known as 'cleansing milk', or impregnated, circular pads called 'Quickies', that came in a tin.

The very pale, almost white, lipsticks, brought in during the Mary Quant era, were accompanied by heavy black eye make-up, including eye-liner and unrealistic plastic false eye-lashes. These were of course for young women. "The older generation deemed too much make-up to be 'fast.'" By the mid-1960s, nail varnishes moved beyond the red, pink and beige spectrum to include, purples, blues and silvers however "only actresses or loose women painted their toe nails." Although manicure sets could be purchased, professional manicures were almost unknown.

"I didn't wear perfume as such at this time but remember tiny bottles of Evening in Paris and Californian Poppy being on sale in Woolworth's and buying some for my mother's birthday. I used bath cubes and talc (French Fern and Lily of the Valley) and had free squirts of perfume from the sample bottles in Boot's when possible. I remember some ladies' rooms at dances had coin-in-the-slot fragrance machines, where you could have a squirt of perfume for sixpence, this included Elizabeth Arden's Blue Grass, Lentheric's Tweed and I think, Coty's L'Aimant."

Accessories

Women always carried handbags. They were usually voluminous leather squares with short handles in brown, black or navy leather. For special occasions, a small, strapless 'clutch-bag' might be carried and this could be silver, gold or white, or might be embroidered velvet. In the mid-1960s, coloured handbags and shoulder bags became popular. "In the late 1960s we used brightly coloured paper carrier bags with plastic handles - 'tote bags'. Adult women carried shopping in string bags[8] or baskets."

Costume jewellery came into its own during this period and was now socially acceptable. "If Granny wore a suit she might wear a brooch with glass stones on her lapel. Both she and my mother wore beads of various kinds, usually in two or three rows. There were also plastic 'popper' beads in many colours. Each bead had a hole on one side and a knob on the other, enabling beads from different sets to be reassembled into necklaces in a variety of patterns." "In the 1960s, 'jewellery' consisted of wooden or glass beads, bracelets and a chunky watch with a wide strap."

Apart from a watch or a wedding ring, jewellery was almost exclusively for women, until the advent of hippy culture when men started wearing chains, beads and bracelets. "In the late 1960s silver identity (ID) bracelets[9] were popular with both sexes and it was considered a badge of office if we acquired the wherewithal to wear a boy's ID bracelet instead of our own. We also had pin badges with slogans such as 'I'm Backing Britain' or 'Ban the Bomb'." "I was at college before I had my ears pierced (too common) and even then I think my mother thought I had sold my soul to the devil. Clip-on earrings were however acceptable (see figure 32)."

"By the time I was born, my mum's tight, wide elasticated belt, a fashion of the early 1950s, was consigned to the dressing-up box." Boys held their trousers up with striped, elasticated belts fastened with a silver snake-shaped clasp. All males might wear braces on their trousers. Some also wore elasticated metal 'garters' on their upper arms to hold shirt sleeves up.

"Children's glasses were inevitably 'National Health'. These were either round, wire-framed affairs in pink or blue, or marginally less hideous plastic frames. The latter were flatter across the top and came in pink, blue or clear plastic. Mine, which I got when I was nine, were blue. Shortly afterwards I acquired a more grown up style with brownish 'wings'. Men would wear glasses with narrow tortoiseshell or black frames. By 1969, I had heavy tortoiseshell frames, which were the new trend."

The Brief

Describe both female and male clothing, for adults and children. What did you and your family wear, how did this differ with age and gender? At what age did your clothing move from children's styles to teenaged (if they existed) or adult styles? How did styles change over time?

Cover ordinary clothes, clothes for special occasions and uniforms. What was considered acceptable/respectable dress (eg. hats, gloves, skirt lengths, ear piercing, ties for men)?

Were clothes home-made or bought? Who made them? How much did they cost? How many clothes did you/your family have at any one time? How often did you have new clothes?

Did clothes rationing effect you and if so, what was its impact?

How often were clothes washed?

Please also mention underwear, swimwear, nightwear and jewellery.

Comment on hairstyles (your own and your family's) and how these changed with age and over time. Who cut your hair? Who went to the hairdressers or barbers? How often? For what? How much did it cost? How often was hair washed?

Comment on attitudes to make-up. What was worn, what was acceptable? At what age was make-up used?

You may wish to recall some of your favourite and not so favourite items of clothing or style disasters.

Chapter 3 footnotes

[1] Jumble sales were the forerunner of car-boot sales, except, in this instance, the beneficiary was a good cause, rather than the previous owner of the items on sale. 'Jumble' would be donated, sorted by willing volunteers and then sold in a church or village hall in aid of charity.

[2] 'Make do and Mend' was originally a war-time government initiative to encourage people to save resources. The Ministry of Information issued a pamphlet by the same name that provided tips and hints on how to be thrifty, whilst still dressing with style.

[3] Marks and Spencer.

[4] Small, round collars, usually white.

[5] In the 1960s, Lesley Hornby was a very thin model, with a short 'pixie' hair-cut. She worked under the name of 'Twiggy' and her iconic style became a trademark of the era. She was associated with the fashion designer Mary Quant and trendy London shops such as Biba.

[6] For school uniforms, see Chapter 6.

[7] A 'perm', or permanent wave, was a chemical process of curling the hair, in what was meant to be a semi-permanent manner. Permed hair did how ever still need to be 'set' (put in rollers when washed) in order to avoid a distinctly frizzy look.

[8] These resembled a fishing net and might be made of a plasticised string.

[9] These were made up of links and a flat piece of silver upon which a name could be engraved.

1

2

3

4

5

6

7

8

9

10

11

12

13

14

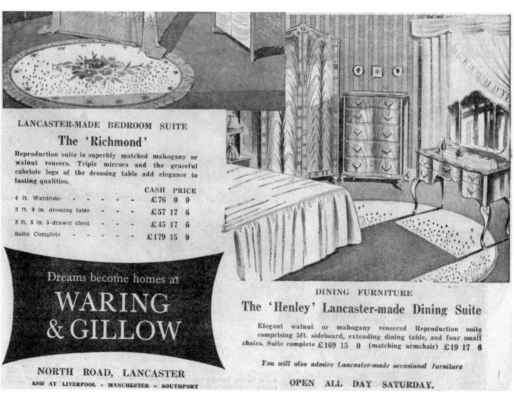

15

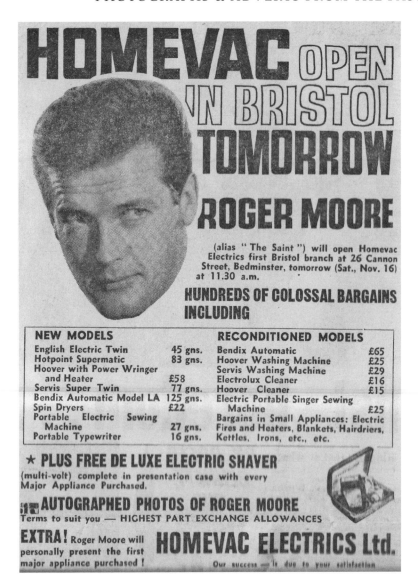

HOMEVAC OPEN IN BRISTOL TOMORROW

ROGER MOORE

(alias " The Saint ") will open Homevac Electrics first Bristol branch at 26 Cannon Street, Bedminster, tomorrow (Sat., Nov. 16) at 11.30 a.m.

HUNDREDS OF COLOSSAL BARGAINS INCLUDING

NEW MODELS		RECONDITIONED MODELS	
English Electric Twin	45 gns.	Bendix Automatic	£65
Hotpoint Supermatic	83 gns.	Hoover Washing Machine	£25
Hoover with Power Wringer		Servis Washing Machine	£29
and Heater	£58	Electrolux Cleaner	£16
Servis Super Twin	77 gns.	Hoover Cleaner	£15
Bendix Automatic Model LA	125 gns.	Electric Portable Singer Sewing	
Spin Dryers	£22	Machine	£25
Portable Electric Sewing		Bargains in Small Appliances: Electric	
Machine	27 gns.	Fires and Heaters, Blankets, Hairdriers,	
Portable Typewriter	16 gns.	Kettles, Irons, etc., etc.	

★ **PLUS FREE DE LUXE ELECTRIC SHAVER**

(multi-volt) complete in presentation case with every Major Appliance Purchased.

FREE AUTOGRAPHED PHOTOS OF ROGER MOORE
Terms to suit you — HIGHEST PART EXCHANGE ALLOWANCES

EXTRA! Roger Moore will personally present the first major appliance purchased !

HOMEVAC ELECTRICS Ltd.

Our success — is due to your satisfaction

16

the Osokool

COLD FOOD CABINET

for Cottage
    Castle, Caravan

NO GAS OR ELECTRICITY!
NOTHING TO GO WRONG.
½ cu. ft. size £4-17-6
Double size £9-2-0

Recommended by:

JOHN R. BUSS & SONS LTD
23 KING STREET · MANCHESTER · Tel. BLA 6675

17

BOROUGH OF BIDEFORD.

JOHN ACKLAND, C.R.S.I., M.S.I.A.
SANITARY INSPECTOR
AND
MEAT & FOOD INSPECTOR.

TELEPHONE:
BIDEFORD 486 (TWO LINES).

Municipal Buildings,

Bideford,
Devon.

August 5th 1947.

Dear Sir,

      re BARTON HOUSING ESTATE,
          BIDEFORD.

      I am directed by the Bideford Town Council to offer you the tenancy of a newly erected house, numbered twelve on the above estate.
      The rental of the house will be £1 . 0 . 0 (One pound) per week inclusive of rates (the rates are estimated at 4/6 per week).   An additional charge of 1/- (One Shilling) will be made as hiring fee for the gas cooker, payable at the same time as the rent.
      Rent and hire of cooker will be payable one week in advance.   All other conditions as per the usual tenancy agreements for Council Housing Estates.
      The fencing at the back of the house is incomplete at present, but will be completed as soon as materials are available.
      Your tenancy will commence from Monday August 11th 1947.
      Will you please let me know by signing and returning the attached slip, within the next three days whether you are agreeable to accept the tenancy of the house on the above terms.

      Yours faithfully,

              J Ackland

           Housing Officer.

18

T. V. CRITCHLEY

~~INVOICE~~

CARPENTER & JOINER

Do-it-Yourself & Woodworkers' Supplies

376 Two Mile Hill Road - Kingswood - Bristol

Telephone : 673718

We Specialise in—
DOORS
WINDOWS
MIRROR &
GLASS WORK
REPAIRS &
ALTERATIONS

25th. June. 1964.

M r. Boyce, 36, Parkside Avenue, Winterbourne, Bristol J9

To erecting double-sided hardboard partition complete with sliding door & serving hatch. Supply & fixing base unit & corner base unit. Supplying & fixing working surface & covering working surfaces with decorative laminated plastic. Supplying & fixing wall cupboards. Cutting away inside wall to make doorway, fixing R.S.J., supply & fixing pair of sliding doors, complete with fittings. All work left in the whitewood. Price for this work, as agreed:-	£137.7. 0.
nett.	

Paid by cheque 487589 30/6/64

19

You'll be
happy
with a

G.E.C.

No wonder everyone wants it!

Look — isn't it amazing how much it holds! Think what it means in safe, delicious food. Plenty of cool, health-building milk. Ices and iced drinks, quick-set jellies, easy-to-make iced puddings. Think of the crisp salads you can have. And how easy to keep meat and fish fresh in hot weather! Space-saving, capacious This is the ideal refrigerator for small

kitchens; table-topped, wonderfully compact. The remarkable new *plastic-on-steel* interior cannot chip, and is framed in cool spring-leaf colour. So cleverly planned that it gives you over 3 cubic feet of storage space, 6 sq. feet of shelving, and 1½ lb. of ice at a freezing.
A 5-year Guarantee goes with the sealed refrigerating system. A 1-year

guarantee with the complete refrigerator. Choose a refrigerator with the famous name behind it—choose G.E.C.

DE31 **£66·0·0** (3 cubic feet)
Other models:
DE32 **£99·1·5** (5 cubic feet)
DE33 **£144·18·0** (8 cubic feet)
(including purchase tax)
Write for illustrated descriptive leaflet DE2785 to Magnet House, Kingsway, London, W.C.2

See them at your local dealer's or electricity service centre   The General Electric Co. Ltd.

20

21

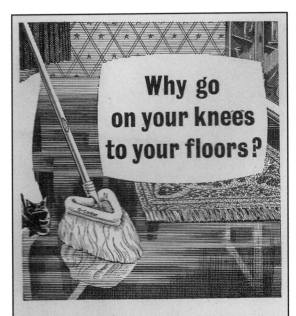

Why go on your knees to your floors?

GET AN O-CEDAR IMPREGNATED MOP
and do your floors *standing up*. It will save you back-ache, and it's better for your figure. The O-Cedar Polish in the Mop Head dusts, cleans, polishes, preserves, and disinfects—all in one easy operation. Lino, parquet, stained, varnished and painted floors come up beautifully —*without toilsome effort—without kneeling*.

THE O-CEDAR IMPREGNATED MOP does not scatter the dust but collects and holds it, thus safely removing dangerous dust-borne bacteria. To maintain the properties of the Mop you stand it periodically, overnight, in its own Can into which has been added a little O-Cedar Polish. This is called refreshing the Impregnation.

The Mop Head is shaped to go into corners, hinged to worm its way into difficult places, cushioned to protect paint, etc. The pad is easily removed for washing or renewal.

O-CEDAR POLISH is the product of years of scientific study. It is an all-purpose polish, excellent for furniture, paint and enamel work, glazed tiles, cars etc. It is sweet-smelling and every drop is made to DUST, CLEAN, POLISH, PRESERVE and DISINFECT.

O-Cedar Impregnated Mops, in special cans and with green cellulose polished metal screwed handles, from 12/3d.

O-Cedar Polish: bottle 1/6d., large economy size 2/10½d. Stocked by ironmongers, hardwaremen, stores, etc.

O-Cedar
IMPREGNATED MOPS AND POLISH

23

24

25

26

27

28

29

30

RIGHT
THROUGH
THE
DAY... **GOR-RAY** skirts one better!

Go 'cotton-picking' for a summer Gor-Ray, prettiest new arrivals on the summer scene. Or wear Gor-Ray slacks this summer with turn-ups or tapered legs —they're so well tailored.

31

32

All-in-one version of a famous girdle — that's *Youthlines Midi Six*

Many women prefer a corselette to a girdle, or need a corselette. For those who do, and who have been casting envious glances at our 'Midi', here's good, good news — Youthlines 'Midi Six' corselette.

It's the same miracle blend of unforgettable leno and satin elastic, designed gently but firmly to control your whole figure . . . to give you a long smooth line on which today's fashions will sit with assurance. See 'Midi Six', in pink or white, at good shops everywhere. For bust sizes 34-40 (odd and even) 159/6.

33

Someone is growing up with perfect feet by way of *Clarks* SANDALS

Width fittings, selected by footgauge measurement for length, breadth and girth. Close fit at heel and instep — with room for toes to grow.

PLAYFREE *Infants sizes 3 to 7½. In brown, blue, red or white.*

PLAY-UP Sandal, *infants sizes 3 to 7½. In brown, blue, red or white.*

SUNWAY *Infants sizes 3 to 7½. In white, blue or red.*

All with "Pussyfoot" soles.

Nearest shop?
Write CLARKS, Dept. CDS, Street, Somerset — and ask for an illustrated leaflet

34

35

FASHIONABLE DIRECTOIRE KNICKERS
AT SPECIAL PRICES.

SMART DIRECTOIRE KNICKERS recommended for hard wear, in good quality rayon satin, well cut shape, garter knee, finished elastic. In Black, Ivory, shades of Blue, Green, Wine, Beige, Beaver, Grey, Pink, Peach and other new shades. In short and medium lengths.

Price
10/9

Outsize, Price 15/9.

In washing crepe satin, 18/9.

Debenham & Freebody
Wigmore Street.
(Cavendish Square) London. W.1

Sent on approval.

Simplicity Pattern

36

BERNAT BOOK NO.59

FASHIONS AND FUN FOR THE "ALMOST TEENS"

37

The Nation's Balance-Sheet

BUDGET ESTIMATES, 1952-53 (Ordinary Revenue and Expenditure)

Estimated Revenue

Inland Revenue—

	£000	£000
Income Tax	1,804,225	
Sur-tax	125,000	
Death Duties	175,000	
Stamps	57,500	
Profits Tax and Excess Profits Tax	452,000	
Excess Profits Levy	5,000	
Special Contribution and Inland Revenue Duties	2,000	
Total Inland Revenue		2,618,725

Customs and Excise—

	£000	£000
Customs	1,043,500	
Excise	772,000	
Total Customs and Excise		1,815,500

	£000
Motor Vehicle Duties	64,150
TOTAL RECEIPTS FROM TAXES	**£4,498,375**

	£000
Surplus Receipts from certain Trading Services	12,000
Broadcast Receiving Licences	15,000
Receipts from Sundry Loans	26,000
Miscellaneous (including Sale of Surplus War Stores)	110,000
TOTAL REVENUE	**£4,661,375**

Estimated Expenditure

	£000	£000
Debt Service		575,000
Payments to Northern Ireland Exchequer		40,000
Other Consolidated Fund Services		10,000
Total		625,000

Supply Services—

Defence:

	£000	£000
Army Votes	521,500	
Navy Votes	357,250	
Air Votes	467,640	
Ministry of Supply (Defence)	98,480	
Ministry of Defence	17,340	
	1,462,210	
Less—Sterling Counterpart of Economic Aid appropriated-in-aid of Defence Votes	85,000	
		1,377,210

Civil—

	£000	£000
I. Central Government and Finance	14,196	
II. Commonwealth and Foreign	92,662	
III. Home Department, Law and Justice	77,041	
IV. Education and Broadcasting	280,934	
V. Housing and Local Government, Health Labour and National Insurance	813,570	
VI. Trade, Industry and Transport	143,201	
VII. Common Services (Works, Stationery, &c)	68,832	
VIII. Non-Effective Charges (Pensions)	91,653	
IX. Supply, Food and Miscellaneous Services	598,379	
		2,180,468
Post Office Vote (Excess over Revenue)		4,498

Tax Collection—

	£000	£000
Customs and Excise, and Inland Revenue Votes	43,386	
		3,605,562
TOTAL EXPENDITURE		4,230,562
SURPLUS		430,813
		4,661,375

38

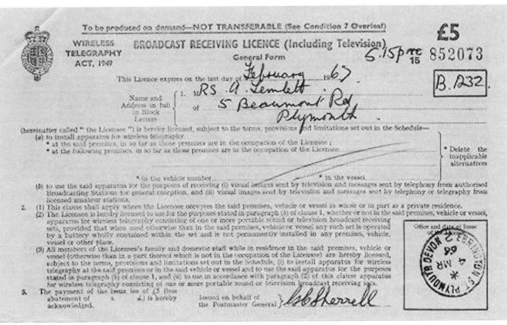

39

40

41

42

43

My husband and I and our one-year-old daughter are living in a cramped and inconvenient house. We could buy a modern, well-situated house, but to meet the expense I should need to return to work as a teacher, and leave my daughter in a day nursery. She would have opportunities to play with other children there, but should I be right to deprive her of my presence during her most formative years?

You have put the issues clearly and I agree that you are faced with a situation which needs to be thought out very clearly.

You are right to value pleasant and healthy surroundings for your child and you must certainly aim to get that modern house. But not at the expense of giving up the personal care of your daughter while she is still a baby. Day nurseries do excellent work for children whose mothers are the sole bread-winners or for those whose home conditions are so unsatisfactory that it is essential for them to be away from home in the interests of their health. Nevertheless, a day nursery is not the ideal environment for very little children. They are not old enough to take pleasure or profit from each other's company; to a large extent they are all rivals for the attention of the adults, who are too busy to give each one the amount of individual attention he needs. Children's speech develops by talking with grown-ups, not in the first place with other children, and they play most happily in their mother's company. A little later, when they are old enough to go to nursery school, the position is very different. I would ask you to keep your daughter at home with you now and let her grow up securely with you. You may well find that you could supplement your income by giving extra coaching in your own home to a few pupils who need it, and so get the best of both worlds.

Decorous

DECOROUS GARMENTS LIMITED

DALLAS ROAD

LANCASTER

MANUFACTURERS OF NYLON OVERALLS
have vacancies for

MACHINISTS

40-HOURS   5-DAY WEEK

Starting Rates :   Age 15 ...   £5/ 0.0
                             16 ...   £5/10.0

Minimum rates for girls with machining experience :

                             Age 16½ ...   £6/10.0
                                17 ...   £7/ 0.0
                                18 ...   £8/ 0.0

With opportunity to earn up to

£12 per week

EXCELLENT WORKING CONDITIONS AND GOOD
CANTEEN FACILITIES .

45

opportunities

Junior Females
aged 16—18 years required in a number of offices.
Arithmetical ability and an interest in figures would
be an advantage.

Experienced Invoice Typist
required at our White Lund Warehouse. Applications
can be made direct to Mr. Paton at White Lund.

Layout Artist
wanted for publicity department. To produce roughs
and finished art work for leaflets and catalogues.

Youth, aged 15-16 years
required for Mail Office duties. This position could
lead to an interesting office career for a suitable
candidate.

Weavers
Experienced on plain Lancashire looms. Also Trainees.
Single day shift. Cotton trade rates and conditions.
Apply — Moor Lane Mills, Moor Lane, Lancaster.

Male Process Workers
Must be keen and active, aged 19-40 years and
willing to work shifts.

Female Process Workers
A limited number of Females are required in our
Queens Mill Department to be trained in plastic
welding. Must be willing to work two shifts 6 a.m.
to 2 p.m. and 2 p.m. to 10 p.m. Minimum height
5'6". Good pay and bonus scheme.

Conditions for all the above vacancies include a three weeks' holiday with pay

at

Storeys OF LANCASTER

apply to: Personnel Department: White Cross, Lancaster

46

CHAPTER 4

Food Glorious Food:
diet and shopping

What we Ate

Food, its taste, its smell and even the product names are all evocative of the era. In the days before universal car-ownership and when lives were more active, there was a need for calories. The diet, especially for those engaged in manual labour, might encompass a fried breakfast and two large meals a day, perhaps with the addition of supper, or a bread and jam, or bread and dripping, tea. "I have always been interested and sometimes confused by the names of meals. Breakfast seems to be the same meal over all the country but after that, chaos! Tea can be just a drink or a mid-afternoon snack (cakes and biscuits) or a proper meal after work about 6.00 pm. If invited to 'come for dinner' it might mean midday or evening, depending on which part of the country one is in and supper might be the same thing or a cup of cocoa and a biscuit at bed-time." In the 1950s, sixty percent of men came home for midday dinner, so the main meal did not move to the evening for most until the 1960s. At this point, midday 'dinner' started to become known as 'lunch'. In the early 1950s, half of all children were having a main meal at school and school dinners are described in Chapter 6.

Breakfast was not a meal to be taken lightly and often included a cooked element, such as eggs, even if it wasn't the full 'fry-up'. Porridge was frequently eaten and processed cereals, such as the popular Kellogg's cornflakes, were available, although the range was limited." "Just as now, cereals were targeted at the young and often had a toy inside the packet. They usually had a game or cartoon story on the back of the box. My favourite was *Zorro* which I think was on Puffed Wheat." "My favourite cereals were Sugar Puffs, Rice Crispies, Shreddies, Weetabix and Cornflakes, often depending on which one had a toy or model in the packet to collect." "We had cereal, toast and marmalade for breakfast and milk to drink, or tea for the older children and adults." Toasters were available but unusual, especially at the beginning of this period. "Toast was usually made under the grill on the gas stove but we loved it when we were allowed to toast it on a toasting-fork in front of the coal fire." Crumpets were also toasted by the fire.

"Bread was un-sliced and Mum never did cut an even slice. One end of a sandwich was a doorstep while the other end looked like it had been cut with a razor blade. Sandwiches only had one filling at a time, cheese, tomato, cucumber, jam and margarine rather than butter." "We also had wedge-shaped processed cheese, wrapped in silver paper, Kraft Dairylea was typical, or Primula." Fish paste was another popular sandwich filling, as was Marmite. "If visitors came for Sunday tea then there would be potted meat sandwiches, tinned peaches or pears with tinned Nestlé cream and plain cake." Home-baked cakes might accompany a packed lunch, or be reserved for Sunday tea. "At least once a week she would cook cakes. This must have been on Friday because it was 'for the weekend'. This was nothing fancy but basic and filling; fruit cake, rock buns, gingerbread, sponge." "A housewife might be criticised for serving shop-bought cakes but these became available, as did packet mixes from which to make things like fairy cakes. Swiss rolls and pink and yellow squared battenburg, surrounded by marzipan, or individual cakes such as cup-cakes,[1] jam tarts, fondant fancies or doughnuts were favourites."

"'Meat and two veg.' was the order of the day for the main meal" "There was a definite routine to the weekly menu. We usually had a roast dinner on Sunday. This was often quite small and sometimes the cheaper cut of meat. Monday's meal would always be the same. Mum would put the meat remains through the mincer and we had this made into a cottage/shepherd's pie, with bubble and squeak[2] from the left over vegetables." "We didn't buy minced meat, we minced the left over meat ourselves using a mincer that was screwed to the kitchen table. Mum made rissoles, which were a little like burgers, made from the minced up meat covered in bread-crumbs." Chicken was less popular than lamb or beef, perhaps reflecting the relative cost at the time.

"Fish was traditionally eaten on Fridays. The only way to have chips was to chop the potatoes and fry them in dripping in a chip pan." "Mum would keep a bowl of dripping in the larder which was brought out each time chips were fried and the dripping was returned to the bowl after the chips were cooked. It was added to whenever we had a roast, which yielded more fat/dripping." "We had potatoes with practically every meal. Rice only appeared in a milk pudding and pasta only showed its face as macaroni cheese." "Another difference between food of today and in the 1950s was that we only had fruit and vegetables that were in season. So eating new potatoes was a real treat and something we looked forward to, as were strawberries, cherries, runner beans, fresh peas. Shelling the peas together, sitting on the back doorstep was companionable and memorable."

Nothing was wasted, quite a feat in times when left-overs could not be frozen. Cheaper cuts of meat would eke out the weekly budget and offal was frequently eaten. "Tripe was served up every three or four weeks, usually boiled in milk with chunks of onion but occasionally curried, which helped considerably! A relative had a tripe stall in Newcastle market and sold about fifteen different kinds of tripe, all of it disgusting (to me)! Sometimes Mum would get a sheep-head, which was split in two and she would use any traces of meat in stews; the brains were spooned out, mashed and served grilled on toast, rather like herring milts. Likewise, half a cow's head would provide meat for brawn and pressed tongue. Bones were slow boiled to give a nutritious stock for soups and stews. Offal was served at least two or three times a week: sweetbreads, liver, and kidneys." "I remember baked heart stuffed with onion but Mum's liver and onions with gravy was my favourite. I remember eating brains on toast once."

Convenience food such as fish fingers, which first went on sale in 1955, were a godsend as they needed no preparation. Even households who did not have the ability to freeze these would buy them to eat on the same day. Vesta packet curries were available from 1961 and other 'instant' foods, such as Smash dried potato arrived in the 1960s. Angel Delight, produced by the Bird's company in 1967, was a powder that became a dessert when milk was added. There was also a broadening range of menus with the coming of 'foreign' food, as a result of overseas holidays and television. "Although we were used to eating boiled rice, the advent of spaghetti was amazing and so risqué!" "Condiments were Cerebos table salt, which came in a packet with a boy chasing a bird with salt, ground white pepper, Colman's Mustard Powder in a yellow tin (mixed with water when needed), HP Sauce and Daddy's Sauce ."

The second course of the main meal was also known by a variety of names: 'pudding', 'dessert' or 'afters'. "Second courses tended to be stodgy, calorific and frequently served with custard. The custard was often home-made, although custard powder, most notably Bird's, was available. Steamed puddings, bread and butter puddings, pies and crumbles were popular as were puddings made with tapioca, sago, semolina or ground rice." In a lighter vein, tinned fruit, often accompanied by a tin of evaporated or condensed milk, blancmange and jelly were served. "Ice cream was a treat, whether a brick to be sliced and shared for a family dessert, or individual ices, wafer sandwiches, as the ice cream was sold in rectangular individual portions wrapped in greaseproof paper; there were also cornets shaped specially to take these rectangular pieces of ice cream. They were either plain vanilla or vanilla and strawberry, half and half. There were choc-ices as well and ice-lollies."

By far the most commonly drunk beverage was tea, made of course from tea leaves in a tea pot and poured into cups through a tea strainer. Although tea bags had been invented in America in the early years of the nineteenth century and introduced into Britain by Tetley's in 1953, in the early 1960s only three percent of the tea market was tea bags. Coffee was drunk more rarely. "Camp coffee was made from chicory and came as a liquid in a bottle; it bore little relation to coffee!"

Children drank milky tea, milk and squash. Robinson's Lemon Barley Water was popular and fizzy drinks were available but these were a treat, rather than a regular drink. "The Pop man came every Saturday and we had a bottle to share. There was Lemonade, Dandelion and Burdock, Limeade, Ginger Beer and Cream Soda but my favourite was Cherryade." Men might drink beer at the pub and making beer and wine at home began to be popular but excessive drinking of alcohol, especially by women, was rare. "Women often drank Babycham, Cherry B or a Pony." In most homes, buying alcohol for home consumption was reserved for parties or Christmas.

Snacking and what is now known as 'grazing', between meals was unusual, especially whilst rationing was in force. Even after these items were more readily available, biscuits, crisps and sweets were eaten sparingly. This was from habit and for reasons of economy, rather than due to any suggestion that these things were bad for one's health. "Smith's plain crisps contained a little blue bag of salt that could be added if desired. I am sure I am not the only person who once inadvertently ate the salt." Cheese and onion crisps became available in the late 1950s, followed by salt and vinegar but there was not a wide range of exotic flavours during this period.

"My grandmother always believed in finishing dinner with a sweet or chocolate afterwards, so we had a sweet tin and everyone had one but only one, which might be one square of chocolate (Cadbury's of course) or one sweet. We had an Easter egg each at Easter, which we ate bit by bit, not all at once. We did have some biscuits but I can't quite remember when we ate them! Eating between meals was not encouraged; it would spoil your dinner." Although some women still made their own biscuits, they were frequently shop bought. These ranged from plain shortbread, Rich Tea and digestives, to brown, sugary bourbons or custard creams. Ginger nuts and Garibaldi biscuits, containing dried fruit, were favourites and Crawford's pink wafer biscuits were often served at parties. The treat that was mentioned most frequently by participants was a Wagon Wheel; these were large, thick, chocolate 'biscuits' with a marshmallow filling. Other popular chocolate treats were Tunnock's tea cakes (dome-shaped chocolate-covered shortbread and marshmallow), Penguin biscuits, Club biscuits, Cadbury's chocolate fingers and chocolate Swiss rolls.

Some sweets were of the un-branded, old fashioned, sweet shop variety and these were usually sold loose: sherbet-filled, coloured rice paper 'flying saucers', liquorish boot laces in red or black and gobstoppers. "Some of our favourites included sherbet dabs, with a liquorice 'straw' to suck through (though this didn't work very well and we usually ate it and then shook the sherbet powder out into our hand to lick up), liquorice all sorts, liquorice torpedoes (especially the red ones, which you could lick and use as a 'lipstick' to colour your lips), sweet tobacco (shredded coconut in cocoa powder), lemonade powder (which you dipped your wet fingers into and licked it off, giving you orange fingers), sweet cigarettes (candy sticks, coloured red at the end, so they looked alight, especially on a cold day when your breath looked like smoke), jelly babies and raspberry drops. Spangles, Polo mints and Rolos came in tubes and my favourite chocolate bars: Mars and Bounty." "There were Black-jack and Fruit Salad chews for ½d and larger ones in orange and purple wrappers for 1d."

Other named sweets and chocolate bars immediately evoke the period "Some popular brands of wrapped sweets of the time included tubes of Lovehearts, Refreshers, Fruit Pastilles, Fruit Gums, Trebor mints or Trebor fruit flavoured sweets, Opal Fruits and Smarties. There were packets of wine gums, Jelly Babies, Basset's Liquorice Allsorts and Dolly Mixtures and chocolate-covered Poppets in cardboard boxes. Favourite chocolate bars were: Milky Way, honeycomb-filled chocolate Crunchies, Milky Bar, Fry's Five Boys, Fudge and Fry's chocolate cream. Fry's also produced a chocolate bar where each segment was filled with a different fruit flavoured cream." "We did have Wrigley's chewing gum and pink bubble-gum. The latter came with cards that you could collect, with pictures of the Beatles."

Rationing

The end of the second world war did not bring an end to food rationing. Families continued to be issued with ration books and had to exchange coupons before they could be served with certain food items. Some form of food rationing was in force until 1954 and in fact, some rations were more meagre after the war than they had been during it. For example, the allowance of cooking fat was reduced from two ounces to one ounce per week, making it difficult to make pastry. The weekly bacon ration was also cut, from four ounces to three. The severe winter weather of the winter of 1946-1947 destroyed crops and resulted in potato rationing. The meat ration in 1951 was five ounces per person per week, hence many families kept rabbits or chickens 'for the pot'. "In the 1940s and 1950s many of our meals were based on starch and carbohydrates to make us feel full and satisfied, such as dumplings, suet pastry, suet puddings, Yorkshire puddings and potatoes. The mainstay of Mum's cooking was the casserole, cooked slowly on top of the oven and often using cheap cuts of meat such as neck of lamb, rabbit or cow heel. As meat was rationed or scarce the casserole would be 'beefed up' with chunks of root vegetables, pearl barley, lentils and split peas."

In the post-war period, it was not just the limited amounts of food allowed that caused problems for the housewife but also the time-consuming queuing that was a result of food shortages. Country relatives would send produce to town-dwelling cousins in order to help supplement the rations. Those eating in restaurants, workers who had their meals in factory canteens and children who could eat dinners at school were able to save their rations. "Vegetarians were given an extra allowance of cheese and my mother registered my younger sister as a vegetarian for this reason!" Despite this provision, vegetarianism, food allergies or other special 'free from' diets were almost unheard of. "We always ate what was put on the table there was never a question, whether we liked it or not. You ate it or went hungry and never left food on your plate." "There was never any mention of particular foods being good or bad for us. We ate a little of everything and we were expected to eat what was put in front of us." "We had no idea that certain foods were to be avoided in large quantities or that processed foods were poorer."

Dripping might replace rationed butter as an accompaniment to bread. "Tea after school was usually 'bread and scrape',[3] sometimes dripping and rarely, a slice of cake." "Bread came off ration in 1948 but was replaced with the 'National Loaf', which was made with the wholemeal and husks; people longed for white bread. When National Bread was abolished, in 1956, there was virtually no demand for wholemeal bread, as everyone wanted white." Chocolate biscuits, treacle, jelly and mincemeat were rationed until 1950. Sweet, milky tea was the universal drink but tea rationing went on until 1952 and it was 1953 before sugar, along with eggs, came off ration. Finally, cheese and meat were derestricted in 1954. By this time, government initiatives and agricultural improvements had increased food production dramatically, availability improved and prices began to fall. "National food was issued by the Ministry of Food, such as margarine and dried egg powder and National Dried Milk, used for cooking and for feeding babies. The egg powder was a substitute for fresh eggs, which were in short supply. It was used to make cakes or puddings and to make scrambled eggs or omelettes but these were very rubbery in texture."

Preparing and Storing Food

Food preparation in the 1950s was a lengthy procedure with the aid of few labour-saving devices. An average of seventy five hours per week was spent on housework and a significant proportion of this was taken up with purchasing and preparing food. "There was a cast iron range with an oven heated by the fire and food tended to be stews that cooked in the oven for most of the day." Gas and then electric cookers found their way in to most homes and were cleaner and more versatile than the ranges that they replaced. "Cooking was done on a gas stove; friends cooked on electric stoves and an aunt cooked on a Calor Gas stove in the country, the gas tanks delivered by van." "Frying, usually using dripping not oil, was common, no one would have thought of grilling bacon or sausages. Salt and sugar were used without a thought for, or conception of, the health implications." Gradually gadgets, that might make cooking less arduous, appeared in the kitchen. "We also acquired a pressure cooker and my mum would cook potatoes and vegetables in that for quickness."

"Milk was kept cool in the summer by standing it in cold water in a cool place. My great aunt had a terracotta saucer, filled with water and a bottle shaped cover, which soaked up the water, to keep the milk bottle in. It was kept on the floor in the pantry. The pantry had slate shelves to store perishable food on as they were thought to be cooler." "Our meat was kept in a wire-fronted meat safe, that was hung in a cool place." "The larder was our only storage for fresh foods but we preserved many items; green beans were sliced and stored between layers of rock salt, crushed with a rolling pin. Apples, onions, potatoes, swedes and turnips were carefully stored on beds of peat, the dreaded marrows stored in a dark cupboard and eggs in crocks of isinglass."[4] "Without frozen or canned foods everything was very seasonal. Imported fruits like oranges were only available at Christmas and English fruit and vegetables were only around in season. We looked forward to them arriving in the greengrocers and really enjoyed them. My family have always kept a store cupboard of non-perishable goods: dried fruit, flour, spices, salt." "Preserving, making jams and chutneys or bottling fruit in Kilner jars[5] was a regular activity." "I remember jam-making with old net curtains full of straining fruit, suspended over a pan to drip."

Various cookery books were in fashion during this period, many of which reinforced the prevailing gender stereotypes and expectations that a woman's role was to serve her husband. "I had not taken a great interest in cooking when living at home so as soon as I was married I had to learn very hastily. This I did with the aid of my *Cookery for Girls* by Margaret Laski, (first printed in 1950). The introduction is very patronising, beginning 'Have you ever said, 'I love it when Mother lets me try making something for tea, but Mother's cookery book doesn't always explain exactly what to do?'.....Well, here is the very book for you – written in simple language which you will understand' but it was in fact an excellent book. It was full of good recipes all accompanied by hand drawn and coloured sketches at each step. I have to admit I didn't make use of the more advanced instructions for bottling, making jams, laying the afternoon tea table (complete with cake stand, napkins, tray cloth, doyleys etc.) and how to feed invalids (from beef tea through to soups and steamed fish). These were obviously thought to be necessary skills for young girls. We were also exhorted to 'Keep an eye on the clock' and serve quickly, neatly and punctually."

"We would choose to prepare something interesting and learnt the techniques from books and practice. We particularly liked Elizabeth David's *French Provincial Cooking* and *Mastering the Art of French Cooking* by Julia Child, *The Constance Spry Cookery Book*, *Cooking* by Philip Harben and *The Times Cookery Book*. When we announced our engagement in *The Daily Telegraph* I was sent a plain little book from Stork Margarine called *The Art of Home Cooking* giving basic sensible recipes for cakes and pastries etc. using Stork." "There had always been cookery books but with the end of rationing and the advent of television in most homes, the celebrity chef began to develop. The earliest of these was Philip Harben, a conventional jolly chef in hat and apron but the one who broke the mould was Fanny Craddock, who always cooked in a cocktail dress, full make-up and jewellery and had her husband, Johnny, running around doing all the menial tasks. All the dishes she made seemed to have elaborate garnish or decoration, with swirls of cream and fruit and nut on sweets. Radishes, spring onions, cucumber all had to be cut to form shapes or flowers."

How we ate was also significant. "Meals when I was a girl at home were taken all together round the dining room table." "There were meal times, more or less and we all ate together as a family, unless there was good reason not to. Dad worked shifts so, for example, he would leave work at 2pm and his dinner would have been kept for him and reheated by steaming over a saucepan of water; no microwave. I know this was the norm because I can remember going to friends' houses and their dad's dinner would be steaming away." "If you wanted pudding you ate your dinner. No food was ever wasted and left-overs appeared next day in some other guise." Manners were important and the idea of eating off laps would have been regarded with horror by many however as televisions became commonplace, some families did start to abandon eating at a table.

Eating Out

Going out to a restaurant for a meal was not part of most people's experience in the 1940s and 1950s and food shortages obviously had an impact on restaurant owners. Food that was eaten out was not subject to rations however and there was much resentment that those who could afford to go to restaurants thereby had access to additional food supplies. In an attempt to counteract this, British Restaurants, were set up by the Ministry of Food in 1942. These provided a three-course meal for 9d and no coupons were required; they remained in operation until 1947.

Although the term was not used until the end of our period, there were 'take-away' opportunities, primarily fish and chip shops. These and other street food stalls, seem to have been used as a source of special treats, rather than substitutes for home-cooked meals. So people would pick up a portion of chips on the way home from an outing, rather than go and get fish and chips to save preparing dinner at home. Pubs were primarily for drinking, not eating and opening hours were restricted. Licensing laws meant that pubs opened at lunch time and again in the evening but they had to shut during the afternoons. 'Last orders' was 10.30pm, except on Saturday, when it was 11.00pm. In some areas of Britain, notably Wales, pubs were shut on Sundays. It was possible to apply for a late or afternoon license for special events.

Tea shops were not new but tended to provide dainty sandwiches, cakes and beverages for the more affluent. These were being joined by the rise of the café, with its associations with youth culture. In 1954, the first Wimpy Bars, selling burgers and chips, opened under the remit of Lyons' Corner House. Eating out became more popular during the 1960s. "There were also pub meals available then, including chicken and chips or scampi and chips 'in the basket' and the sixties saw the growth of speciality eating pubs like Berni Inns, where for 12s 6d you could have a three course meal, typically melon boat or prawn cocktail, followed by fish, gammon or steak and chips, with Black Forest gateau, ice cream or cheese and biscuits to finish. There was also a limited wine list and in the early sixties we tentatively tried out cheaper bottles of wine at home, such as Blue Nun, Bulls Blood, or Niersteiner Domtal. By the end of the sixties most of us had learned to be a little more discerning!" Other popular wines were Liebfraumilch and Mateus Rosé; the latter came in unusually shaped bottles that were often turned into table lamps.

"We ate out sometimes with my husband's Luncheon Vouchers[6] and went to Lyons' Corner House, where for 5s you could have soup, as much salad, including quiche and ham, as you could eat and a pie with ice cream." "We also went out to eat on special occasions, for example, my twenty-first birthday (1967) was celebrated, by the two of us only, with a meal at a pub. I remember we paid £5 per head for our three-course meal which included Gaelic coffee but we didn't have wine."

Shopping

Food shopping was a huge part of family life. Not only was about a third of a working family's income spent on food in 1950 but shopping was a frequent activity. The difficulties of keeping food fresh meant that many housewives shopped daily, at least until they acquired a fridge. In 1950, only three percent of the population had managed to save enough money to purchase a fridge, the cost of which might represent ten weeks' wages. Until car-ownership became common, purchases were also limited by what you could carry, or put into a wheeled shopping basket, old pram or push chair. This meant that even once the storage problem was solved, frequent shopping trips were still necessary. "We didn't have a car, so I had to shop on two consecutive days because I had to carry the shopping home on the bus." Some shops were willing to deliver to customers' homes. This was usually done by teenaged boys riding bicycles with large baskets on the front. A few corner shops might open on a Sunday but they were only allowed to sell a restricted range of goods. In general, shopping was not a Sunday activity. Legislation, designed to help shop workers, also instead on half-day closing once a week. All the shops in a particular town had early closing day on the same day, usually Tuesday, Wednesday or Thursday.

As well as shops who delivered what you had chosen during a visit to the store, some foods were routinely delivered to your door as part of a round. "Milk was left daily by the milkman. Mum would leave a note out if there was any change to the usual daily order and paid him weekly when he knocked for his money. There was gold top, with all the cream and silver top milk, with less cream content, all in pint glass bottles. We might find the birds had pecked a hole in the foil top to drink the cream off the top of the milk." "The milkman delivered every single day, in his green coloured Morris 1000 van, including Christmas day and Easter Sunday, although in later years, after George had retired and his milk round was taken over, that all changed and the normal order was doubled up on a Saturday, or bank holidays and also Christmas Eve, so that the milkman could have the relevant day off." Milkmen often delivered other dairy items and sometimes bread or carbonated drinks, although the latter were usually the preserve of the Corona man. "We had cockles or winkles that were bought from the man who came round on his bike on a Sunday afternoon. The milk was delivered by horse and cart." "A local firm, Sergeants, made their own ice cream and came round the village in a van at Sunday dinner time. We raced out with a bowl into which was placed a spoonful of ice cream, one for each of us." Many recalled the ice cream van passing through the locality, with it's chimes ringing out to let potential customers know that it was in the area.

The paper-boy was another regular visitor to all but the most remote homes and many people ordered their daily paper and magazines from the newsagent, for home delivery. Some might offer a twice daily service, so that evening papers could be provided as well. Certain newspapers reflected particular political standpoints and stereotypical associations between newspapers and their readership did have a basis in truth. "The professional classes might be more likely to read *The Times* or *The Telegraph*, whereas *The Sun* (famous for its pictures of topless models on page three) and *The Mirror* were regarded as working class papers. *The News of the World* was a widely read Sunday paper, notorious for its focus on sexual scandals and the lives of celebrities."

Except in very isolated areas, it would be possible to purchase most everyday food items at a shop that was within easy walking distance. There was the local High Street, with its comprehensive range of food and other shops and there was the 'corner shop', frequently literally sited on a corner, at the end of a row of houses, which sold practically everything that might be required on a regular basis. Apart from these, very small, very local, 'general stores', most shops specialised. As regards food, there would be the butcher, the baker, the grocer selling dried goods and tins and the greengrocer to provide fruit and vegetables. There might also be a dairy, selling milk, butter, cheese and eggs and a fishmonger. Markets, typically held weekly, provided another chance to purchase food, often at prices that were cheaper than those in the shops. Fruit and vegetables were commonly bought at markets but there might also be meat or fish markets. Other salesmen might have individual stalls selling take-away pies, beverages or chestnuts to passers-by in the street. "Sometimes on a Saturday we had a pint of shrimps bought from a stall in the High Street. We had to shell them ourselves but they were lovely."

Shops all had a very individual feel and most shopkeepers knew their customers by name. "During the hostilities people had to elect the butcher, grocers etc. that they wanted to use, so as to ensure foodstuffs were fairly distributed. Often these choices were adhered to after it was no longer necessary." Goods would be weighed and packaged for each customer in turn. "There were big slabs of butter in the earliest days from which pieces were cut and placed in waxed paper and also cheese was the same. Later it came pre-packed and we had Summer County Margarine and Anchor Butter." "Salt came in a large block about a foot long and four inches across. My job was to chop it up with the bread saw and put it in the salt jar." "Our Sainsbury's in those days was what we would now call a Delicatessen, selling cold meats and cheese, with shelves containing a very sparse array of tins of things like spam[7] and tongue. I never liked Sainsbury's, mainly I think because it was tiled and shady."

Most shops displayed their wares openly, so huge joints of meat would be hung up outside butchers' shops. "In those days all butchers had sawdust on the floor and there was a very distinctive smell." "Meat was not packeted, so you had to know what cut to ask for." "The grocer's floor was covered in large sacks of flour, sugar, biscuits, and dried fruit. Vinegar was dispensed from a barrel into the bottle you had taken with you. The loose goods were weighed out and put into brown paper bags, the grocer made a hand written list of the purchases and added up the cost. If it was too much to carry, the grocer had a delivery boy as did the butcher. They had large black bicycles with a huge basket on the front. Milk was delivered loose from the farms in churns. The milk was ladled out into your enamel jug. The farmer's sons came around with an old van with fruit and veg. and the baker called a couple of times a week." "Many items needed wrapping on the spot, because they were sold loose from a sack, or cut from a whole item, such as a cheese. Cheese was always Cheddar, from Mr Mullins; he would have a large round cylinder of it, wrapped in cheese-cloth and he cut it as required and wrapped it in greaseproof paper. Sugar was scooped from a large sack and weighed and put in a blue paper sugar bag. Biscuits were kept in large biscuit tins, often with transparent lids, so you could see what they were and make your choice. There was a special tin for the broken biscuits, they were sold off cheaply and were quite a good buy."

Although shops might wrap goods, you were expected to provide your own bag or basket. The expectation was that purchases would be made with cash, except for very expensive goods, such as furniture, when a cheque might be written. "Some shops had a cashier who dealt with the money and accounts and there might be flying cylinders on high wires that sent your money to the cashier's office and then returned your change."

Non-food shops on Britain's High Streets did include chains, such as Boot's the Chemist, which then just sold health products and toiletries, W. H. Smith's for books and magazines and Woolworth's, which was famous for sweets, records, toys and miscellaneous items at cheap prices. Large towns had department stores selling clothes and household items but rarely food; these were usually independent stores. The haberdashers sold cotton, ribbons, buttons and other trimmings and there might be a newsagent's, a tobacconist's and an ironmonger, selling pans and do-it-yourself items.

As regards food, the most significant change on the High Street during this period was the rise of the supermarket. Although names, such as Tesco (1924) and Sainsbury (1869) have a long history, the concept of serving yourself and one-stop shopping was still a novelty. The first shops that would be recognisable as 'supermarkets' arrived when the Co-op opened ten 'Q-less shops', in 1947. Chains of supermarkets, on a much smaller scale than today's large stores, selling a variety of goods, really took hold during the 1960s. Until 1964, a practice known as 'resale price maintenance' allowed manufacturers to dictate the price at which shops sold their products. Once this restriction was removed, supermarket chains, with their buying power, were able to discount goods. Lower prices and the convenience of having everything under one roof, began to win over customers, who preferred this to the personal service of the old-style shopping experience. Supermarket chains might also offer the incentives of schemes such as Green Shield Stamps. "Green Shield Stamps and Pink Stamps were given away by Tescos, other stores and petrol stations. You stuck them in a book then could exchange them for 'free' items when you had collected enough." By the very end of the 1960s, towns were creating shopping precincts, along the lines of the American malls. "In 1968, the Whitgift Centre opened. This concept of pedestrianised shopping centres was very new." Shopping had now moved a long way from the dependence on the small, independent, specialist shops of the 1940s High Street.

Growing your own

Many families, in urban as well as rural environments, grew their own food in gardens or on allotments. This was often a necessity, especially in times of food shortages. "As children, we saw where our food came from and knew that it was the result of people's labours. We followed the horse and cart down the street with a bucket and spade and knew that the dung was needed for the garden." The keeping of bees, chickens, rabbits or even pigs, to supplement the diet, was rarer and mostly confined to country-dwellers but still part of many people's lives. "Chickens and ducks were kept to provide eggs and also a pig was kept and killed in the spring. Neighbours would give food scraps to help feed the pig and in return would be given a plate of pig's fry, consisting of liver, kidney, sausages, bacon and suet (whatever needed to be eaten quickly as there was no refrigeration). A piece of bacon or ham would be given later in the year after hanging, drying from the ceiling."

Home production meant home preparation. This could be anything from shelling peas to wringing the necks of chickens and plucking them. "When my parents wanted a chicken to roast Father would go down to the chicken pen to get one. I don't remember him ever killing a chicken in front of me but I was allowed to go and watch him while he plucked the feathers out and got it ready for roasting. Once he had plucked the bird he would bring it into the kitchen and draw the insides out to get it ready for stuffing. When the chicken was prepared he would peel the potatoes that he had grown in the garden."

For some, foraging was essential, especially when rationing was in force. It gradually became more of a leisurely accompaniment to a day out, rather than a necessity. "On Saturdays in the summer, we sometimes went 'cockling' or 'winkling' on the beach when the tide went out. These were soaked in a bucket overnight with a sprinkling of flour 'to encourage them to spit out the sand'. They were then boiled up to eat with bread and marge for Sunday tea, fishing the winkles out of their shells with a pin! Another form of foraging was for blackberries for pies or jam in August and nuts (hazelnuts and chestnuts) and sometimes mushrooms in the autumn. There was also the scrumped[8] apples and pears which my brother and I took from the disused orchard behind the garage two doors away but there wasn't much of this and it was often under ripe!" "My brother caught eels in the local river which Mother jellied." Thus the 'food for free' concept was often a source of supplies that were less mundane, or considered to be a special treat.

Summary

This era took us from ration books to ready meals. It was still regarded as the woman's role to see that meals were put on the table. Male involvement in cooking was unusual, even in families where the wife worked full time. Diets were heavily weighted in favour of carbohydrates and 'filling up the family' was the priority. Certainly at the start of this period, a significant amount of what was eaten was home grown or home produced. As people brought back ideas from foreign holidays, the range of food stuffs began to expand. With the exception of workers' lunches, eating out was still regarded as a rare occurrence, reserved for special occasions.

The arrival of convenience food, which really took hold in the 1960s, was welcomed by most as a labour-saving blessing. Our High Streets and shopping habits were evolving, with the dawn of the self-service supermarket and the beginning of one-stop shopping. Increasing numbers of working women had less time to spend buying food but had acquired fridges and cars, making daily shopping unnecessary. Labour-saving gadgets made food preparation less arduous and pre-prepared foods also meant that the housewife did not have to spend such a large proportion of her time purchasing and cooking food. Expectations were changing and many 1960s' women were becoming increasingly reluctant to devote long hours to producing meals that were cooked from scratch; they might have careers or hobbies to pursue. How food was eaten was also starting to change and becoming less formal; there were glimpses of a future of TV dinners, eaten on laps.

The Brief

Write about food and meals. What made up a typical menu? Refer to snacks and food treats.

Include comments about cooking methods and food storage; mention rationing if applicable.

How much food went uneaten? How was waste regarded?

How often was food shopping done and in what type of shop? What products were delivered to your door? Mention prices if possible.

What food was home grown or home produced? Include fruit and vegetables as well as keeping bees, chickens or rabbits. Mention the use of allotments and foraging for food in the countryside.

Chapter 4 footnotes

[1]   These were small sponge cakes with a thick layer of soft icing on-top.

[2]   This was made from frying up left over vegetables and it frequently featured cabbage.

[3]   A very thin covering of butter. It would be spread on the bread and then all the excess 'scraped' off with the knife.

[4]   Gelatin from the swim bladder of fish. This coated the eggs and prevented bacteria from permeating the shells.

[5]   A glass jar designed for this purpose, which had a glass lid with a rubber seal, that would be held in place by metal clips.

[6]   These tokens were issued, from 1946, by many employers as a tax-free perk of the job. A number of restaurants would agree to accept them in lieu of payment.

[7]   There are numerous suggestions as to the origins of the word spam, which is believed to be an acronym. Amongst these are, 'Specially Processed American Meat' and 'Shoulders of Pork And Ham'. It is a, much reviled, tinned meat product, consisting primarily of spiced pork and ham.

[8]   Fruit that was 'acquired' without the owner's knowledge.

CHAPTER 5

Rags to Riches: work and money

Currency and the Value of Money

This was the time of the guinea, the florin, the 'tanner', the 'bob' and the ten shilling note; when calculating monetary sums required more than an ability to work in multiples of ten. Lsd meant pounds, shillings and pence, not an hallucinogenic drug. There were twelve pence (d) in a shilling (s) and twenty shillings in a pound (£). Coins in circulation (see figure 44) included:

¼d a farthing; this was withdrawn in 1960.

½d the 'happeny'; this was withdrawn in 1969.

1d a penny. A penny was just that, a penny; although you would never say 'one pence', multiples of pennies were referred to as pence, never as a 'pee'. Pence was normally pronounced 'punce' and run together with the number, so 2d would be 'tuppence', not 'two pence'.

These three coins collectively were 'coppers', as that is what they were made from.

3d a twelve-sided, brass coloured coin, known as 'thruppence'.

The remaining coins were silver.

6d sixpence, spelt with the two words put together to make one and pronounced 'sixpunce', referred to as 'a tanner'.

1s a shilling, also called 'a bob'

2s still sometimes referred to as a florin. Whereas 'tanner' and 'bob' were slang, florin was an archaic term.

2s 6d two shillings and sixpence or 'half a crown', although crown coins no longer existed.

Notes in common use were those for ten shillings (also written as 10s or 10/-), a pound (£1) and £5; until 1957 the latter was white.

A guinea had long since ceased to be a coin but equated to £1 1s; luxury items in particular were often priced in guineas.

Although the currency was not decimalised until 1971, new coins were issued from 1968 in preparation for this. Thus the sixpence was replaced with a similar looking 2½p coin, the shilling with 5p and the two shilling coin with one designated 10p.

It is very difficult to equate monetary values of the past with meaningful present-day sums. Average wages can also be misleading. Government figures suggest that the average wage for a male manual worker in 1953 was £9 5s 11d. This was considerably more than that for females, for whom the average was £5 0s 2d. By 1962, these sums had risen to £15 17s 3d for men and £8 0s 10d for women.[1] The following figures relating to earnings for 1960 can be found in Hansard.[2]

Civil Service Clerical Officer	£789 per annum
Civil Service Principal Officer	£2375 per annum
Professional Footballer aged over 20	£8- £20 a week in the playing season
Industries covered by the Ministry of Labour	£14 2s 1d a week

Data from the Office of National Statistics gives £960 as the average household income in 1961. An article in *The Guardian* by Darren Lee, about life in 1962, stated that, "The annual inflation rate was 1.1% ..... and unemployment was negligible. The average house price stood at £2,670..... The average yearly pay was £799."[3]

Varying proportions of household income have been spent on housing, fuel, food, clothes and non-essentials at different times. The following figures have been quoted for 1969:

Food 26.1%
Transport and vehicles 13.9%
Housing 12.4%
Alcohol and tobacco 9.4%
Clothing 8.9%
Services 8.9%
Other goods 7.2%
Fuel 6.6%
Durable household goods 6.3%
Miscellaneous 0.3%[4]

This would vary enormously from family to family, depending on circumstances and disposable income.

Household accounts provided by a participant show annual expenditure for 1951.

	£	s	d
Food, clothing & household expenses	213	11	0
Rent & Rates	68	9	10
Fuel & Lighting	51	2	6
Life & Fire Insurance	59	15	4
Interior decorations & Repairs	17	17	0
Furniture (Nursery)	11	15	0

Newspapers & Professional Periodicals	12	6	9
Hire Purchase (Furniture)	44	5	10
Telephone a/c	7	4	7
Bank charges & Cheques	7	6	6
Allotment rent & outlay	6	2	0
Poultry outlay & food	5	19	8
Subscriptions & donations	5	5	10
Technical books	3	4	6
Balance c/f. 31. Dec.	41	5	8
Total	£555	12	0

A different household spent the following in January 1967:

	£	s	d
Bed	54	18	0
4th Coal	3	10	0
31st Coal	2	2	0
Skull's Plumbers	11	3	0
Parkray Heating system	279	16	0
Car Tax	17	10	0
Car 10,000 mile service	6	4	3
Papers 7/1 to 10/2	1	16	0
Telephone	4	8	1
Electricity	5	19	3
Rates	19	4	6
Vet's bill	3	5	6
House contents insurance	3	15	0

Managing the Family Budget

This was a time when many people, were paid weekly and in cash. Shop and factory workers would certainly not expect to receive a cheque and having a bank account was not universal. Even those who did have access to a cheque book would only use it for expensive items or bills, not for everyday payments or food shopping. Cash machines and credit cards were not introduced until the late 1960s. A common practice would be for the man to pass the majority of his pay-packet to his wife, who was frequently in charge of household finances. "He handed over his weekly pay packet to mother, who gave him spending money." She would then put appropriate amounts of cash in various jars or tins, in anticipation of specific expenses. "My husband would give me a sum of money each week from his wages. I had a pile of coloured, bank, paper money bags, one each for rent, electric, gas, phone, catalogue etc. and I would put an amount in each every week so that it covered the bills when they arrived. I would try not to ask for more from my husband. I used what was left and my family allowance and my wage (I always worked) to pay for the food, clothing, children's bits etc.." Money was not often discussed within families and it was not unusual for a wife to be unaware of her husband's wage. "Whatever money my husband had left in his pocket and I never knew how much that was, he spent as he pleased." "Money always seemed to be a mysterious topic in our family. Money was something my father never talked about. I never really knew whether we were rich or poor and whenever I dared to ask the question I was always told that it was no concern of mine." Although women were often responsible for the bill paying, the ultimate authority was that of the main bread-winner. "Father managed the household expenses with a weekly sum given to Mother to buy food and I think if any of us or Mother needed new clothes or shoes the man of the house had to be asked."

Apart from 'cash under the bed' there were other ways for those without bank accounts to save; Post Office accounts were a favoured option. In the days before the lottery, premium bonds were purchased, with their potential for life-changing returns. Unlike lottery tickets, with premium bonds, you could always reclaim your capital. For this reason, buying premium bonds was seen as saving, not gambling. "Mum also saved for premium bonds for us, you had coupons on Red Wing flour and tea and after you had collected so many, you could apply for a premium bond." The perception was that betting on horse or greyhound races was the preserve of the working classes. The most common form of gambling was 'doing the pools'. This was a method of betting on the outcome of football matches; several companies operated 'pools' and would collect coupons from those who played. The pools man was just one of many callers at the door who needed paying and their coming might cause consternation. "The football pools man collected my Dad's coupon and payment weekly and I think the insurance man also came weekly for payment, as did the tallyman (for payment for goods bought from the catalogue). When money was short, one of us was sent to the door to say, 'Mum's not in', whereas she was really hiding behind a door, or even under the table, with her fingers in her ears and her eyes closed!"

"There were no cheque books or credit cards (usually only professionals had bank accounts) and wages were normally paid in cash weekly, so transactions were 'cash in hand' and such things as milk, bread (both delivered, for convenience of paying as well as shopping) and the rent, were paid weekly, after payday. We paid for gas and electricity by coin-in-the-slot meters and Mum kept the coins in a jug and tried not to spend them on anything else during the week." The gradual change to monthly pay and the increasing use of the cheque book, was beginning by the end of this period but was rarely welcomed. "My father managed the household budget. He gave my mother money for housekeeping each week which she kept in a wooden box on top of one of the living room cupboards. When the utility bills came in she had extra money to cover these and paid in cash at the Gas, Electricity or Water Board offices. This was the way she liked it. When my father was paid monthly into a bank account he tried to show her how to write a cheque but she hated it and he still had to give her cash." "When the company wanted to pay monthly, there had to be a bank account set up; there had been no need before. The first year was a thirteen month arrangement to help people cope with the change."

Working children, who were likely to be still living at home if unmarried, would be expected to make a contribution towards family finances. "I earned £10 a week. After tax this left about £8.15s a week, then I paid my parents £5 a week for my keep and had the remaining £3.15s to pay my fares to work (about 10s a week) and buy clothes and anything else I needed. I opened a bank account with the National Westminster Bank for this, I was interviewed by the manager to make sure I was acceptable."

Some families were vehemently opposed to the use of credit. "We were firmly brought up that you didn't have anything unless you could afford to pay for it, the only exception being a mortgage for a house. You didn't borrow money, or have anything on credit or hire purchase. If you hadn't enough money, you saved up until you had, or did without whatever it was." Despite the lack of credit cards, many families relied on some form of credit to balance the books. This might be the occasional pawning of a valued item, running up credit (or 'tick') at a local shop, or paying for expensive items in installments by a hire purchase agreement, known colloquially as 'the never never'. Catalogue purchases were also a form of credit. A shopkeeper's daughter wrote, "Our regular customers were allowed to 'run a book' whereby everything was written down over the course of a month and the bill settled at the end of that period. This applied to all the villagers, whether they were farm workers, builder's labourers or the 'better off' commuters and land-owners; however, it was always the lower paid villagers who settled their accounts first and the relatively wealthy who had to be reminded to pay their dues!" "I remember our next door neighbour, rather a nervous woman, coming around in tears saying she was hiding from the rent man as her husband would 'kill' her, I think he would probably have hit her, if he found out she didn't have any money left. My mother gave her a gold and garnet pin, just about her only jewellery, to 'pop' at the local pawnbrokers for the necessary rent money."

Credit normally had to be taken out by men. "Buying on credit could not be done by women well into the 1960s and beyond. You had to get your husband's permission and even then you could be refused." "When my mum bought a fitted carpet in 1968 and needed hire purchase my brother-in-law had to be guarantor, even though she was in full time employment managing a factory of sewing machinists and had no other credit." One volunteer wrote that she had to get her father to stand guarantor for a hire purchase agreement, because she was under twenty-one, even though she was earning more than her father. Mortgage arrangements also disregarded the woman. "Around 1960, a maiden aunt with a regular health visitor's salary had experienced considerable difficulty in getting a mortgage in her name." "Obtaining a mortgage then was not as easy as it has been in recent times and entailed an interview with the manager of the building society, who not only asked for the amount of John's annual salary but quizzed us on our future plans as to having children. This was besides the fact that my salary would not be considered when deciding on the amount of the mortgage, (He said that I may give work up at some time in the future). It seemed that we could only borrow two and a half times John's annual salary, which at the time was just over a thousand pounds."

Unexpected expenses could play havoc with carefully balanced budgets. "My parents used the tobacco tin method for budgeting, payday was Friday and in the evening, the money was allocated to the various tins with a special thrupenny bit tin for holiday savings. There was also a magic ten shilling note, which lived in my dad's wallet; the emergency fund! I recall the hurried discussions on a Thursday evening in school term when my brother, who was about seven, had kicked the toe out of his school shoe and a replacement was urgently needed; the ten shilling note was produced and new shoes bought from a nearby late-night shop ready for school next day." If the bread-winner lost their job it was a real crisis. Fortunately, this was a period when unemployment rates were very low and obtaining a new job was normally fairly easy. There was also an abhorrence of being unable to support yourself and your family. "Unemployment was anathema to my parents' generation. When my father was made redundant from the gas works, he was straight down to the employment office and would have taken any job they offered him, no matter what it was, because it would have been better than being unemployed. To be in employment and thus provide for your family was a matter of pride."

Pocket Money

Many children were given small weekly sums of pocket money; sometimes this was in return for performing chores. "Money was always tight at home but I did have pocket money. Pre-teenage this was 6d a week. For this I was expected to help in the house and had my own jobs of cleaning the brass on Fridays and brushing the stairs down every day. I could spend this money how I wanted; 6d could buy a 3d comic and about 2oz of sweets, when they became available, or I could spend it all on Saturday morning pictures.[5] I also saved it sometimes to buy books. Five weeks' pocket money would buy me a copy of a Regent Classic book from Woolworth's."

There were different expectations about what had to be financed from pocket money. "I first had pocket money at the age of eleven when I started secondary school. The sum, I think, was two shillings. I paid my Girl Guide subs which were 2d per week, Saturday morning pictures 6d. I had my own sweet coupons and I would buy sweets on my way to or from school. If I wanted to buy anything else it would have to come out of my pocket money." "I did not have pocket money until

I was about twelve (1948) and this started at one shilling per week and was about two shillings and sixpence (half a crown) when I was sixteen (1952). I did not have to do chores to receive this money but the previous week had to be free of misdemeanours!" "I had pocket money given to me by my mother, from about the age of five. The princely sum of 6d was placed in my excited palm each Saturday morning. I was allowed to walk the one hundred yards with my brother, to the newsagents at the end of our Avenue. I was always clear what I would buy, a delicious, refreshing, Orangemaid ice lolly!"

Occasional gifts of money from visiting relatives, or given as birthday or Christmas presents, were always welcome. "My uncle would give me 2s or even 2s 6d when he came to visit. 2s 6d was great because it would buy a book. If money arrived from far-flung family members it was often in the form of a postal order, which was safer to post than money and could be cashed at the post office."

Some children were expected to save money, either that acquired as presents or a proportion of pocket money. This might be achieved by use of a piggy bank, or perhaps a Post Office account. Many schools ran a scheme whereby National Savings Stamps could be purchased. "I remember that National Savings Stamps were on sale at school; my sister remembers buying some, she thinks spasmodically and I remember selling them, as a teacher, later in the 1960s. (I remember what a pain this was on a Monday morning, when I also had the dinner money to collect and total up and wished the stamps could be sold on a different day!). They had pictures of Prince Charles (2s 6d each) or Princess Anne (6d each) and were stuck in a small book to be cashed later, ideally when the book was full. My sister also remembers the stamps being given as prizes on school sports days!" "I was given a small amount of pocket money every week, although I don't remember any regular tasks or chores to qualify for the money. I know I was very excited and proud when I asked the post office assistant for either a sixpenny or a 2s 6d savings stamp, which was carefully stuck into a small rectangular savings book, although I can't remember what the pocket money was eventually used for."

Jobs for Children

Many school children earned sums of money by doing jobs outside the home. Often this would be an informal arrangement and might well be in contravention of the laws relating to the employment of children that were in force at the time. Jobs included newspaper rounds, collecting empty Corona bottles to return, or selling garden produce 'on the knock', i.e. door to door. "We lived in a holiday area and children from the age of ten or eleven would queue up at the station as the tourists arrived, hoping to get money for transporting suitcases to guest houses using converted prams or pushchairs." Sometimes the children's contribution to the household income was vital. "In October each year local schools closed and all the children, including me, worked at potato picking, earning eight shillings a day. It was back breaking work and the money was given to my mother for house-keeping. I think in 1948 a bill was passed in Parliament stopping child labour. This was met with absolute horror in our village as the money earned was relied on."

In rural areas boys, in particular, would be expected to help with farming or fishing tasks. This might be seen as their contribution to the family business, or might be paid work. Girls also helped with harvesting. "There were traditional jobs performed by school children including potato picking, singling beet, strawberry picking and sprout cutting. Generally you were expected to get yourself to work which would be by walking or on a bike. The furthest I travelled was about three miles on a bicycle before and after work. I think the day's wages for me in about 1965 was 10s."

Many teenaged girls worked in shops or cafés before leaving school. "I started a Saturday job at Woolworth's as soon as I was fifteen. I also worked for one summer school holiday too. The pay was eight shillings for the Saturday." "When I was fourteen I got a job in the local grocer's. It was after school every weekday, from 4.30 to 6.00pm. I was paid half a crown a day. So on a Friday I got 12s 6d and on Saturday I spent half of it on the latest hit record at 6s 3d." "For about three and a half hours work, spent up to my elbows in hot, greasy water, I was paid the princely sum of 7s 6d, quite a lot of money for me in those days, at least a 45 rpm[6] single a week!"

Girls who would now be regarded as children themselves were employed as babysitters. "When I was eleven years old I baby-sat for local couple on Saturday nights. They paid me two shillings which seemed fantastic. The children were very young and slept most of the time." "When I was about ten/eleven years old I used to look after very young twins, taking them out for walks in their twin pushchair to give their hard working mum a break. I didn't get money for this but as the mum was a hairdresser, I had a most awful perm from time to time!" Some were entrepreneurial with their baby-sitting services. "We charged two shillings per hour and we had a massive response, often being double-booked and having a baby-sitting job each on the same evening, as well as having to pass on our bookings to other local girls if necessary. We must have done a good job as our 'clients' often recommended us to their friends too, so we built up quite a clientele. Despite our claiming to be responsible, experienced child-minders we in fact had had very little to do with young children and absolutely nothing to do with babies but luckily for us and for the parents and their children, our charges were usually asleep and settled when we arrived and rarely woke while they were in our care. Just as well really as we were invariably on the home-owner's phone to our friends, reading their 'naughty' books such as *Lady Chatterley's Lover* as I recall, or smoking our illicit menthol cigarettes and hiding the dog-ends and tell-tale ash in matchboxes to drop in the litter bin on our way home, or next day if we were offered a lift."

Working Women

This was still a time when many unmarried women sought a job, rather than a career, as the expectation was that this was a stop-gap between school and marriage. "My best friend learnt typing and shorthand at her secondary modern school but found that factory work was more lucrative. She changed jobs frequently but was never out of work. Neither of us gave much thought to the future, vaguely assuming that we would marry, have children and not continue to work full time." "At school we had a careers interview; I said I would like to train to be a journalist. The teacher laughed and said that it was not likely to happen and I should be happy to have an office job rather than a career. I was fifteen years of age so didn't argue, thinking he was probably right and considering I had learned office skills from the age of thirteen, these skills would keep me in work. Our school was next door to *The Barnsley Chronicle*, perhaps I should have called in and asked whether there would be any way I could get a job there. The reason I did not approach them is that I did not want to be laughed at again."

Although many married women did supplement the family income in some way, full-time work for married women was still thought of as unusual, especially when the children were small. "When my school friend's mother started work in one of the shops in the village a lot of negative things were said, especially about her husband. I knew he came in for a lot of criticism for not being able to provide for his family. There were some people who thought it was disgusting that he had sent her out to work." "I was often asked if my husband 'allowed' me to work. I would smile broadly and say, 'Yes and I allow him to work too'." "My first name is also used by males, so sometimes there was confusion. One of my favourite encounters on the phone was with a man who asked to speak to Mr M****. I explained that it was probably me he wanted to speak to and I was Mrs M****. 'Oh', he said, 'Are you the Director?' 'Yes,' I replied and then he said 'And are you a woman?' I delighted in responding by saying, 'Well, I was the last time I looked'."

Most women who did work took jobs that fitted in with their families; this often meant menial and poorly paid work. "I did early morning cleaning (4.00am – 7.00am), bar maid, forecourt attendant, delivering newspapers and leaflets and knitting Aran sweaters. My husband and I often crossed at the front door but my children went on all the school trips, including two of them on educational cruises. One job was manning a washing-up machine at the cattle market. I reeked of cooking oil when I finished and walked home rather than stink the bus out." Some did piece-work at home. "In 1968 mum took up home working. She worked for a local lampshade maker, making up the shades. She would have to bind the frames and then fit and stitch pre-sewn shades onto the frame. I would help her to bind the frames. I remember she didn't get very much for each shade. I think it was 4s for the smallest up to 10s for a standard lamp shade." "In 1967, both my mother and my aunt next door took on evening work of an unusual sort. The London Rubber Company, of Durex fame, employed lots of women on a part time basis and they joined these ranks. My mother's job was to test the Durex on a machine, i.e. blow it up to check it didn't have any holes."

Women were discriminated against in the workplace but this was not generally seen as unacceptable. Job adverts could specify whether they wanted male or female employees and a woman's pay might be as little as half that of a man doing the same job. "It was generally accepted that female wages would be lower than those of their male counterparts but the beginning of discontent that this engendered was just starting to become apparent. One married couple were incensed when they realised that her salary was less than her husband's, even though she was his line manager!" Some employers expected women to resign on marriage. The civil service had officially removed the bar on equal opportunities for married women in 1946 but attitudes were slow to change. "My mother-in-law was quite high up in the civil service but left as soon as she married in 1952." "It was usual at this time for women to leave work if they became pregnant. There was no maternity provision or right to return to your job once you had a baby. Also, unlike today when women work to very near their confinement date, it was usual for women to leave work when they were about six months pregnant; pregnancy was still something to be hidden from view. If you wanted to come back to work after having a family, you had to start again by applying for a job."

One of the traditional employments for women was secretarial work and young ladies struggled with an increasing variety of office equipment. "I would take shorthand notes and type up letters throughout the day on an Imperial 66 typewriter. Any copies needed were on carbon paper, so it was essential not to make mistakes or they needed to be re-typed. This was in the days before computers or even Tippex. Neither did we have photocopiers, fax machines or calculators, although we did use a book called *Ready Reckoners* to help calculate charges for quantities of items being invoiced." "In the basement a room was set aside for the Gestetner machine. Minutes, programmes and other papers were typed onto flimsy, waxy paper, backed with a carbon sheet and a backing sheet, which when the typewriter was used would pierce the flimsy sheet so making the master for printing. If you made a mistake you had to use a pink fluid that smelled like nail varnish to block the piercing, wait for it to dry and then make the correction; a very tedious process." Telex machines, using similar technology to the telegraph, would deliver printed messages on long strips of paper. Although fax machines, which allowed a document to be copied in one location and sent through the telephone network to be printed at the other, had been invented, they were not in general use until the 1970s. Xerox's 'easy to use' 914 photocopier became available in 1959; most photocopiers were cumbersome objects that printed on to rolls of smelly, shiny paper. Secretarial skills were considered to be a passport to a job and there was no shortage of available of opportunities in offices. "It was very easy to find temporary work if you had a secretarial training and experience and I worked in a variety of places."

Grammar schools might encourage their pupils to consider training for a profession and secretarial or shop work was regarded as inappropriate. "At Camden School for Girls (Frances Mary Buss Foundation) there was a formula and if you were seen to be bright you would be encouraged to become a teacher and go to teacher training college, the middling to train as nurses and the not so bright to train as secretaries." "Our teachers used to threaten us when we were on the run-up to 'O' Levels, 'If you don't pass your exams, you'll end up behind the counter at Woolworth's!' Which, for a grammar school girl, was clearly considered to be 'A Fate Worse Than Death'."

The World of Work

"In a time of near full employment, it was comparatively easy to get a job. School leavers might work for the same employer as their parents, or hear of an opening through family or friends. Alternatively you looked in the local paper, or on notice boards, for news of vacancies, only resorting to the Labour Exchange[7] in desperate cases." Parents might have a considerable influence on their children's job opportunities. "I had wanted to go to Teacher Training College and become a teacher of English and Geography but my father refused to allow this, insisting that I join the Civil Service and do a 'respectable' job until such time as I married and of course, I had no option but to do as I was told." Written applications might consist of a brief letter, or you were interviewed by your prospective employer. "In those days it was considered the right thing to do to dress formally for interviews. So, I had to buy a suit, hat and gloves and a pair of court shoes." Sometimes however all that was needed was an informal chat because you or your family were known and there were plenty of vacancies.

Working conditions varied. The traditional office hours were 9.00am to 5.00pm with an hour for lunch. Paid holiday was restricted to two or three weeks a year, plus bank holidays and flexi-time[8] was not yet invented. Many industrial towns had a 'Wakes Week', when all the local factories shut down at the same time and holidays had to be taken then. Some companies treated their employees very well. "The company was very relaxed about many things. I had an extra week's holiday because I used one for Girl Guide camp and this was the same for Scouting or Territorial Army leaders." "One of the perks of working in London was Luncheon Vouchers, which were part of any salary negotiation, they were valued at 2s 6d in the main, although I think there were higher value ones but I never managed to get them. We used to save them up and then go out for a posh meal and pay with our wad of vouchers."

Although aggressive trade union activity is more often associated with the 1970s, trade unions were working to improve conditions and there were some highly publicised strikes. In 1956, workers at British Motors' plant at Longbridge went on strike for six weeks following large scale redundancies. The following year the Amalgamated Engineering Union secured wage increases for engineers and shipbuilders. In 1958, it was the turn of the Transport and General Workers' Union, who organised a London bus strike. There were between nine and ten million union members in the 1950s, nearly half the working population.[9] "We all had to join the Printers' Union and were obliged to attend one union meeting a year after work. These were deadly dull and seemed to consist of middle-aged men calling each other 'brother' and spouting endlessly. There were no female 'officers' the only women there were us poor typists. Union dues were collected weekly by a man who came round the offices."

Seniority was important in most workplaces. "Clerical staff got a single-pedestal desk and a chair without arms and a shared extension on the switchboard. Admin. staff got a double pedestal desk and a chair with no arms. Executive staff got a double pedestal desk, a chair with arms and their own extension telephone. Executive staff in charge of a section sat at the top of the room containing their staff and furthest from the door." "Although it was comparatively easy to change jobs, promotion within the same company would often mean waiting for a retirement, when everyone moved up one."

Some participants were able to provide specific detail about wages. "In 1959, a newly qualified male teacher, having completed a two year certificate course, would earn £475 a year, females earned £430. The men's wages increased by £25 for every year's service, whereas that of the women only increased by £20, so the differential was increasingly wide." Nurses reported a monthly salary of £6 during the first year, rising to £7 in the second year and £9 in the third. Their accommodation, food and uniform was also provided; they were paid monthly in cash. A letter of 1965 reads, "I can give you some proper facts about fishermen's earnings in Brixham now. I had it from the skipper of one of the small trawlers working out of Brixham at present. The first ship grossed £400 for that (part) week and the full following week, the skipper receives 8% of that figure, that would be £32 for his two weeks' pay, his crew gets 6% so theirs would be £24. She was about the top earner that fortnight. Now the *Concord*, she was working from Newlyn, she grossed £180 one week and £120 the second week, that's £300 for the fortnight. Skipper £24 crew £18. Of course you know enough about fishing and trawling to know that earnings vary more than in any calling." In January 1964 a farm worker was being paid 5s 2d per hour, with overtime paid at 7s 1d per hour, which rose to 6s 9d per hour in 1967, with overtime at 9s."

Summary

Cash was king in the post-war years. Wages were normally in cash and all but the largest payments were made in a similar way. The use of credit, although not the credit card, was frequently the only way to make ends meet. Volunteers gave the impression that even families where the wage-earner was in a higher status job had to be careful to live within their means. For some families, the smallest unexpected expense had serious consequences for a carefully balanced budget. Saving was seen as desirable but this was just as likely to be under the mattress as in the bank and many did not have the disposable income to save.

Unlike their parents, who might be expected to have a job for life, those new to the world of work after the second world war, had the luxury of plenty of job opportunities and might move to new employment frequently. This did not normally mean a change of occupation and most stuck to the same kind of work; career changes or re-training in a completely new field were rare. Women's work choices were restricted by societal expectations and married women were still likely to sacrifice career for family. Women did not enjoy, nor for the most part did they expect to enjoy, equal opportunities with men.

The Brief

Write about the world of work, your own and that of the bread winner(s) in the family.

Did you have pocket money/an allowance before you were old enough to work? How much was this and what was it expected to cover e.g if you had an allowance as a teenager were you expected to buy all your clothes from this? Were chores expected in return for pocket money? Mention childhood savings.

Consider work for school children. Was it expected that teenagers should have a Saturday or holiday job? What type of work might that be? Include work done within the family or for a family business. Were you expected to contribute to the family budget from any earnings from Saturday/holiday jobs or paper rounds?

Who managed the family budget? Was this rigorously adhered to or was budgeting more casual? Who contributed to the family income? Were wage earning teenagers expected to contribute to the family budget, if so, to what extent? Were pawn shops, loans or credit part of the family's financial management strategy?

When it comes to permanent work, was their a wide choice of jobs, or was a certain career path expected? Was there any careers advice? Was it expected that a job would be for life? How easy was it to change jobs/ careers?

For each job, your own or that of the family bread winner(s), describe as much of the following as you can:- interview process, training, conditions, duties, wages, uniform, tools.

Comment on retirement and pensions.

What were the attitudes to unemployment and to working women?

Highlight any gender differences in the above points.

Chapter 5 footnotes

[1]   House of Commons Debate 21 March 1963 Hansard vol 674 cc100-1W via http://hansard.millbanksystems.com/written_answers/1963/mar/21/manual-workers-average-weekly-earnings.

[2]   House of Commons Debate 29 November 1960 Hansard vol 631 cc42-3W via http://hansard.millbanksystems.com/written_answers/1960/nov/29/national-average-wages.

[3]   Lee, Darren Life in 1962 (The Guardian 13 January 2004) accessed via http://www.theguardian.com/uk/2004/jan/13/past.comment.

[4]   Williams, Sally Family Finance: price comparison (Daily Telegraph 12 January 2010) accessed via http://www.telegraph.co.uk/finance/personalfinance/6973290/Family-finance-price-comparison.html.

[5]   The 'pictures' was the cinema; also sometimes referred to as 'the flicks'.

[6]   45s first appeared in 1949 to replace the old 78 records. This new format of 'single' record needed to be played at 45 revolutions per minute (rpm). LPs, with multiple tracks were played at 33rpm.

[7]   The forerunner of the Job Centre.

[8]   The trademark 'Flextime' was registered by the Haller company in 1971.

[9]   TUC History Online www.unionhistory.info/timeline/timeline.php.

CHAPTER 6

School Days: education

The School System

Not surprisingly, the education system did not escape the wave of change that swept Britain between 1946 and 1969. The school leaving age was raised from fourteen to fifteen in 1947 and was set to rise again, to sixteen, in 1972. Statutory education began at the age of five, so pupils usually started school at the beginning of the term closest to their fifth birthday. The wide-ranging, 1944 Butler Education Act had required local authorities to provide nursery education for the under-fives but attendance at a nursery was very unusual. Pre-school education was more likely for those who went to nursery as a preliminary to being enrolled at an associated private school. With the exception of some private schools, boys and girls were normally taught together at primary level. After the age of eleven, single sex schools were more common and grammar schools were almost exclusively segregated.

The divisions of the school year have remained largely unchanged since the start of compulsory education in 1870. The year began in September and was divided into three terms of roughly thirteen weeks each, with private schools normally having shorter terms. This might be compensated for by longer school days and Saturday morning classes. Each term was usually divided by a week long 'half-term' midway through. There would be a two week holiday at Christmas and Easter and six weeks off in the summer. Easter weekend was traditionally in the middle of the two week Easter holidays, meaning that the spring and summer terms might be of unequal length, depending upon the date that Easter fell.

In 1951, General Certificates of Education (GCEs) in the form of 'O' (ordinary) levels and 'A' (advanced) levels replaced the School Certificate. School Certificates could be gained in a variety of subjects and reaching the required standard in the appropriate range of subjects led to 'Matriculation', an essential qualification for university entrance. "In July 1950 I passed the Cambridge School Certificate with credits in English language, English literature, British and European history, French, elementary mathematics and biology, with passes in geography and art. This meant I had reached Matriculation standard." The new GCE examinations were designed for the top twenty percent of the ability range and students typically sat eight subjects at 'O' level when they were sixteen, some going on to sit three 'A' levels two years later. Those wishing to attend university needed to ensure that

117

their 'O' levels included, English, mathematics, a science, a foreign language and either history or geography. The top universities also expected an 'O' level pass in Latin. Although it was possible to sit 'O' levels in less traditionally academic subjects, such as needlework or domestic science, these were often frowned upon as being somehow less acceptable. Assessment was by a terminal examination at the end of two years' study. Almost all subjects required essay style answers to three or four questions, normally with some element of choice. 'A' level papers, typically two or three per subject, were usually three hours long; 'O' level examinations might take two hours. Intensive revision was required for success in these examinations. "I remember learning pages of quotations for my English Literature and History 'A' levels." Grading was done using a curve of natural distribution, so a fixed percentage of candidates were destined to fail. At 'A' level, only the top ten percent of candidates were awarded the highest A grade and thirty percent of entrants failed to achieve any form of 'A' level pass.[1]

GCE examinations were normally taken at the ages of sixteen and eighteen, so were not part of the lives of those whose education ended at the statutory school leaving age. It was still the exception, especially for girls, to continue with post-compulsory education. In 1965, Certificates of Secondary Education (CSEs) were introduced, designed for the less able pupils attending secondary modern schools. A grade 1 at CSE (the top grade) was considered to be equivalent to an 'O' level pass. These too were taken at the age of sixteen, so necessitated staying on at school for an additional year.

In 1944, the 'tripartite' system of secondary education had been cast in the tablets of stone that were the clauses of Butler's Education Act. Prior to this, the majority of children attended the same school for the whole of their school career. The new system was underpinned by the principle of selection at the age of eleven, by means of the 'eleven plus' examination. The results of this test determined the school to which pupils would be sent. The twenty percent of pupils who performed best were destined for a grammar school education and the majority of the others for a 'secondary modern'. In between were the technical secondary schools, who were supposed to offer a more practical curriculum. This third strand of the system, never took more than five percent of pupils and was soon largely subsumed by the other two providers of secondary education. "For bright children the fifties and early sixties were a Golden Age of education. Those who passed the eleven plus exam and went on to grammar school, received a traditional, thorough and sometimes inspirational education, as well as the opportunity to study the arts and music and to take part in competitive sport. The brightest percentage of these pupils, who then went on to university, had their tuition fees paid for by the state and received a (means-tested) maintenance grant from the Local Authority, which did not have to be repaid. For those who failed the eleven plus and went on to a secondary modern school, expectations were lower and career prospects narrower. Many felt written off at the age of eleven. The technical schools, which were intended to teach practical and vocational subjects to the less academically-minded children mostly did not materialise." In some areas, children were allocated to grammar schools considerable distances away, in order that they could attend the one that was deemed to be correct for their level of ability; secondary moderns were more likely to be closer at hand.

The eleven plus was sat in January and consisted of papers in English, including exercises in grammar and punctuation, comprehension and essay writing; Arithmetic and a third paper, which was basically an IQ test. The main failing of the eleven plus was that levels of coaching dramatically influenced performance. Some people reported intensive 'teaching to the test', whilst for others the eleven plus came as a complete surprise, with no preparation having been done. "Each week, under the teacher's watchful eye we did practice papers for the eleven plus. I later found out that the B stream had no practice whatsoever." Some parents, perhaps encouraged by teachers in schools for whom results mattered, purchased practice papers for their offspring, so the drilling continued at home. "J. did a fair number of tests, mainly Arithmetic. I paid her 1s 9d for each of them. On the day before August Bank Holiday, I told her that since the next day was August Bank Holiday she could do an English test instead! She was thrilled to bits! (Actually she got 91%). She used the *Scholarship Home Tutor* published by Odhams. She always grumbled mightily and on one occasion she produced tears but mostly she got 60% or 70%." Others remained in a state of blissful oblivion that might affect the rest of their lives. "Our class spent weeks before the eleven plus rehearsing a play to celebrate the Coronation of Queen Elizabeth II. Even at the time, I could not understand what Samuel Pepys and King Charles II had to do with events in the 1950s. The outcome was that we had lost a large amount of lessons and were given absolutely no idea of what the eleven plus was about. For example, we had never been able to answer 'Don't know', nor had we used tick boxes. As a final consequence nobody passed the exam that year, although the average pass rate was fifteen children."

"At age 11 years, it was time for the eleven plus exam. I did fine until it got to the arithmetic. Most of that was O.K., as I used my fingers to count on but when it came to the applied stuff I couldn't cope. We had not done much of this before and when the paper asked if it took one man three days to dig a hole how many days would it take for two men to dig the hole? Well, I just didn't have enough information! My poor brain was thinking about what if it rained? Would they carry on digging, because the hole would fill up with water? Or maybe they could put a sort of tent over it to keep the rain out etc. etc.."

Some of the eleven plus questions would seem daunting to the modern eleven year old. One year, candidates were expected to write a paragraph about four of the following: "Everest, Westminster Abbey, The Gothic, William Shakespeare, Queen Salote and The Maoris". Longer essay titles included: "The Adventure of a Submarine", "An Ant's Adventures in Crossing a Garden", "A Market Day in a

Country Town" and "Eggs". The Arithmetic papers required pupils to solve problems such as, "If a motorcar covers a distance of 42 miles in 1½ hours, how long at the same rate should it take to complete a journey of 147 miles?". Calculations ranged from, "Divide 2268 by 78" to "7·42 - 0·156 + 8·007".

Some areas became sensitive to the inadequacies of the system. "Continuing unhappiness with the eleven plus saw the West Riding introduce what became known as the 'Thorne Scheme', from the mid-1950s. This was a means of allocating grammar school places to the ablest primary school children on the basis of teachers' recommendations. This scheme, which was judged to be no less reliable than a formal examination, was operational in two-thirds of the county by 1964."[2]

The most sweeping educational change of this period was the introduction of the comprehensive system, which began being rolled out in 1965. This put an end to the eleven plus in all but a few areas. Instead, at the age of eleven, children transferred to a mixed ability comprehensive school. Although these schools normally adopted a rigorous system of 'setting', or sub-dividing by ability, crossing those divides was at least possible, whereas, under the previous regime, one was permanently labelled at the age of eleven.

Streaming was not new and had gone on at both primary and secondary level under the old system. "From the age of eight, in the second year (today's year four), we were set by ability. These sets were cast in stone and I don't remember anyone moving from one set to the other. They weren't called the A and B stream but I think we were all aware that that is what they were." Once streaming was in place, "there was no attempt at differentiation; teachers delivered their material and pupils either got it or didn't." "We were seated according to ability. It was never openly acknowledged but those in the back three rows were expected to gain places at the most prestigious grammar schools." "At the end of the school year (aged twelve), following exams, we were streamed according to results. This could have a considerable effect on your future ambitions. Those who entered Lower 4A would learn Latin and French, Lower 4B would learn German and French, whilst forms Lower 4C and 4D would just learn French. You needed to have the ability to do translations in two languages to get into an Oxford College, even for science subjects." "There were three streams in the school, according to ability. The top stream did Latin, the middle stream did Spanish and the third stream did Domestic Science. There was little if any movement between streams. In the Latin stream we did a little cooking and sewing in the first year but after that we only did academic subjects."

For all its failings, the eleven plus did provide educational opportunities for those whose backgrounds may once have held them back. "The Grammar School had four or five classes for each year up to the age of sixteen. I think they had more or less sorted us ability wise, as my class were all about the same level. The majority of us were from the local council estates and thinking back now, it was an excellent opportunity for us to achieve something in our lives, which our parents could only dream of." There was however a stigma attached to attending both grammar and secondary modern schools. Grammar school girls from poorer backgrounds found themselves neither fish nor fowl and families struggled to afford uniforms, equipment and school trips. Anyone who attended a grammar school was considered 'snobbish' or 'posh' by those who did not. Secondary school pupils might be looked down upon by their grammar school counterparts. The eleven plus system allowed some of the brightest pupils to attend what were essentially private schools under the 'direct grant' system, whereby the council paid the fees. This sometimes led to resentment and differentiation between fee paying and 'free place' students.

Memories of private and boarding schools reveal an education that was often more formal and academic than that provided by many of the state schools. At primary level though, private education might be delivered by unqualified, well-meaning ladies, in a fashion that could lead to an unbalanced curriculum. "The head teacher 'entertained' us by putting on the radio for schools programmes, whilst she sat at her desk knitting her stockings." "There was little on offer beyond the 'three Rs'[3] but my goodness were they well taught. I did not repeat the maths I learnt as an infant until I was in secondary school. We all, whatever our ability, learnt our tables up to twenty twenties. The teacher would call out 'seventeen eighteens' and point at someone who would give the answer. I don't remember anyone not knowing instantly. The only form of physical activity was skipping in the concrete playground, with the teachers turning the ends of the rope. I don't recall anything that could constitute, science, geography or history. 'Art', for infants only, consisted of colouring in Bible texts." "Once a year, in early summer, the whole school was allowed into the headmaster's private garden (which was normally out-of-bounds). The teachers were there too and the purpose of this unusual occurrence was for the staff and the headmaster in particular, to be able to listen to a horse race being broadcast on the radio. (It would have been the Derby, I think). Even as I write, the whole thing seems peculiar, couldn't the headmaster have delegated his classes for the afternoon? Or why would he think his pupils, aged between five and twelve, would be interested in a horse race? Did he have significant money resting on the result? Maybe it just highlights the eccentric teaching philosophy of a small private school in those pre-curriculum days."

Boarding school regimes were rigid. "The bell went at 6.45 and you had to get up at seven. There was a five-minute quiet time, when we were meant to say our prayers! Then it was prep time or music practice until breakfast at eight. School started at nine. We were back for tea at four when we could eat as much bread and jam as we liked, with cake at weekends. Prep was at 4.40 and piano practice for half an hour. We had fifteen minutes Chapel at 6.40; I often played the piano for the hymn. Supper at seven was a light meal but we could eat as much bread and butter as we liked afterwards with jam that we had brought from home. After that, in the common room, we could have sweets or chocolate from our tuck boxes. The young ones went to bed early and that time got later as we went up the years." "At this Catholic boarding school the girls in the senior school were of mixed ability and nationality, some being children of diplomats and army officers. This was comprehensive education in every sense. The equipment list was specific, including knicker liners and twelve pairs of shoes for differing uses, silver Christening mugs and cutlery, plus a pair of sheets."

Termly fees, quoted for day pupils at private junior schools in the 1940s, ranged from £3 to £6. Fees for boarders at a minor prep school in the 1950s were £70-£150 a term. "The fees (for a junior day school) started at £5 15s 6d a term for a full day for a five year old and increased with the child's age. There was an extra charge of 5s for text books, stationery and handwork materials. The Kindergarten (mornings only) cost £4 14s 6d and they only paid 3s 6d for their handwork. Extras were on a sliding scale. Music lessons cost two guineas for twenty half-hour lessons and group dancing and elocution lessons cost a guinea for ten lessons. Swimming cost 12s 6d per term (including transport and tuition). At lunch time you could have two-thirds of a pint of hot milk at 6d a week or cold milk at 5d a week. You could go for a third of a pint of hot or cold milk at half price but it is not clear if these prices included the lunch as well, probably not."

Unless a family member attended, special schools were not something that the general public were aware of. Integration of those with learning difficulties or physical disabilities was unheard of and even quite mild physical problems would result in special education. Schools for those with learning difficulties (not a term in use at this politically incorrect time) were divided into those for the 'educationally subnormal' (ESN) and the 'severely subnormal' (SSN). Provision at these establishments often focused on caretaking and had little aspiration in traditional educational terms for the pupils.

Class sizes were large by today's standards, particularly in primary schools where forty, or even fifty, pupils per class was the norm. Secondary school classes were typically thirty pupils, with smaller classes in the sixth form. One of the selling points of private schools was often their smaller class sizes and here classes of less than twenty might be found. Many schools, at all stages, divided their pupils into 'houses' or 'teams' to encourage competition. This was a system beloved of the private sector but which permeated its way into state schools, particularly those with aspirations to offer a pseudo-private ambiance. "Team points were awarded for work and other meritorious activities and were displayed on a board in the school hall." Pupils often had fierce and long-lasting allegiances to their houses.

The school day usually ran from 9.00am to 4.00pm, even for the youngest children. This was to allow for a lengthy lunch break, in some cases as long two hours, as many children went home for a cooked meal at midday. Once out of the infants' department, at the age of seven, most children walked to and from school unaccompanied, even if this involved crossing a main road. There might be assistance with crossing roads at normal school opening and closing times. "The crossing patrols, who held out their lollipop shaped sticks that said 'Stop, Children Crossing', were known as lollipop men and women." In general, children were considered capable of looking after themselves. "Anyone taken ill during the school day was smartly dispatched for home; few people had phones so teachers didn't know whether there would be anyone at home to receive the child but I know of many children who, at a very young age, arrived home saying that they didn't feel well."

The Buildings

Although the late 1950s and 1960s did herald a wave of new school buildings, most were still Victorian edifices, with high windows and dark classrooms, devoid of decoration. "I remember the rooms as being cold and the windows too high to see out of. The room was heated by a large coal-burning stove with a heavy guard around it. It used to smoke when the caretaker filled it up." "My memory is of high ceilings, high windows and tall cupboards and a long window pole to open the windows." The sanitary arrangements evoked many memories that were, without exception, unpleasant. "The toilets were the worst element of the school, a brick shed across from the main school, with little toilets for the infants and three larger ones for the older girls, with creaking wooden half doors for modesty, no roof over the little alleyway, it was dire and of course frozen up in the winter. The smell was horrid, full of leaves and slippery in the autumn. It was not on mains drainage and a lorry used to come to clear the cesspit." Only at the very end of this period were primary classrooms likely to include anything that might be termed visually stimulating. "The classroom was on the first floor. On the walls were pictures of the 'Little Princes in the Tower' and 'Christ the Light of the Word' and a large World Map. I still remember the smell of the red carbolic soap in the cloakroom and the mixture of inky and milky smells of the classroom."

Pupils habitually sat at pairs, or rows, of desks facing the teacher. "We sat at double desks with ceramic inkwells and lift-up lids. Inside we kept our exercise books, pencils and dip-in pens and any personal 'treasures' such as marbles or skipping ropes. There was also an old Oxo tin with a knob of Plasticine in each desk. This began term as two or three new and separate colours, which blended into a muddy grey-brown with use." The, often blotting paper filled, inkwells were remembered by many and several recalled the use of a slate, rather than paper, particularly in the infants. "Children sat in rows in paired desks with a lift up seat. There was a shelf under the desk where we kept our chalkboard, tin of chalks and a small board rubber. The teacher sat at the front at a high desk with a step up to it. The desks had sliding brass covers over the inkwells and the inkwells themselves were white porcelain. I was ink monitor for a time and had to refill the inkwells every morning using a metal can with a long narrow spout." "We had no locked desks or lockers and didn't take round with us what we didn't need. There was never any problem with this, I never ever heard of anyone taking anything that wasn't their own."

In 1957, the delights of a brand new comprehensive school were extolled in the local paper under the headline, "Sedgehill's £604,000 investment in education." "Take thirty four normal classrooms, five gymnasiums, six art rooms, four geography rooms and three history rooms and you'll have an idea of the size of Sedgehill comprehensive school. But to get a full picture you must add to this impressive list, five woodwork shops, two metalwork centres and an engineering room, ten laboratories, six housecraft and bedsitting rooms, two needlework rooms, one trade needlework room, a kitchen, hall, library and a staff administration block. The school, which cost about £604,000 to build can accommodate 2,000 boys and girls. The first pupils arrived last September and Sedgehill opened with a roll of 1,164, drawn from local secondary and primary schools.

During their first three years at Sedgehill, all pupils take a common course of study. During the third year pupils are interviewed with their parents, talks on careers are given, and the courses to be followed in the fourth and fifth years are chosen. Both boys and girls are encouraged to stay on for advanced work, which will prepare them for entrance to universities, technical or training colleges. Out-of-school activities include clubs for art, ballroom and country dancing, drama, badminton, chess, table tennis and handicraft. School journeys and camps in the British Isles and on the Continent are arranged.

The site of the school is L-shaped. Hard pitches and play areas have been provided and the slope of the ground has made it possible to form an open air theatre. The central teaching block is three floors high while the workshop and gymnasia blocks are single-storey. Linked to the main building by a common main entrance hall is a two storey administration block. The large assembly hall can be sub-divided into five separate halls by means of sliding wood partitions."

The Curriculum

In general, the teaching was much more formal than that of the twenty-first century, with pupils being expected to work in silence, unless invited to speak. Rote learning was common, or children were required to copy out large chunks of text from books, or from the blackboard. Text books themselves were full of continuous text and had few illustrations. "Text books for all the subjects for the year were issued at the beginning of the term and all had bookplates at the front in which you wrote your name and form number, crossing out that of the previous owner above and you looked after those books until you handed them in at the end of the year. Two (brand new) books you had for the whole of your school life and in fact you were given them on leaving, namely, your hymn book (*Songs of Praise*) and your atlas. Exercise books were issued, a different one for each subject and a different colour."

For infants at least, there were signs of a dawning realisation that learning might be achieved by less rigid means. "We just seemed to play but we must have been learning. I particularly remember playing with the taps in the low set sinks and filling up containers and then emptying them again. We had sandpits and a Wendy house, with little tables and chairs. We also used to play games with small bean bags, throwing them to each other and catching them, sometimes we did this to music." An afternoon rest was a feature of many infant classrooms. "I clearly remember the afternoon naps we were forced to take. Little camp beds were put out with scratchy brown blankets on them and we were expected to sleep for an hour. I just wanted to play." "We had mats in the classroom where we would nap. There was a sandpit raised up to our waist height and the teacher had a large board and squeaky markers. She would write two words a day for us to learn, things like 'this' and 'that'."

Schools were obliged to conduct a daily act of collective worship or 'assembly'. There was no suggestion that this would acknowledge any faith apart from Christianity and Anglican Christianity at that; the only exceptions were in schools that were Catholic or Jewish foundations. Parents had the right to ask for their child to be withdrawn from assembly and the compulsory Religious Education (RE) lessons. "The one Jew and one Catholic in the school just missed assembly." "Daily assembly for the whole school took place in the hall. The hall had a very distinctive smell, a stage and a shiny parquet floor with white tape marking out a grid. We had to parade into assembly in height order. There would be prayers, notices and a hymn from a blue covered hymn book." "As my parents were Christian Scientists, they wanted me to have education in our religion and not that of the recognized church. So early morning, twice a week, I went along to one of the Christian Science teachers, who lived just a little out of the way from my usual route to school, for an hour and then joined my class for the next subject. I got a little questioning and singling out but after my classmates knew I was also taking religious classes, it was accepted."

The '3 Rs' were paramount and reading was often taught from a series of books about 'Janet and John'. Less modern texts were also used "The books from which we learned to read had first been printed in the 1890s and were based on the presumption that the shorter the word, the easier it was to read. This gave rise to sentences such as, 'Lo, here is the big red ox' and 'Let us sit on the sod'. Each day we had to read a new page. I don't know what happened if you couldn't read them as I don't remember any actual instruction. Once you got to the end of Primer Two you were on your own."

Many schools taught 'joined-up' handwriting from the outset. "Each lesson we would concentrate on a different letter, doing rows and rows of 'f's or 'g's keeping within the lines. Then we would be allowed to do a 'handwriting pattern' at the bottom of the page, a series of loops or minims that were letter-like but not actual letters. These could then be coloured in." Several left-handers were still being encouraged to use their right hands. "My main difficulty was that I was naturally left handed but this was seen by the school as a sign of moral weakness and I was forced to use my right hand." "I was left handed and although never encouraged to write with my right hand I can remember a female teacher shaking me because I wrote my fives and sevens the wrong way around when I was about six." Once the basics of writing were established, pencils were supplanted by pens. "Soon we entered into the realms of dip pens and ink and using inkwells. What a messy experience that could be! There was a ridge at the top of the desk where the pen could sit and it would become a river of ink at times, as we first learnt to grapple with said object. My fingers were permanently stained with dark blue ink and my mother was never pleased to see ink on our clothes. I can still recall the smell of the ink and blots and smudges. Were it not for the fact that I loved handwriting and became very good at it, I would have given up altogether I think. Anyway, before too long, my father bought me a fountain pen of my own and my first bottle of Quink and I managed much better without the horrid dip pen!"

"Junior School history consisted of working our way through four books, one per year, by, I believe, R J Unstead. We started with cave men in the first year and arrived at the Victorians in the fourth year. 'History' of course did not then extend into the twentieth century." "I do still have a copy of a year 4 (eleven year olds) geography test, duplicated in purple ink on a Banda machine. Questions included: 'Describe briefly what is needed in a country for the free flow of world trade' and 'Give a brief account of the cultivation of rubber or jute or tea'."

Diversions in the form of radio broadcasts were greeted with enthusiasm. Occasionally a visiting projectionist would arrive with a film that might be educational or, at the end of term, entertaining. Schools' television arrived in 1957 but many schools did not acquire television sets until the late 1960s. "Each term a new *Time and Tune* magazine came out to accompany the BBC radio programme of the same name. Further up the (primary) school we graduated to *Singing Together*. The repertoire of these programmes is best described as 'traditional British', *Raggle Taggle Gypsies*, *The Oak and the Ash*, *Cargoes* and others of that ilk. There was also an issue that centred round London street cries that was particularly unforgettable."

PE was often limited in scope and either loved or loathed in equal measure. Many junior school pupils listened to the BBC's *Music and Movement* radio broadcast, which involved a great deal of 'finding a space' and floating around pretending to be trees. Primary children often did country dancing. Children of both sexes took part in gym but football was exclusively for boys and netball for girls, with cricket and rounders replacing these sports in summer. Rugby and lacrosse were traditionally associated with grammar schools but opportunities to play hockey, tennis and athletics were more commonly provided. Particularly evocative, for all the wrong reasons, were the communal showers that often formed a compulsory part of senior school PE.

Not every subject was open to all. Apart from some, such as Latin or a second language, being reserved for the more able pupils, gender dictated what were acceptable fields of study. The boys did woodwork and metalwork; the girls did needlework and cooking. "We had cookery and housecraft lessons, even rooms made up as lounges, kitchens, bedrooms and bathrooms, so we would know how to look after them, only girls mind. I swapped with one of the boys to do woodwork lessons as he wanted to learn cookery; we got swapped back and told not to be so silly!" "One of the boys wanted to learn shorthand as he had ambitions to be a reporter but he wasn't allowed to as he was a boy." Even when certain subjects were available, there were preconceptions about which were suitable for girls. "I opted for Biology rather than Chemistry or Physics, as the latter were regarded as more masculine subjects."

Homework was a feature for secondary school pupils, notably those at grammar school, where up to three hours a night might be expected from older pupils. "Homework was compulsory and onerous. There were at least two subjects to be completed every night and three at the weekend." "Each subject carried homework and the teachers were relentless about setting it, according to the homework timetable. We used to try to appeal to the teachers to modify their homework requirements, as it seemed to us that they had no idea of the burden but they didn't ever relent. I certainly felt the pressure; my father wouldn't budge on his idea of when I should go to bed and I often hadn't finished my homework, having spent all evening on it." Not all families prioritised homework however, especially for their daughters. "In the third and fourth years homework started to become a problem at home. There was a lot of it and concentration was needed. I was the eldest of four children and there were no concessions just because I had to do homework."

Staff

Staff were predominantly teaching staff, with the school secretary, caretaker and dinner ladies hovering in the background. Classroom assistants were unheard of, although secondary schools might have laboratory technicians to help with science. Large, usually private, schools might employ a librarian or a nurse. Parents invariably upheld any decision by the teaching staff and were often in awe of them. Parental involvement in education was minimal; this was before the days of active parent-teachers' associations. A few mothers helped with such tasks as making costumes for drama productions but most parents were unaware of what went on in school. The education of many parents was such that they were unable to help with schoolwork and even general encouragement was not forthcoming from some. Children, of all ages, invariably treated staff with respect, would be wary of speaking out of turn and would dread the possibility of falling out of favour. "The relations between pupils and staff were formal." "If a boy met a teacher in the street he had to raise his cap." "Manners were most important from the outset and we were expected to stand if any adult entered the classroom. The usual greeting of, 'Good Morning Reverend Mother' or 'Father' on days when the priest came to visit, or 'Mrs' or 'Miss' when it was another member of staff, was strictly adhered to. If we were spoken to individually, we always replied with a 'Yes, Sister', or similar." In general, staff were an aloof crowd who did not allow themselves to be on friendly terms with their pupils. "One only knocked on the staff room doors in emergencies, which, when opened, allowed thick clouds of tobacco smoke to issue forth! All the staff wore academic gowns but not mortar boards and on speech days these were augmented with the silk academic hoods."

Punishment

There were no qualms about punishment being physical, humiliating or both; boys in particular might be beaten. Lesser punishments included the writing of lines, standing in a corner or being kept in after school. "At seven years old I was made to stand on the desk, others had to stand in the corner wearing a dunce's hat.[4] Boys were frequently hit round the ear and caning of boys took place regularly." "Our headmaster was a committed disciplinarian and favoured corporal punishment for almost anything." "I loathed handiwork, girls did knitting and I got smacked for making a mess of mine." "I remember, when I was in my second year infants, the teacher slapped me for not knowing that four times zero was zero." "You soon learned to keep your hands off the desk to avoid a rap across the knuckles with the narrow edge of the ruler. We were normally very well behaved, although the head-mistress did give my friend Patsy the cane for carving her name on the desk and Sidney had his mouth washed out with soap after swearing." "I do remember being smacked on the bottom with a wooden spoon! I think I had finished my work and I was kneeling on my chair talking to someone in the row behind. The only thing that hurt was my pride."

"Punishment at school was occasionally writing lines but more often a detention, taken after school on Friday afternoons. Teachers devised their own punishment to suit the 'crime'. When some fifth formers had reduced a new biology teacher to tears, Miss Field punished them by making the whole class sit a biology GCE 'O' level paper until everyone got one hundred percent. It took six months and no one ever forgot it." "During prayers, when we were supposed to be silent, somebody behind me hit me quite hard on the head with a book and I cried out. Without asking for an explanation, Miss Cox called me to the front and I was given the stick on both palms." "I recall crying in her class and she took a mirror out of her drawer and made me stand in the corner to look at my stupid face."

Playtime

Most schools had a break between lessons in the morning and sometimes also in the afternoons. The possibility of spending these breaks indoors was rare, whatever the weather. Most recalled the third of a pint bottles of milk that were issued. Frequently the memory was of those that had been stood near the heater to warm, consequently putting the recipients off milk for life! "Milk came in one third of a pint bottles with a cardboard lid, which had a hole to punch in the middle for the straw and was usually given out just before morning playtime. In the summer the milk was sometimes warm and almost on the turn, whilst it was sometimes frozen in winter and pushed through the lid. I was lucky to have one of these 'ice creams' once." Other refreshments might be available. "At morning break we had the delights of buns. Every morning, large trays of freshly baked (still hot) buns arrived from the local baker's, jam doughnuts, long iced buns and Chelsea buns. Jam doughnuts cost 3d and the others 2½d".

Playground games were uncomplicated and came and went in phases. "Playground activities seemed to be on a seasonal rotation. That is, marbles came into favour for a while, then no-one played marbles after we had swapped and bartered different speciality marbles. Other games included skipping and tag but these weren't ongoing through the year." "We played skipping, 'swaysies' and 'overs'. I could never get the hang of the timing to run in when the rope was turned over and could only manage if I started standing next to the rope before it began turning. There were many skipping rhymes. I preferred French skipping, which involved jumping on and twisting elastic that was round the ankles of two 'enders'. Hopscotch was also popular. There were four brick panels, interspersed with windows that were the perfect width for handstands. We used to rush to 'bagsy' one of these spaces in the hand-stand season. Often one girl (it seemed to be a girl thing) would do a handstand and then move her legs apart to allow another one or even two girls to handstand up in front of her. It didn't seem to matter that his revealed our knickers, although sometimes we tucked our dresses into them first."

"Running around, chasing games of various types involved someone being 'he' or 'it', This person was chosen by the use of a 'dip' rhyme, such as 'Ip dip, sky blue, who's it? Not you.' Sometimes followed by 'O U T spells out and out you must go'. One word was said as you pointed to each person in the circle to determine who was chosen. Another dip began 'One potato, two potato, three potato, four'. With some of these dips it was possible to employ mathematical skill to work out where you needed to stand in relation to who ever was calling the dip, in order to avoid being chosen. Games that followed dips included Off Ground He, where you were safely 'home' if you were off ground and Stuck in the Mud. In this game, if you were caught you stood still with your legs apart and another player could free you by crawling under your legs. I can't quite recall how the role of catcher changed. Grandmother's Footsteps involved creeping up on someone who had their back turned. They would turn round frequently and if they spotted you moving, you would have to go back and start again. If you were the first to reach the person with their back turned, you took their place. One of my favourites, whose name, if it had one, I've forgotten, involved making one's way down a course following instructions such as 'if you have an R in your name move 2 lamp-posts', 'a giant step if you have a brother', or '2 pigeon steps for those with hair ribbons'.[5] It was obviously perfectly simple for whoever was doing the calling to fix the winner of this game."

"Less energetic pastimes came and went in 'crazes'. These included games, such as Jacks, Conkers or Cat's Cradle and collections, involving swapping with friends. Most years bead collecting took its turn. Beads from discarded costume jewellery would be collected and swapped. Sparklers, paste stones prized from rings or brooches, were particularly popular, with rainbow sparklers being the most highly valued. Bead swapping was banned after I think someone swapped the family jewels without permission! Nowadays it would be banned in case someone swallowed one, or tripped over one, or stuck it up their nose but no one thought of that in our day. We also had autograph books. Collecting autographs was usually an end of the summer term craze, when you needed to collect the signatures of those about to leave. People would write fairly awful rhymes in each other's books."

School Dinners

Although many children, especially primary aged children, did go home to lunch at this period, school dinners were usually provided for those who wanted to stay. They were stodgy and unimaginative, lacking in any choice and invariably the expectation would be that nothing would be left on the plate. With a few exceptions, school dinners were not greeted with enthusiasm. For several, the smell of over-boiled cabbage was an abiding memory of school. "School dinners were my bête noir. At intervals my mum decided that I should try them again and there was the added attraction that I didn't lose play time walking home and back but it never lasted long. I just detested everything about school dinners, especially as we were expected to eat a significant proportion of them. There was never any choice of menu; things like vegetarianism were unheard of. My pet hates included mashed potato, which used to be served with a large scoop, now more commonly used for ice cream and always had awful lumps in; I still can't stomach mashed potato. Then there was semolina and jam that we mixed together and turned pink, when we could get away with it." "I remember fatty meat, cabbage and potatoes followed by semolina, rice pudding or something stodgy. I suppose it was balanced and filled us up. You had to eat it all, fat included. If a girl did not want her rice pudding she had to sit there until it got cold, with tears no doubt!"

Table manners were important and dinner supervisors ensured good behaviour whilst eating. Silence might be expected for at least part of the meal. Although the provision of free milk persisted throughout our period,[6] free meals for all were short lived. In a Britain that was still suffering from rationing, all school children were offered a free school meal until 1951, with about half taking up the opportunity. From then until the end of the 1960s prices gradually increased from 7d to 1s 9d a day.

Extra-Curricular Activities

There were few extra-curricular clubs associated with the schools of this period, although some schools, notably those in the private sector, had quasi-military

Combined Cadet Corps, or allowed pupils to work for Duke of Edinburgh's awards. "A chess club was very popular, mostly for the boys. On a Friday night we had a pop session where we used to bring in our 45rpm records and LPs to play on the record player and we would all dance to it. I used to sing in the school choir and a couple of times a week we practiced in the lunch hour."

School visits became more adventurous during the 1960s and the residential trip became a feature. "A visit to The Commonwealth Institute in London in the fourth year was a highlight. We also had a day trip to Portsmouth in 1967, at the end of our primary school careers. Our parents paid 21s for the trip. We went on the train and allegedly went by launch round the harbour, looked over *The Victory* and had 'a set tea' somewhere." Some schools gave pupils the opportunity to go abroad; girls who attended private schools mentioned skiing trips and cruises. By the 1960s, even primary schools might run trips to France for their eldest pupils. "During the year when I was 10 (1956) the school organised a three day trip to London for that third year group (today's year 5). We saw all the major sights and stayed in a very nice hotel." Health and safety had not yet cramped the style of teachers wishing to take their pupils out of the classroom. "Because we behaved well it was possible for the headmistress to take about thirty children on a school trip entirely on her own." All these activities had a cost implication and some children were excluded because of this.

Uniform

Although some primary schools had no uniform, many did. "School uniform was dark green for infants' school. A pinafore dress, known as a 'tunic' with a blouse and tie was worn in winter and a green and a white gingham dress in summer, both with hand knitted cardigans. This was accompanied by a green beret, a gabardine, belted raincoat and a leather satchel (see figure 47). A fleecy lining could be buttoned on inside the raincoat when it was particularly cold. All our school clothes had to be named. We had 'Cash's' embroidered name tapes that lasted a lifetime, as they would be carefully unpicked from discarded clothing and reused. Knickers, some with hanky pockets, were thick knitted cotton in regulation green or blue, colours that used to adhere to one's person when they were new." A primary school uniform cost £5 in the mid-1960s. Many ladies, even those from more wealthy backgrounds, wrote of the financial hardships that accompanied the necessity to acquire secondary school uniforms. These often had to be obtained from specific suppliers and with all the sports wear and accessories, represented a significant outlay. "The gabardine raincoat was £7 (in 1958) and the blazer a similar amount, even the wretched beret was 7s 6d and it was a lot of money."

"In secondary school, tunics were replaced by navy skirts that were supposed to reach the floor when we knelt down, although never did. In any case, skirts could be and were, wound up at the waist until they reached a more fashionable height. This resulted in an unsightly roll round one's waist but it was the length that was key. Skirts were accompanied by white blouses, green ties and regulation, never hand-knitted, jumpers." "In my first year (1967-8) we were supposed to wear velour hats in winter and straw 'panama' hats in summer but these were abandoned as a lost cause and I don't think I ever had a panama hat. Uniform rules relaxed as I went up the school, skirts certainly got shorter and shoes and coats acquired more individual styles. In the sixth form we could wear our own clothes, including trousers. Technically these were supposed to be trouser suits but I don't recall ever seeing even the most 'square'[7] girls wearing anything resembling a trouser suit." "Clean blouses or shirts were not a daily affair; once or twice a week only." Boys wore short trousers to primary school and sometimes into the early years of secondary school, moving to long trousers when they were twelve or thirteen.

PE kit for primary school girls was commonly a vest and knickers. "At secondary school PE kit consisted of divided skirts, or culottes and aertex shirts for outdoor PE. I think the wearing of knickers, without shorts over the top, for indoor gym went on until we were about fourteen." "Younger children wore black plimsolls with elasticised sides that were easier to put on and take off. As they got older they had white lace-up plimsolls, that had to be whitened with 'Blanco'."

Post School Education

For girls in particular, the post-war period was still a time when education beyond statutory school leaving age was not seen as worthwhile, or was impossible on economic grounds. Most parents expected girls to aspire to marriage and a lifetime as a housewife but this was an era when the daughters of the house were less willing to conform to this stereotype. "I remember a poem we learnt in domestic science, which started, 'I have done angel's work today; yes, such an honour came my way', which just summed up to me the attitude of the time we lived in."

Going to university, although an option in principle, was restricted to a very small minority and it was not just a lack of academic aptitude that held young women back. "It was not so common for people to go to university in those days and my parents were not very enthusiastic. When I came back from my summer job of waitressing in a hotel, just three weeks before going to university and said how much I had enjoyed it, my mother asked if I really wanted to go to university, because it would save them a lot of expense if I didn't go and I 'would probably get married anyway'." "Mothers couldn't accept that things were different and resented, or saw no need for, new educational opportunities that were now available for girls." "In 1963, when I left school, going to university, even for my friend who had nine 'O' Levels, just wasn't thought of for us. We have discussed it since and we never thought of it as a possibility; even fifteen years later I had to be persuaded that it was an option. The majority of boys who went to Chorlton did not consider university. They went into industry becoming apprentices as draughtsmen, engineers, or into banks, building societies, insurance companies and would take internal examinations. At that time, even in the bank where I worked, banking exams were for boys and men, not girls and women." "I left after getting nine 'O' levels much to the disappointment of the teaching staff as I'd been among the top half-dozen achievers in the top class. This decision was taken after a rather heated discussion with my mother who demanded to know what I would want to do with a degree, to which I had no answer. Her argument then was that I might opt for a career that didn't require a degree, so perhaps I should get out and find that career now, remembering that my brother would be expecting to go on to tertiary education and that there weren't funds for both of us."

Several girls had their plans thwarted by a combination of parental disapproval and economic constraints. "My plans to become a teacher were shattered but thinking back, that is all they were, dreams." "I caused the Headmaster some grievous disappointment by not pursuing an expected Oxford scholarship, as a result of lack of parental enthusiasm for something 'too ambitious and costly'. Consequently, I was obliged to follow my interest in medicine by another route." Girls' career options were limited by expectation. "The school had quite a rigid approach to possible careers; nursing, teaching or secretarial work were the only options offered." "I had long known that I wanted to teach, so when it came to choosing my path, I already knew the direction I wanted to take. This doesn't mean that I hadn't considered the other options apparently open to me as a girl at the time: nursing (I decided against that emphatically after a stay in hospital, secretary or typist, air hostess (you needed languages for that!), librarian or shop assistant." The range of acceptable careers for girls gradually widened and the influence of grammar schools helped in this respect. "We once had a visit from a Careers' Advisor from outside school, on which occasion one of the girls in my form made the mistake of saying she wanted to be a nurse. This evoked the horrified response of, 'Not a nurse, not with a grammar school education!'".

Financial limitations were also weakening. "At the time, further education was funded by Local Education Authority grants in conjunction with parents' contributions, which were means tested." One volunteer wrote of the grant that she received as a trainee teacher. "Because of my family's financial position, I was given the full grant at the time of £77 9s 0d which was to be paid in three instalments of £26 9s 8d, one at the beginning of each term." She also had free board and lodging. "Evening classes were free if you were under eighteen and after that just a few shillings a year. Classes were available in a wide range of academic subjects. Between 1963 and 1969 I gained 'O' Levels in History, Maths, Biology and Sociology at evening classes after work and later went on to pass three 'A' Levels." Despite this, many women of this generation were left to fulfil their academic aspirations in later life. "I was lucky enough to live through times of free education and second chances. I missed learning and began studying for 'O' and 'A' levels to attend Teacher Training College and then University in my mid twenties and early thirties."

With the arrival of several new universities and the introduction of Polytechnics, offering a more vocational, degree level training, the 1960s increased the options for post-school education. There were other possibilities. "One of the ladies my mother knew had sent her daughter to a 'finishing' school, Montesano, in Gstaad, Switzerland for a year. It seemed an exciting idea so I was enrolled just for the spring term. Lessons were in French though most of the girls were English with a sprinkling of German, Italian, Brazilian and Spanish. Several girls came just for the one term and we lived in a typical chalet in a little village called Rougemont with the handsome ski instructor who I fell in love with from afar! We skied every afternoon and all day on Wednesdays but there were late afternoon school lessons as well (see figure 54). It was good to have teachers who were actually French, German and Italian and hear the proper accents. We learnt French, read books and did oral work. I particularly enjoyed the History of Art lessons. I also kept up the German and started to learn Italian." "I started a nine month secretarial course at a very respectable establishment for young ladies, run on firm but friendly lines. Punctuality and good manners were expected and we worked hard. I learnt Pitman's shorthand, speed typing, how to prepare a whole range of documents, French shorthand, civics and office management. We learnt to type methodically and eventually were practising to strict tempo dance music to get our touch even."

Summary

Between 1946 and 1969 the education system opened up greater opportunities, particularly for working-class pupils. Some children were however still held back by societal expectations and gender stereotypes. Teaching methods were formal and often uninspiring, with little or no consideration for the range of ability levels or different learning styles of the pupils. Discipline was rigorous and respect for staff was paramount. Children viewed school as a place where they should behave and study, even if they did not enjoy the experience. Testing was an inherent part of the post-war education system and pupils had to be prepared for failure as well as success. Nonetheless, the perception of the participants was that most pupils of the 1950s and 1960s left school with a good grounding in the basics and that those who had attended a grammar school acquired a sound level of knowledge across a range of subjects, as well as being equipped with study skills for later life.

The Brief

Describe your school(s). What type of schools were these (secondary modern, grammar, fee paying, single sex or mixed)? For fee paying schools, what were the fees?

Describe the curriculum. Was this the same for boys and girls? Which subjects did you enjoy or dislike and why? What were you good at, or less good at? If there was a stage when you had a choice of subjects, were there expectations about which subjects you would study?

Think about memorable (for good or bad reasons) teachers and lessons. What were relationships with teachers like? What about parent/teacher relations?

How much homework was expected, if any?

Mention class sizes and the times of the school day?

Write about school examinations such as the eleven plus, school certificate, RSAs, CSEs and GCE 'O' and 'A' levels. How were you prepared for these? How was revision handled? What were the expectations?

Was there pressure to leave or stay on beyond statutory school leaving age? How did this vary with gender or class?

The comprehensive system began to be rolled out on 1965, how did this effect you?

What about playtimes and break times? Did you stay at school for lunch? What were school dinners like? Can you remember playground games or activities?

Mention school trips or outings.

Describe further education or training, if this applies to you. Was this something you wanted to do, or perhaps fought for, or was it undertaken because it was the done thing? Did you have to leave home for this? Was this daunting or part of the appeal?

You may want to look out school reports or timetables, school magazines and programmes for school events or photos.

Chapter 6 footnotes

[1] In 2009, 26·7% of candidates were awarded an A grade at 'A' level and a far higher proportion of young people sat 'A' levels in 2009.

[2] Crook, David Local authorities and comprehensivization in England and Wales, 1944-1974 History and Philosophy Group (undated).

[3] Reading, 'Riting and 'Rithmetic - but clearly, from this, not spelling!

[4] A tall, conical hat with the letter 'D' on.

[5] A giant step was a large stride, a pigeon step was putting one foot in front of the other with the heel of one foot touching the toe of the other. A lamppost involved lying full length on the ground and then standing up again at the point where your head reached.

[6] The provision of free school milk to secondary age pupils ceased in 1968.

[7] A derisory term for someone who was old-fashioned.

CHAPTER 7

I Feel Fine: health and hygiene

Personal Hygiene

Washing and bathing were infrequent by today's standards, showers were not yet popular and not all homes had plumbed in baths or indoor toilets. "Personal hygiene depended on the domestic facilities available. In my parents' home in the 1950s the bathroom was very primitive and the W.C. was downstairs, reached through the porch at the back door. There was no hand basin there, so washing of hands had to be done at the kitchen sink." "As a child, baths were weekly with a minimum amount of water. It never occurred to me that it was possible to have water that covered my legs when I was sitting down. I think this was a hang-over from the water-saving regime of the second world war." "Hot baths and hair washing were done on a weekly basis, supplemented by a daily stand up wash with hot water, soap (red Lifebuoy) and flannel. My cousins occasionally travelled out of the city to our house to have hot baths because they had no bathroom but they usually paid to use the public baths in their neighbourhood. In some families, the children were bathed together or used the same bathwater with the cleanest being bathed first!" "Up until I was eight, we did not have a bathroom, so the weekly bath was taken in a tin bath, which hung on the back of the door when not in use. This bath was put in front of the fire and filled with hot water. Dad bathed first, then mum and then the children. Our hair was washed in the bath and the shampoo rinsed off with a jug of warm water." "Daily washing, if you did not have a bathroom, was either done in the kitchen sink or you had a jug and bowl in the bedroom and you washed in this. It was not always hot water either, because this was not piped and had to be boiled in the kettle on the stove. So often we got up on a chilly morning and the water was ice cold, it certainly woke you up."

"I used to go with a friend of my mother's to Manor Place Baths. Here there were cubicles with big Victorian baths and you had an allotted time to take your bath. There were constant calls of 'more hot water in No. 6' and 'more soap please'." "There was the washhouse where you could have a bath. I think it cost 6d. There were lots of cubicles containing baths, set in surroundings of polished wood and the partitions were of polished wood, the floors were tiled as were the walls which weren't partitions. The taps were operated from outside the bathroom door by a woman employed for that purpose who turned the taps on and off with a type of Allen key. She also cleaned the bath after every person had a bath. She had big buckets of cleaning materials and scouring solution and it was always spotless. She filled the bath, with as much water as you wanted and you tested whether it was hot enough. The outside operation of the taps was so you could have the bath topped up with cold water at the start if it was too hot or you could ask for hot water if it cooled down and you wanted to soak. You took your own towel and soap, like going to the swimming baths."

"Bars of soap were used; there was no liquid soap or shower gel. Popular brands of soap were Palmolive, Camay and Imperial Leather. Cussons' soap was considered luxurious and often given as a present but it was highly scented and made my skin tight, so I didn't like it. We did also have soaps encased in thin layers of sponge. As an economy measure, tiny pieces of soap would be soaked to make them soft, then squeezed together, sometimes using a mould, to make a new bar of a usable size for the kitchen." "There were bath cubes and bath salts that dissolved in the water leaving an oily scum and what was supposed to be a pleasing aroma. Talcum powder was liberally used." "We had Radox crystals and sometimes I had Matey Bubble Bath as a child." "Moisturisers used were inexpensive ones such as, Pond's Cold Cream, Nivea and Astral, usually used in the winter months to protect against the cold winds."

It was very unusual to wash hair more than once a week. "Shampoo was mostly a medicated one, Vosene and on special occasions, Sunsilk. My mother always had her hair washed at her weekly visit to the hairdressers, for a shampoo and set and a perm every two or three months." Perms were usually a job for the hairdresser, although home perms, such as those by Toni, were available, if not always successful. Ladies who had their hair shampooed and set weekly at the hairdressers normally wouldn't wash it in between. Going to the hairdressers was not viewed as a luxury and even some women from poorer backgrounds went to the hairdressers each week, not considering the possibility of washing their hair themselves. In the 1950s, ladies paid between 3s 6d and 5s for a mobile hairdresser to provide a shampoo and set at home.

"I washed my hair in Lin-co-Lin beer shampoo (sachets shaped like a beer barrel, made especially for dark hair, there was a lemon version for blondes) and rinsed it with vinegar in the water to make it shiny, I must have smelled like a chip shop." Vinegar was not only used to promote shine but also to keep nits at bay. Highly inefficient dry shampoos were available, or talcum powder might be used as a substitute. The powder was sprinkled over the hair, left for a short time and then brushed out. It was virtually impossible to remove all traces of the powder and it never seemed to make the hair any less greasy. Split ends might be kept at bay by singeing the ends of the hair. "Shampoos included Amami, Vosene and Silvikrin and setting lotions were used to induce curls and waves with grips or curlers. Rinsing of shampooed hair was done using jugs of hot water, later there were rubber spray attachments for taps. At this time, home perms were popular. Hair lice were treated with a blue ointment, or even by complete shaving of the head." "The whole family had to be treated for nits with liquid paraffin and I remember us standing on newspaper, which was burnt later, in our knickers one by one, to have our hair combed through with the nit comb."

There were a variety of tooth cleaning products, including Eucryl powder, especially designed for smokers. Popular brands were Crest, Colgate and Gleem. Advertising concentrated on the whitening properties of the product: 'You'll wonder where the yellow went when you brush your teeth with Pepsodent'."

Toilet paper might be home-made from squares of newspaper or purchased brands such as Izal or Bronco, which were hard and shiny, a little like tracing paper. Especially for those with no indoor toilet, chamber pots, also known as 'guzunders' or 'pos', were kept under the bed for use at night. Softer, tissue-like toilet paper, arrived in the 1960s along with tissues to replace cotton handkerchiefs.

Deodorants, including vaginal deodorants, were in use in the 1950s. "Deodorants first appeared in a jar as a cream (Odorono and Mum) (see figure 58) and then in solid stick form, followed by roller ball containers and sprays." "The first deodorant I remember was a tube with a plastic ball on the end of it that rotated to pick up the rather sticky product. You had to wave your arms around after applying it so that it would dry, otherwise it would stick to your clothes and leave a deposit that dried to a white residue."

Shaving underarms, legs and occasionally the bikini-line became the norm. "Women did not have dedicated shavers in the 1940s, 1950s and 1960s; mostly women of my mother's age did not shave at all. We used Dad's razor which was a Rolls' Safety Razor and came with a 'strop' in a box which you fixed the blade to and pushed it up and down and it made a 'clap, clap' sound each time you passed it back and forth. We were for ever getting into trouble for using this and blunting his blades. Before that he had used a cut-throat razor and sharpened it on a leather strap or strop and I can remember as a child being fascinated, watching him use a lather and brush and then shaving himself. Eventually, disposable razors arrived and we used them and then in later years there were razors that ran on batteries or electricity to aid women's shaving." "As razor blades were expensive I resorted to a kind of sandpaper mitt from Boot's, which removed the hair but also took off the top layer of skin and any sun tan I'd managed to achieve." "Underarm and leg hair was removed using cream called VeetO. I think the 'O' was meant to stand for 'odourless' but it was anything but."

Men were expected to be clean and neat but products had to be 'manly'. "My father used Old Spice aftershave, Brylcreem and Gillette razor blades." "Excessive attention to personal grooming on the part of a man was regarded with suspicion as effeminate."

Medical Care

Illness was seen as an inconvenience, "We were too busy to be ill." "There was pretty much an attitude of 'get on with it'." "Ailments were initially treated by the patient being told to stay indoors and rest, with glasses of water. If this did not work, then temperature and pulse were taken. If these measurements were raised, bed-rest and Milk of Magnesia or Lucozade (see figure 57) were the order of the day. If symptoms persisted, without a recognisable rash, then a scrub up, clean clothes, manners polished and a visit to the doctor was arranged. The doctor asked about bowel habits, food partaken and generally sent us home to be brought back for another visit, if the patient did not show improvement in the next few days." "Home visits seem, in retrospect, to have been easier to get. This must have been partly due to transport problems and very few people having a car. Our mums couldn't just bundle us into the car and drive to the surgery, we had to wait at the bus stop, get the bus, then walk to the surgery." "I do remember that there was quite a hullabaloo when the doctor was called, hot water and clean towel at the ready and anything he said taken as gospel." The doctor was often well known to the family and revered as a person of status in the locality. "We had what was universally known as a 'family doctor'. My parents, my brother and I all 'belonged' to Dr Harden; my grandad was a patient of his partner, Dr Miller. It was very common at this time for the doctor to come to see you, rather than vice versa."

Feared ailments of the period included those that have now been conquered. "When I was little, polio was very common and it was not unusual to see children and adults with callipers on their legs because they had suffered with polio and it left their muscles wasted. In very severe cases they were put into 'iron lungs', a bed covered by a container over the patient, with just their head showing and an apparatus which the patient was enclosed in, that helped them to breathe because their own muscles did not work anymore. Polio vaccination was introduced in 1955 and I can remember having the nurse come into the school and we were given a drop of the vaccine on a lump of sugar." "The big scare in the early fifties was polio and Mother wouldn't let me go to a public swimming pool for a couple of years because of this. In fact I believe the government closed some pools."

"A problem that still existed when I was little was rickets and to help with this I remember that we went to a building that had a very large sun-ray lamp in it. The lamp was in the middle of a room which had a balcony around the lamp and our mums sat on seats at the back and the children all stood or played near the lamp. We all had to wear green glass goggles to protect our eyes. This was when I was in London and about seven years old, or younger. I don't know if this practice was carried out countrywide."

Illnesses were treated with a combination of home remedies and proprietary brands. "Syrup of figs for constipation, whole cloves on an aching tooth, eucalyptus for stuffy noses, bicarbonate of soda for indigestion and Vick rubbed on chests." "I must have suffered from constipation because I had to take syrup of figs occasionally and my grandmother would give me Andrew's Liver Salts when I went to stay with her. Both of these things tasted awful." "I can remember being given Fenning's Powers, which came in a folded paper oblong about two inches long, on a teaspoon in milk and there were Fenning's Little Healers, which were like white peppercorns only slightly larger."

"My grandmother was in charge regarding home remedies, which were tried before our GP was involved. Angier's Junior Emulsion or Petrolagar for children's purgatives, Germolene for grazes, warm olive oil for earache, oil of cloves for toothache, Junior Aspirin for headache or fever, glycerine and blackcurrant pastilles for sore throats. Threadworms were common in children in the 1950s and 1960s and a bottle of vile pink medicine was obtained from the doctor." "Favourites for treating stomach upsets were Indian Brandee and Kaolin and Morphine, there was always a bottle of Milk of Magnesia, which was favoured by my Mum." "When I had a cold I used Metholatum on my hankie, or up my nose, to help me breathe, or I sucked Tunes ('Tunes help you breath more easily' went the advertising slogan). Obridges was for coughs and Lucozade was drunk to aid recovery, although I drank this on a regular basis, regardless of my health. Savlon or Germoline were used on cuts and grazes."

"The joke in the village was that the same pink medicine was given for all ailments, whether young or old. Pre National Health Service the people used their own remedies such as Andrew's Liver Salts if feeling liverish, Calamine Lotion for burns or skin ailments, cloves for tooth problems, dock leaves for nettle stings, Reckit's Blue Bag for bee stings, vinegar for wasp stings and rolled soap pellets up the rectum for constipation. High temperatures were dealt with by applying a cold flannel to the brow and replacing it regularly." "Inhalations of Friar's Balsam for colds and stuffy noses; Vick vapour rub; lemon, honey and glycerine mixture for sore throats and plenty of Ribena to drink." "I was fascinated to hear my Grandfather talking about using Wintergreen Oil or Horse Embrocation to treat his rheumatism; apparently the Horse Embrocation worked best!" "Chilblains in winter were a common occurrence and treated with Wintergreen ointment. I think another cure was to put your feet in a potty of urine but I don't remember anyone doing this." "Gee's linctus, or Boot's honey and lemon were the favoured cough medicines, with Glycerin of Thymol pastilles for sore throats, Meloids in case of losing one's voice and catarrh pastilles for catarrh (you had to feel pretty bad to be willing to take those). Liqufruta herbal cough medicine was garlicky and black." "Brimstone and treacle for constipation. I remember the lovely yellow colour, though that was the only lovely thing about it. Pripsen for worms was not lovely in any way!" "A remedy for arthritis was melted wax. This was kept at home in a shallow bowl and placed in the top of the warming oven, heated by the fire. When the wax had melted, my mother placed her hands and forearms in the bowl and then removed them after a while, when they would be encased in a wax layer, which could be peeled away like a pair of gloves."

Although keeping healthy was not then the preoccupation that it was to become in the twenty-first century, there were various preventatives that were used, particularly for children. "I was amongst the first children to feel the benefit of the free orange juice for the vitamin C and cod liver oil, which was obtained by going to a shop in town who stocked these items, for free distribution in exchange for a coupon. I loved the orange juice but only managed to get the cod liver oil liquid (no capsules in those days) down me by holding my nose and rapidly swallowing! Another preventative was California Syrup of Figs, a gentle laxative, which was administered every Friday evening." "I remember weekly dosings of liquid paraffin to 'keep us all regular', whether we needed it or not!"

"When I was a baby I had been vaccinated against whooping cough, diphtheria and tetanus. At the time I received them they were given separately; when my own children were vaccinated (1967 and 1968) the three were given in one injection; the injections being given three times at three monthly intervals, if I remember correctly. I also had a vaccination for smallpox which was a very common disease then and I still bear the mark on my arm today."

Serious illness was not discussed beyond the immediate family and often medical staff would not tell the patient, or their relatives, that an illness was considered to be terminal. Hospitalisation, especially for children, could be a traumatic experience. Care concentrated on medical, rather than emotional, needs and rules were strict. Stays were often lengthy and visitors were not normally allowed in children's wards. "When he was a child, my husband was in hospital for 6-8 weeks with a heart condition and was allowed no visitors during that time apart from the local priest. The feeling was that it would be too upsetting for a child to see his parents, only to have to say goodbye again! When he was readmitted at the age of eleven, he was put into an adult ward, so that he would now be allowed visitors." "Those were the days when a small child was delivered to the hospital and the parent(s) were told to go home and return in a week to collect the child, as constant visiting just caused upset for the child and the nurses. I felt utterly abandoned and went on hunger strike and fought the anaesthetic like a tiger, to the point where it was necessary to call in extra staff to hold me down so they could get a mask on me. My mother used to take a forty five minute bus ride to the hospital every day and stand in the car park in the hope I would look down from the third floor and see her waving, I never did."

"My younger brother and I had scarletina, I was six and he was three. We were taken to the isolation hospital. It was on the ground floor and as our parents weren't allowed to come in, they could see us through the windows. We had injections in the bottom twice a day. I knew the other children in the ward because we were all from the same school. My only other memory is getting into trouble because I didn't hand my books and toys in for fumigating before we left. My brother has a far more traumatic memory of being pushed in his cot into a bathroom and being left because he wouldn't stop crying." "The 'fever ambulance' was an unnerving sight in the neighbourhood. It was black and carried children away with diphtheria, scarlet fever, polio and suspected TB to isolated fever hospitals, where parents could only rarely visit and could only communicate through closed windows. Some TB patients were nursed in beds on verandas outside the wards."

"Going to the Dentist was a dreaded experience and treatment was very primitive, usually undertaken only when toothache made it necessary and little preventative work was carried out. Teeth cleaning was not as thorough as it is today and it was very common for youngish adults to undergo dental clearance in favour of false teeth." "Most adults seemed to have a lot of bad teeth. Both my parents had all of their teeth out in one session even though presumably some of them must have been alright. They then had full sets of dentures; most people of their generation did." "Visits to the dentist were quite unpleasant. We all had to have fillings, I can't imagine why because there weren't many sweets around. Teeth were extracted using gas. This involved big blocks of rubber being put into your mouth to keep it open and then gas being applied until you were unconscious."

"The dentist was only visited when one had toothache and he would remove the offending tooth. Prior to this, Tincture of Myrrh would have been taken from the first aid cabinet and a tiny amount of this horrible tasting liquid put onto the aching tooth with cotton wool and if this didn't work, a trip to the dentist was the answer. Toothache was miserable; I don't remember anyone going for regular checkups." "Teeth were brushed morning and night. Not that I had many. Apparently I had a very thin enamel on my teeth and my first teeth were very rotten. As we had just moved and I had just started school mum took me to the school dentist. He took out all my top teeth in one go using gas and air, which didn't put me out properly and mum could hear me screaming. They wouldn't let her in with me until he had finished and when they let her in I was leaning over a sink with blood pouring out of my mouth and tears rolling down my cheeks."

"When our milk teeth came loose, we were encouraged to wiggle them looser and pull them out by the promise of the Tooth Fairy coming, who left a silver threepenny bit under pillow (later a sixpence). If the tooth refused to come, Dad tied a cotton thread round it and attached it to the door handle, which he then shut (Mum didn't approve of this I think, as she said it would come in its own good time). We tried extra hard to pull the teeth ourselves after that!"

"The advent of the National Health Service made a huge difference to healthcare. Doctors were consulted much more easily and many of the home remedies gave way to prescribed medicine, often made up by the doctor himself in a side room to the consulting room." "Before 1948, all visits to the doctor had to be paid for and consequently my grandparents were very cautious about consulting the professionals, in spite of there being a very sympathetic GP who often 'forgot' to send a bill. Some people contributed to small insurance benefit schemes each week in order to pay the unexpected bill when they had to 'go on the sick'." "I remember that mum used to have insurance to pay for our spectacles and also she belonged to a Friendly Society, dad paying weekly through his wage packet and this meant that if he was off work and did not receive his wage then he could claim a weekly amount from the Friendly Society."

Growing up

Reaching puberty was a process that was frequently a shock and accompanied by excruciating embarrassment and old wives' tales. Menstruation was a matter for shame and methods of coping with it were basic. "Sanitary products were never discussed, Dr White's towels were bought discreetly at the chemist and handed over as a brown paper parcel." "If I had to buy supplies I was told to ask the local shopkeeper for 'one off the top shelf' where packs of pads were discreetly pre-wrapped." "In the late forties and early fifties, menstruation was rarely spoken about, being described as 'the curse' sometimes, or being 'not very well' and more vulgarly as 'having the rag on'. This referred to the use of protective rags fastened to a belt by safety pins. These rags were washed and reused but soon commercially produced sanitary towels (Lilia) became more widely available. Then tampons[1] came on the market, causing much questioning of their suitability for unmarried young women who in the fifties were still largely virgins." "Along with this information (about menstruation) came other things like not being allowed to wash my hair while I was 'on' as it was called, always make sure that I sat correctly so nobody could see the towel, no swimming etc., basically forget your life for a week. A couple of years later I discovered Lillets tampons, although my mother was horrified with this, I ignored her and my life reset itself, allowing me to do everything I wanted to do and I ignored the non hair washing advice too, apparently I would catch a chill, I never did of course!"

"The sweaty, plastic Nikini sanitary belts and towels were uncomfortable and would show through the tight trousers we had started to wear then, so you felt very self-conscious." "My mother explained the very basics and showed me a Kotex sanitary towel, all bulky cotton-wool wadding, with loops to clip them to a sanitary belt, plus a pair of plastic pants to wear over my own knickers to prevent any leakage of potentially embarrassing stains." "The sanitary towels we used were Dr White's and were quite thick. These were very uncomfortable to wear; you were always aware they were there and they had to be changed regularly. Mum found it hard to pay for the towels and as often happened when there are women living together, our cycles coincided and it was a rush to be the first to the cupboard for the towels because if there were none left then we had to use pieces of cotton material held in our knickers with a safety pin. Apart from being far more uncomfortable than the towels; they smelt and it was most embarrassing when washing day came and on the balcony, where everyone could see, were the washed, stained pieces of cloth. One phrase I remember to explain that you were on a period was, 'I have the decorators in this week', because people found it embarrassing to talk about." "Although sanitary towels were available they were much too expensive for our family to buy, we all used rags in our knickers which were boiled between uses. I don't think I used proper towels until after I had my second child in 1955."

As ever, teenage girls suffered from spots and took measures to alleviate them. "I was very lucky when I was a teenager and did not suffer with acne but I did have blackheads. After I had my bath mum would squeeze out the blackheads on my face and back." "Clearasil cream was the usual treatment of teenage spots, it was flesh coloured but a bit hit and miss if matched your own skin. It seemed to work by drying up the spots."

There was some pressure for women to conform to a fashionable body shape. The popular curvy figures of Marilyn Monroe and Diana Dors in the 1950s had given way to the need to emulate the boyish shape of Twiggy by the 1960s. This did not however resemble the media driven obsession with body image, with its accompanying bullying and lack of self esteem, that is associated with the twenty-first century. It was also confined to older teenagers and adults and did not extend to pre-pubescent girls. "I never felt under any pressure to change my weight or body shape and was too busy to ever think about it."

Being overweight was the exception rather than the norm. In fact, for many growing up in post-war Britain, with rationing still in force, the pressure was more likely to be to gain weight. Nevertheless diets, for women never men, were beginning to be advertised. "In the early 1960s people began to think of body image and weight so began to diet. Women's magazines had much on this subject. The grapefruit diet and the cabbage soup diet were popular. As well as the amphetamines prescribed by the GP, there were slimming tablets available from health food shops, which were springing up."

What in the modern world would constitute sexual harassment was commonplace in the 1950s and 1960s. "Remarks which might be considered inappropriate these days, were often made by boys and men about my appearance. Wolf whistles were allowed in those days." Such behaviour in the workplace, or in public, was accepted as normal and only the most ardent of feminists would think of objecting; for many it was considered a compliment.

Sex Education at this time was minimal and normally only undertaken when necessary and amidst much embarrassment. "Words relating to bodily parts or functions were avoided and 'coy' expressions were substituted; female genitalia, 'down there'; pregnancy, 'expecting a baby' and I was aware of this disinclination to use correct terminology beyond my family, indeed amongst all my acquaintances." Schools might provide basic information but this was restricted to the mechanics of the process. Emotions, sexually transmitted diseases or contraception were rarely covered by parents or teachers. Family discussions about bodily changes and reproduction were often confined only to the girls; the commencement of menstruation meaning that it was more difficult to ignore. Apart from the school 'biology' lesson, boys frequently relied solely on playground rumour. "My parents avoided the subject completely and to my shame, when my mother gave birth to my sister when I was almost fifteen, I had no idea that she had been pregnant. It came as a huge surprise when my grandmother put the baby in my arms during my lunch break. The school teacher who was expected to tell us about the birds and bees turned beetroot red before she started and we were all totally embarrassed and still clueless afterwards." "My mother gave me a little Family Doctor booklet about the reproduction methods of banana flies and it really didn't tell me anything at all about human reproduction!" "When I started Senior School at eleven we were given 'sex education,' in fact what it was was a biology lesson. The boys and girls were all told together about the reproductive sections of the male and the female. Nothing was said about how a girl became pregnant. In answer to my question, 'How does the male sperm get into the female body?' the female teacher went bright red and said, 'You will learn about that later'."

"I do remember the condom on the cucumber lesson especially well. It was the first time I had heard the correct names for the female anatomy, which somehow added to the surreal nature of the lessons. These lessons were given when we were about fifteen and were laughable in their delivery. If we hadn't learnt about sex from our elders by this stage, then we must have been living in a cave! We also had the classic 'bad' girls in the school, who delighted in regaling us with their latest adventures, frankly I was too scared of my mother to even think about 'doing it'."

Although contraception was no longer frowned upon it was, until the very end of this period, unequivocally for married women only. "I wasn't able to get any birth control advice until I was twenty-two years old; you had to be engaged or married (or very bold) to get it at all. I wore my engagement ring to prove that I was to be married in six months time, in 1967." "We had a family planning clinic on our estate and when I became engaged and wanted to get their advice, I had to have a letter from my GP informing them that I was engaged before they would help me. I first used a 'Dutch cap', which had to be coated with something called 'K' or 'KY Jelly'." "I needed effective contraception and was able to obtain a Dutch cap at a London clinic in 1966 by pretending to be a married woman, false name, false address, no one checked up."

"Marie Stopes opened birth control clinics, advice was given and women were able to take control. They were shown how to use diaphrams (caps), which fitted over the cervix, lubricated by anti-spermicidal gel. Only married women or those about to marry were given this advice but it later became available to all, which reduced illegitimate births and abortions greatly. A little later the contraceptive pill was popular but dosage was trial and error and there were side effects such as migraine, dvts[2] and weight gain. Women did not realise the pill did not work with certain antibiotics, or if they had a stomach upset." "It was the age of sexual revolution and freedom but nobody told us how to avoid becoming pregnant (or catching syphilis) and condoms were kept under the counter at the chemists, many of which refused to sell them to a female, as I found out to my mortification! I eventually obtained the Pill by concocting a story about heavy and irregular periods but my GP was reluctant even then and flowing tears were involved if I remember correctly, mine, not his!" "By 1967 in London it was possible to get the Pill, we used to go to a sympathetic doctor in South Kensington."

Disability and Mental Illness

Disability, whether mental or physical, was another matter for secrecy and a cause of shame. There was little attempt at integration; many who were institutionalised would have been living at home and being educated in mainstream schooling in the twenty-first century. Those who were in the community seem to have been treated with a form of benign condescension. "We were largely unaware of life-limiting illnesses, especially in children. Those with serious disabilities were segregated and were referred to using terms that would now be considered politically incorrect. Disability was still something to be slightly ashamed of in the 1960s." "I had an aunt who was mentally disabled who lived in a mental hospital. She was not talked about much but she would be brought out of the home for things like Sunday lunch." "Living with them (grandparents) was an uncle who as a teenager had fallen off a load of hay and sustained a head injury. This uncle lived in a downstairs room and I never saw him. My brother and I once tried to see him through the window. My brother saw him but I did not and we were reprimanded and shooed away."

"Because of our family experience of disability, we met other families who also had members with disabilities. This happened a great deal in 1949/50 when my mother set up the Dover branch of what is now MENCAP; then it was called the Society for the Parents of Backward Children. Many of the children were not taken out in daylight. Sadly, the attitude from some people was that giving birth to a baby with a disability was a punishment for the past sins of the parents. There was very little support for such families then and hurtful comments from the general public made it an ordeal to go out."

Those with mental illness, which could encompass anything from serious psychosis to post-natal depression, were often treated by long-term incarceration. Milder instances of depression were considered to be signs of personal weakness. "Mental illness or depression was never mentioned and apart from the lady up the road who had what I now know to be dementia, I was aware of no one of with any form of mental illness or melancholia. If you felt miserable you 'pulled yourself together' and got on with it. Talking therapies were almost unheard of and if anyone did go for counselling, it would certainly never be spoken of." "Depressives were labelled as shirkers." "There was a mental hospital outside of a nearby town and as children we were frightened of being near there at full moon."

Medication was often the option that was preferred to counselling. Although the latter was available to some, receiving this form of treatment was not something that would be advertised beyond the immediate family. "At about the age of twelve (1958) I started suffering from bad nightmares and also when I was walking, my legs suddenly started to give way. After a hospital visit I was referred to a psychiatrist and up until the age of eighteen I visited him every six months. I was put on Phenobarbitone. My mother did not like me telling anyone about my visits to Mr Morgan." "My father died suddenly when I was nine (1965); no one, least of all me, considered that I might need any form of grief counselling, such as would be offered to bereaved school children in the twenty-first century."

"Major mental illness was referred to as a 'breakdown' and some people were said to 'suffer from their nerves'. In the 1950s, tranquillisers made their appearance and the pharmaceutical companies flourished, producing a huge number of new products." "In the mid-1960s many women were taking Valium for their 'nerves'. I was horrified when my five year old was given a 'calming medicine' when he developed a pronounced stammer and I found that that also contained Valium. I threw it away." There were also more invasive therapies for depression. "My mother suffered bouts of depression after the death of my father and often went into hospital for treatment, which sometimes included electric shocks to her head." "My aunt had what was commonly referred to as a 'nervous breakdown' after the birth of her second child in 1954 but was most likely to have been suffering from post-natal psychosis. She was hospitalised in a 'mental institution' for almost a year, where she was subjected to a leucotomy operation, whereby the 'offending' part of her brain was removed."

Smoking, Drinking and Drugs

By the 1940s, it was acceptable for both men and women to smoke and it became commonplace for those beyond school age. There was no restriction on smoking in public places and very little awareness of any impact on health. In fact, many teenagers had been encouraged by their parents to take up smoking to alleviate stress during the war. "Smoking cigarettes was often suggested for 'calming the nerves' and cigarettes were certainly considered to be a sophistication of adulthood." "The majority of people in my family smoked and pubs and dance halls were smoke-filled. We just accepted it as the norm. I can't remember any information being available on the health aspects of smoking. Dad, when he joined the army, had a cough and the doctor said that smoking would clear his lungs and make it better! It was not done for a woman to smoke in the street as this is what prostitutes did and it would make you look tarty."

"Cigarette advertising was everywhere but this is not what encouraged me, as a fourteen year old, to try one, it was peer pressure, availability in the home and the fact that little was ever said about the dangers." "I started smoking at the age of twelve, along with my school friends, we used to buy single cigarettes from the local shop on our way home and smoke down the alleyways. Then, as I got older, I got bolder and used to buy whole packets of ten from a 'friendly' shopkeeper.

One day my mother discovered my packet and matches in my swimming bag and went ballistic, what did I think I was doing? I wasn't old enough to smoke, no concern for my health in those days! I continued until I was sixteen and I was given a lighter for my birthday, it didn't seem rebellious then, so I stopped!" "I experimented with cigarettes when I was at the end of my time at senior school. Then you could buy cigarettes in packets of five. I thought I was the bee's knees in my red velvet, tight dress and the cigarette holder which I used for Sobrani cigarettes. These were strong smelling and came in black with a gold tip or pastel shades of blue, yellow or pink."

There were incentives to smoke that went beyond peer pressure and social norms. "The coupons that came with each pack of Kensitas cigarettes, delivered weekly with the groceries, were collected avidly by my mother, to exchange for gifts." Smoking could be a hazardous activity and not just for the detrimental effects on health. "I experimented with smoking only once, setting my then fashionable 'bouffant' hairdo on fire with a cigarette in a holder; I never smoked again. It seemed a social thing to do at the time (smoking not setting one's hair alight!)."

Attitudes to drinking had changed during the second world war. It was much more acceptable for women to be seen drinking in public and the consumption of alcohol became an established part of social occasions. Underage drinking[3] in pubs was common but binge drinking or drinking to excess on a regular basis was rare. Although it was illegal to be drunk in charge of a vehicle, no legal limit was set until 1967, when breathalysers were introduced. It was not socially unacceptable to drink and drive. "I began drinking once I started work at fifteen, the pubs didn't seem so concerned about your age in those days, although we were usually in a large group and the males would buy the drinks. Drinking and driving wasn't an issue either, we used to do pub crawls around Essex for fun." "My introduction to alcohol came one Christmas at age thirteen, when I was allowed to have a Snowball (advocaat and lemonade) or a Babycham. For the most part, the adults' social life centred on the local pubs. A friend and I had a cider party in the local park at age fourteen, having managed to find the one local off-licence which didn't give a damn about selling booze and fags to under-age kids but we were careful not to be caught."

For many, drinking at home was an occasional activity, confined to celebrations. "Going to the pub was frowned upon in our family and thought of as a bit common. My parents had a glass of sherry at Christmas and weddings. In my teens, I remember having a glass of Babycham and there was a bit of peer pressure to try an alcoholic drink. I never learned to like the taste of alcohol and subsequently became a bit of a social pariah because I wouldn't drink." The increase in foreign travel in the 1960s meant that wine drinking at home became more popular and home wine-making boomed. "My father took up making wine at home. He had all the paraphernalia, the demijohns and large plastic bins, the tins from Boot's, the sulphites and the campden tablets and the vinegar fly, the exploding bottles and the many wines which tasted rather like cough mixture." "Making wine and beer at home became very popular in the 1960s and having restricted herself to an occasional glass of sherry all her life, Mum joined in with an almost industrial production of booze."

Awareness of illegal drugs depended very much on where people lived and their life stage between 1946 and 1969. Those who were in urban areas, or at university, in the 1960s were much more likely to come into contact with a variety of non-prescription drugs. "Flower Power and the sixties produced more awareness of the use of drugs, in particular marijuana with its significant smell disguised by the use of joss sticks. One knew of course, that cocaine was used by the smart upper classes in London." "I became aware of illegal drugs when I was nineteen (1966) and going to night clubs and coffee bars in Manchester. At that time I seem to recall they were mainly pills; you did see those changing hands in coffee bars. It would have been a few years later when I became aware of cannabis being used. I did smoke and would confess to trying an occasional joint but I was always worried about breaking the law rather than becoming addicted." "At the age of fourteen, I had a friend a year older who had experimented with most of what was available and with whom I shared the occasional joint. Availability depended on the dealers, who were mostly to be found at rock concerts and places such as Kensington Market, a sort of 'souk' for the hippie culture and the roof gardens at the nearby Biba store in the old Derry and Toms building. Other than that, my friend had friends and friends of friends and she could usually find someone who could oblige her." "It was comparatively easy to acquire illegal drugs. Most of the boys I went round with experimented with cannabis (pot), marijuana (grass or weed) or amphetamines (speed) but no-one I knew well progressed to heroin. The girls seemed to steer clear."

Many felt that the 'swinging sixties' passed them by and were unaware of the drug culture that was taking hold amongst young people in the cities and universities. It was however not just illegal drugs that were used. "In the early 1950s amphetamines were prescribed for weight loss by GPs. My mother was prescribed some and she would sit up half the night knitting. I took some of the tablets to the hospital and some of us took them to stay awake at night. We were working in theatres at the time and the Superintendent was told. We were called in to the office and reprimanded as well as being warned of the dangers." It seems that although drugs were increasingly obtainable, they were confined to a comparatively small section of the population and that their availability depended very much on where you lived.

Body Enhancements

Sunbathing at this time was not considered to be something that should be done with care. Sunscreen, even for children, was almost unheard of and it was considered healthy to have a tanned skin. "Before the war, ladies were expected to have pale delicate skins and a sun tan indicated a lower social class who worked outdoors. After 1946 sunbathing became popular and this was encouraged to help children avoid rickets. It then became desirable because it indicated that one could afford foreign holidays." Many people took acquiring as dark a tan as possible very seriously. Coconut oil was used to enhance a tan and some people even sunbathed on sheets of silver foil, in the hope of reflecting the sun's rays. Although mechanical aids to enhancing a tan were not yet in common use, fake tans could be purchased. These were not very successful or realistic. "I experimented with fake tans but these resulted in orange skin on my knees and elbows and an unforgettable perfume that stayed with me until any orange colouring had completely worn off."

Tattoos were for men and then usually only those who had been in the armed services; they would be confined to the arms, hands and chest. "Defacing one's body permanently by tattooing was considered only for sailors." "Most of my uncles who had been in the forces had a tattoo. There were not many women that had them then. One fad in senior school in the early 1960s was for the girls to draw on their knuckles, 'love' on one hand and 'hate' on the other. One of the girls thought she would be clever and scratched her hand and put the ink from the inkwell in it so it would last. Needless to say she got some sort of blood poisoning."

"Body piercing was unheard of, except the well accepted practice of ear piercing, which ran the gamete of socio-economic groups. Ear piercing was not for children, in fact it was most popular in married ladies. Big gold rings in the ears were for gypsies only." Other piercings, with the exception of ladies of Indian origin, who might have a nose piercing, were beyond imagination. Male earrings were confined to sailors or gypsies.

Death and Mourning

The reticence that was evident in other areas of health and hygiene extended to death, which was another taboo subject. In many cases funerals were still an all male affair. Whilst the public face of grief was observed, with, for many, mourning clothes still being worn, curtains drawn and cortèges respected, talking about death as a means of coping with bereavement was rare. "My mother hid her tears and my father maintained a stiff upper lip." "In my extended family there were no mechanisms for handling grief."

The deceased were frequently kept at home so that family and friends could pay their respects. "My uncle died about 1962 and as he died at home he was left there and his wife still slept next to him on their bed." "People were laid out in their own front room and dressed in best clothes or night attire. Curtains were kept drawn until after the funeral, when everyone wore black and went back to the house after the service for tea. As the cortège went to the church all the traffic stopped, all the people bowed their heads and men removed their hats. The family wore black for six months after the funeral and then purple for another six months." "A custom, not always adhered to these days, was that on the day of someone's funeral, every householder on the street would draw their curtains together as a mark of respect, until the funeral cortège had left the street. As the cortège passed, any men on the street at the time, would doff their hats and bow their heads, also crossing themselves if they happened to be Catholics. Ladies too, would stop and bow their heads as the funeral procession passed by."

To a large extent, children were excluded from the grieving process. Death was not discussed and children would not normally attend funerals; perhaps this was seen as a way of protecting them. "In my extended family women and children did not attend the cremation or burial service. In 1957, at fifteen years of age, when my father died I just stayed home alone and waited." "If someone close to you died then you just had to deal with your feelings of loss yourself. I suppose if you were a regular member of a church then there might have been some help there. I think the way most people dealt with it was at the wake, which children did attend, when family just stood around and just remembered the person and what they had and had not done." Despite the practice of shielding children from death in some ways, many mentioned being expected to view an open coffin, even at a young age.

Summary

In some respects it might be expected that the years 1946-1969 would see many changes in approaches to health, hygiene and death. After all, this era witnessed the arrival of free medical care, in the form of the National Health Service, the widespread availability of life-saving antibiotics and many advancements in medical knowledge. In the home, hot running water was now the norm and more families had the spending power that allowed them to acquire an increasing variety of grooming products. Despite this, these issues were often approached in the same way as they had been for decades. Much less time and money was spent on keeping clean and healthy than is usual in the twenty-first century. Personal hygiene practices were adequate rather than excessive, home remedies still prevailed and illness was seen as a self-indulgence. Bodily functions, death, disability and serious illness were, to a large extent, private matters. There was a reluctance to discuss such issues, even within the family. Mourning processes were ritualistic and whilst this may have been comforting for some, for many, grief was not well handled.

Attitudes to smoking, sunbathing, tattooing and body piercing have revolutionised since this period. With only glimmerings of the celebrity culture that was to develop after the 1960s, there was much less concern about body image and outward appearance. The idea of personal grooming for men, beyond looking smart, was only just beginning to emerge with the teddy boys and mods. Whilst there was a lack of awareness about things that were not conducive to good health, active lifestyles and a post-rationing diet were much more beneficial to well-being than those that were to come in subsequent decades.

The Brief

Think about attitudes to ill health, was it mentioned? How were aliments treated? At what stage was the doctor involved? What remedies were used? What about preventative measures such as cod liver oil or vitamins? Was it expected that children would be immunised?

For those who can remember, what was the impact of the arrival of the National Health Service in 1948?

Write about attendance at the dentist and dental treatment.

Include attitudes to mental illness and disability.

Was there a personal hygiene regime? Mention frequency of bathing, washing, hair washing. How much water was used in the bath? Were several people bathed together or in the same water?

What 'products' were used? Include such things as deodorant, soap, moisturiser, shampoo, toilet paper, tissues and sanitary products.

Comment on body image, was there pressure to be a certain weight or shape? Did people feel compelled to diet?

What about the removal of body hair? Was this expected? At what age? By what method?

How were teenage spots treated?

What about attitudes towards and ways of dealing with menstruation? What euphemisms were used?

Was there any sex education? Was this delivered at home or school? What did this consist of? At what age was it provided?

What methods of birth control were available/acceptable?

Comment on attitudes towards smoking and drinking, at what age were these acceptable?

Were you aware of illegal drugs? How easily available were they?

Mention attitudes towards and prevalence of, sunbathing, tattoos and piercing.

How was death and bereavement handled? What were the mechanisms for grief and mourning?

Chapter 7 footnotes

[1] Tampons had been patented in 1931 but it took several decades for their use to be widespread.

[2] Deep vein thrombosis.

[3] Although the age of majority was twenty-one until 1969, the legal age for drinking in public was eighteen, or sixteen if it accompanied a meal.

CHAPTER 8

The Young Ones: childrearing, childhood and youth culture

Pregnancy and Childbirth

Pregnancy was not something that was discussed, even within the home. "In June 1946, I woke up to the sound of a baby crying in my parents' bedroom. This was the first intimation to me that my Mum was having a baby. I was five, so perhaps it was understandable that I hadn't been told but the same applied at the birth of my other sister in 1947 and also of my younger brother who was born in a nursing home in August 1949. I may have been naïve not to catch on but we had no pets that had young and there was nothing in the films at the Saturday morning pictures that would have given me a clue as to why my Mum was putting on weight!" "In 1969, when visiting one of my great-aunts with Dad, Auntie Hilda was in all sorts of difficulty trying to tell Dad that her son and daughter-in-law, after twelve years of marriage, were expecting their first child – without letting 'the children' (i.e. us, then sixteen and twenty-one respectively) know what she was talking about. We thought it was hilarious."

There were various euphemisms for pregnancy, some, such as 'in the family way', were more acceptable in polite company than others. "More delicately, the couple would be expecting 'the patter of tiny feet', or 'a little stranger', or the girl was in a 'delicate condition'. If older children were told anything it was that the stork was bringing a baby, or that one had been found under a gooseberry bush." "Other expressions for pregnancy, which I learned later at school, were 'fallen for a baby', 'bun in the oven', 'up the duff' and 'in the pudding club'; to have an illegitimate baby was to 'get into trouble'."

There was help for pregnant mothers from health workers. "The local clinic had classes once a week, in addition to seeing the GP and your allocated midwife at increasingly regular intervals through the pregnancy. The classes were quite solemn by today's standards; the emphasis was on the role of the professionals. The main benefit was meeting all the midwives, so that whoever was on duty when the baby arrived would not be a stranger." "The National Childbirth Trust was getting established and they held antenatal classes where we learned helpful breathing techniques and other handy hints to ease labour pains."

The fashion for giving birth at home, rather than in a nursing home or hospital, came and went. "In the late forties, as the National Health Service became established, most babies were born at home, in the care of the local midwife and doctor. Only the complicated pregnancies (such as those with toxaemia or other difficult histories) were delivered in hospital. Mothers were kept confined to bed for up to three weeks post-delivery. I have heard it said that babies with malformations were not stimulated into breathing by experienced midwives and there was certainly very little provision for premature babies. Fathers were not expected to be present at the birth but waited in another nearby room." "In the 1950s children were born USIB (Up Stairs In Bed, as mum used to say). When she went into labour someone would run to get the midwife from her home, or to the phone box to call her. Dad wasn't even allowed in the house at this time, not that he wanted to be anywhere near! After baby was born Mum stayed in bed for a week with Nan helping out."

By the 1960s, husbands were more likely to be present. "Our second child was born in 1969. Fathers were encouraged to be at the birth and assist by cutting the umbilical cord." "When my two boys were born, in the 1960s, ideas of gender equality were being furthered by more women working and therefore 'new men' shared housework and supported their partner's pregnancy, birth and child care. My husband was present at both births, rubbing my back and as they were both home births, providing the practicalities of tea etc.. The thought was that, unless there were physical or practical contra-indications, births could happen at home." "When my first daughter was born, in 1966, it was just beginning to be accepted that fathers could be present at the birth. My husband was keen to be present but the hospital was still getting used to the idea and we could tell they felt fathers would get in the way of the job in hand."

One volunteer described her own birth through the eyes of her mother's diary "She finally went to the nursing home at midnight and I was born at 1a.m.. For the first four days she had a room to herself at the nursing home and was then transferred to a three bedded room and comments that she was allowed to walk the ten feet between beds! She was allowed up after a week and given a bath the following day. She was also allowed to watch me being bathed on day eight. She went home on day ten (a Saturday). Nurse came on the Sunday to bath the baby and came every day for a week. My mother bathed me herself for the first time when I was two weeks old."

Increasing geographical mobility meant that expectant mothers were less likely to have extended family on hand to help. It may be that this made hospital births more desirable. After a few days hospitalisation, mothers might be transferred to a nursing home for another ten days or so. "On arrival at the maternity home, I quickly sensed that the regime here was by no means informal. In the hospital the babies were left with the mothers, unless the staff decided it would be best for the mother to sleep but here my precious bundle was whisked away to the nursery and only returned to me at scheduled feeding times. This was explained as giving the mothers time to rest but also meant you returned home with a baby you scarcely knew."

Although, even in the late 1960s, some employers were still refusing to hold jobs open for women who became pregnant, there was financial help for expectant mothers from the government. "The maternity allowance had been raised in October 1967 from £4 to £4 10s a week and in November 1969, it was increased to £5 a week. There was extra for dependants and the earning limits for these was also increased. At the same time, the maternity grant was increased from £22 to £25 for confinements occurring on or after 3rd November 1969."

Routines

After the second world war, various childrearing theories held sway. The inter-war guru was Truby King and his methods continued to be advocated well into the 1950s. By today's standards these seem harsh and uncaring but there was a fear of 'spoiling' the child by seeming to pander to a baby's demands. "On the advice of my grandmother, I was raised according to the Truby King regime; a strict four hourly feeding schedule, separate room at night, no picking up and cuddling between feeds and any crying ignored. Consequently, I was a fretful baby and my mother had a more relaxed attitude to the next three babies. The only part of the regime followed for all of us was to put us outside in the pram after the 10am feed, if it wasn't too wet or cold." "The feeds were given rigidly at four hourly intervals and the nappy was changed. The nappy was towelling and the baby was put outside in the pram to sleep for the next four hours, so that mother could get on with the housework. Tough if the baby cried and the pram would be moved further away so that the crying could not be heard." "Four hourly feeds were the norm and my mother tells of how she once dipped a cherry in honey and wrapped it in a muslin nappy for me to suck until she could give me my feed!" "Once babies were starting to sleep through, it was thought bad practice to lift them, if they cried in the night, for fear of 'spoiling' them. Most mothers took no notice of this as it was easier for both mother and baby to get back to sleep after checking that all was alright." "We were not picked up just because we cried, as long as there was no reason for the crying we were allowed to cry, it was at that time thought that you were just 'exercising your lungs' and no harm would come from it."

"Toddlers and young children were expected to have an afternoon nap each day. Dummies were frowned upon and rarely used, only a bad mother would resort to a dummy. Toilet training began and it was training. The child sat on the potty until it produced however long it took and were smacked if they got off the pot." "In the 1940s and 1950s, muslin nappies were used for tiny babies and these were then used as liners in terry towelling ones for solid waste. By the 1960s, special liners were available and Napisan powder for sterilising them. I was surprised to be asked by a friend of my mother-in-law if I ironed my nappies! Disposable nappies were around in the 1960s and were welcomed by some mothers but on the occasions when I tried them, overnight, I found that they leaked and I ended up washing cot sheets instead of nappies, so went back to terry towelling again."

King's methods were superseded by the, less rigid and more child friendly, theories of Dr Spock. "By this time, Dr Spock was the popular adviser on caring for babies and whilst he was reassuring in that parents would soon recognise the difference between cries: hungry, wet, need a cuddle, I did not find this easy and said to the health visitor that it was a pity that babies did not come with a selection of notices to say what was needed. Both boys were demand fed for the first few months and the transition to a more regular pattern seemed to happen quite naturally. I did most of the feeding with bottles but my husband would do this if he was at home." "When Dr Benjamin Spock's manual of childcare was published, in 1946, it recommended feeding on demand. Much discussion followed about 'discipline' and the formation of bad habits."

Immediately after the second world war, bottle feeding was in the ascendance. This was partly because bottles could now be sterilised safely. In addition, with food on ration, bottle feeding meant that the mother did not need the extra calories that breast feeding required. "My mother may have thought bottle feeding would be better for us as she was on food rations and also it may have been recommended by the District Nurse. The crescent-shaped glass bottles were double ended with a rubber teat, which stretched over one end and a rubber valve-cap at the other. I remember that these were removed for sterilising, with the bottle, by putting them in cold water and bringing them gently to boiling point."

Using condensed milk for bottle-fed babies was going out of fashion and National Dried Milk and orange juice were obtained from baby clinics. "Mum never breast fed, she always used bottles of National Dried Milk. These were only ever made up by the women and fed to baby by the women. Dad had no involvement at all in the changing, dressing or feeding of the baby. Mum returned to work when the baby was tiny and Nan cared for it." "We used National Dried Milk, which was in a tall tin container; orange juice and also a malt extract, which mum used to use to make toffee apples to get us to eat it. In the late 1960s, when my own children were born, you could still purchase these items and also they used to have 'A & D' drops, which were added to the milk. Advice was given either verbally by the nurse or from a collection of booklets and leaflets available. There was also a paediatrician on hand and you could make an appointment to see them at the clinic if you were concerned about your child's health."

"In the 1960s, breast feeding was beginning to be adopted again and was usually confined to the home but some hippies made a point of feeding wherever they were." "Mother breast-fed all her children for a few months, always in the living room and on demand." "Breast feeding was expected and sometimes was continued for many months, even to the second birthday and beyond. This was hoped by some to be a way of postponing the next pregnancy!"

Some form of solid food might be given as early as two months. "I started by giving them Farley's Rusks or Farex cereal, morning then evening, then adding lunch consisting of potato, vegetable and gravy mixed together, which was then liquidised or mashed to a smooth paste using a 'Baby Mouli'. As time progressed and my baby had teeth, textures became coarser until the baby was able to eat the family's meal." "I used tins and jars of baby food in the weaning process, not realising until too late that it would have been healthier to have purchased a liquidiser. Gadgets such as this were on the market but not yet in common usage." "None of us ever had a dummy and when teething I was given of all things fried bread to bite on, my own children had something called 'Bickie Pegs' which came on a ribbon that you attached to their clothes so they couldn't choke on it by putting it too far in their mouths."

Caregivers

Parental involvement frequently revolved round physical care, feeding and keeping the child clean and warm. Playing with children, particularly very small children, was rarely part of the regime. "My relationship with my parents was not close and physical but I knew they cared for me because of all the sacrifices they made for me and the respect they gave to me. I don't remember either of them playing with me or my brothers." "My parents were not distant or uninterested in my every-day doings but they very seldom participated actively in play. Children were expected to amuse themselves and initiate their own interaction with other children nearby." "I have little memory of playing with my mother, except for the occasional game of cards or Ludo. She was always at home as she didn't go out to work but in general children were left to their own devices, without activities being planned for them and without adult supervision most of the time."

Fathers, in particular, were distant figures. "My father was the antithesis of the modern hands-on Dad. He did no practical childcare of any kind. I'm sure he never changed a nappy in his life. He would have regarded the day-to-day management of his daughter as his wife's role. I have little memory of playing with him in any way; he seemed to be always working. Seaside holidays were the exception, when both parents came to the beach and helped to build sand castles."

Older siblings, female of course, were often involved in childcare, even at quite a young age. "1946 was the last year that I had no housework duties; I was three years old living with my parents before the birth of my sister in 1947. At this time I became assistant mother and chief fetcher and carrier of things for the baby. If she cried, I rocked her outside in the pram or gave her a bottle. One of my duties was running errands to the corner shop eleven doors away. When my second sister arrived in 1949 my work increased." "I often baby sat, although only ten years of age. Up to that time I had gone to Sunday school and church every week. I was told I couldn't go as I had to help with the baby. My duties had now increased to the whole of the housework including laundry, dealing with nappies catering for many visitors. When I did the grocery shopping, I had to take at least one other child." "As the eldest, I was meant to look after my siblings. When Mum asked, 'Who did that?' If I replied that a sibling did, she usually said, 'You shouldn't have let them!'"

The extended family and neighbours also had a role to play. "My grandma and granddad helped in my upbringing and I often went to stay with them. Our neighbours all had an unofficial open doors policy and I could go into any of the houses for help, so they were a big part of my early years." Au pairs or nannies were rare but not unheard of. "After the twins were born in 1953 life changed a great deal as we employed a resident nanny who wore a uniform with a starched apron. There was a succession of nannies, some more memorable than others and I think they only stopped when the twins started school aged five. I remember them as being quite bossy; some were more fun than others."

Children were expected to keep themselves out of harm's way. "One aspect of child-rearing which has changed drastically is the attitude towards physical safety. There seemed to be far less recognition of possible hazards. Our house had a huge open fire without an adequate fire-guard; it had a set of iron heating pipes running along a wall at knee height, hot enough to burn a child's skin. And anyone with a car travelled without seat-belts and with the children happily bouncing around in the back, or worse the front, seat. Playgrounds had unforgiving tarmac surfaces and cycle helmets had not been thought of."

Punishment

Then, as now, concepts of good behaviour varied from family to family but in general, children were expected to conform to adult expectations, without question. There was an emphasis on manners and showing respect for 'elders and betters'. "The guiding principle of discipline seemed to be that a child was expected to do as it was told, full stop, without the benefit of the reasoning or explanation that most modern parents favour. The assumption was that an adult's word would not be challenged. If I queried why I should do something, my father's usual rejoinder was 'Because....' implying, 'Because I said so is reason enough'." "Children were expected to be seen and not heard in the 1940s but by the 1960s this was changing" and children's views were beginning to be heard in more progressive families.

Punishment for wrong-doing was frequently physical. "Misbehaviour was dealt with by a smack. This was universal and my mother used to smack my bottom with a hairbrush if she felt it necessary." "He had strict rules about how we all ate together at the table; with clean hands, no talking, laughing or arguing. Mother was actually quite cruel to me and I still have scars where she scratched me, she often hit me on the head with a wire brush which bled but never when dad was in. When I was very young she made me sit on the stairs, which were unlit and I was scared." "My chief offence, as I got older, was answering back or 'speaking out of turn', this was often punished with a slap across my bottom, the back of my legs or arms, sometimes quite hard. I remember the last time Dad hit me, just before my sixteenth birthday; Mum said, 'You won't be able to do that again, she'll be counted as an adult from tomorrow'.

Toys and Leisure

For the majority of this period, most homes did not boast an abundance of toys. Toys were acquired, in small numbers, at Christmas, for birthdays, or were rare purchases that followed the diligent saving of pocket money. This was as much a consequence of expectations, as it was the result of post-war shortages. A lack of exposure to media advertising meant that there was little peer pressure to obtain the latest 'must have' toy. "We didn't have lots of toys, as my grandchildren do today but what we had we treasured. With no endless television adverts for the latest toys and games to tempt us, we were generally satisfied with what we had and were grateful to have them." "The main exposure to advertising in the 1960s seems to have been in the shops themselves, with displays of goodies in the windows and Christmas section."

Many toys were designated as being suitable for either boys or girls and it would take a brave adult to buy something that was intended for the opposite gender. In families where there were children of both sexes, there was of course the opportunity for girls to play with 'boys' toys' and vice versa. Children from single sex families however had their range of playthings limited by societal attitudes. Only the most enlightened parents crossed the gender divide when providing toys. Whilst it might be just acceptable, by the late 1960s, to buy a toy car for an all-girl family, giving a boy a doll would be a ridiculous concept, unless it was an Action Man.[1] "My toys were very much 'girl appropriate': dolls and prams, a cot which had beautiful drapes, I also had a doll's pushchair." A few volunteers were fortunate enough to be provided with toys designated for boys, despite lacking brothers. "I did have a dinky/matchbox car collection and there was no suggestion that this was inappropriate for a girl. Dad made me a roadway by sticking a cardboard road layout onto two large sheets of hardboard." "Although we were all girls we didn't just have 'girls'' toys. We had a large collection of wooden bricks; when I was older I had Bayko, this was a building toy with bases, metal rods and different types of bricks to thread onto the rods to build houses. I had a Meccano set and added to it from time to time, my younger sister had a clockwork Hornby Train Set."

The use of the environment and imagination as an aid to play has already been mentioned in Chapter 1. "A lot of playing didn't involve anything at all but we seemed to be out most of the time. I would go out in the morning, come home for dinner at midday, go out again until teatime and then out again until it got dark. This must have been during the summer holidays. Nobody had a watch but we seemed to be able to accurately gauge the time." Many playground games, mentioned in Chapter 6, translated to streets and gardens and playing outside was a feature of most childhoods. This might involve having 'adventures' or making dens but bikes, trikes (often made by Triang) and roller skates featured, as well as home-made go-karts. "At primary school, the girls played hand stands, two-ball and skipping. I prided myself I was good at all these and had some of my own balls and a rope to use at home. I also remember hopscotch, Simon Says and What's the Time Mr Wolf?." Parties were the opportunity for different games and these are described in Chapter 9.

For most of this period, play was very much the preserve of children, with adult participation being rare. Occasionally, board or card games might be a whole family activity. "With no television in the 1940s we spent a lot of time playing board, dice and card games in the evening, when friends came for tea in the winter or when it was wet. I spent hours playing Patience. Our favourites were Rummy and Canasta which I picked up early. We played Cribbage using a special wooden board with holes and pegs to record scores." Card games were played including, Snap, Happy Families, Whist, Patience and Rummy. Board games, such as Draughts, Snakes and Ladders and Ludo, were unsophisticated by modern standards. A 'compendium' containing a variety of such games was a prized possession. "I loved playing Tiddlywinks and also Chinese Chequers with my Mum. We also had Dominos which was quite fun. When older, my brother taught me to play Chess but I quickly became disinterested as I could never beat him!" Games produced by Waddington's, such as Monopoly, were becoming popular. "Careers was produced rather handsomely by the people who made Monopoly and it cost 21 shillings. In this game, the players would make a life-plan around money, love or accolade and then travel round the board hoping to collect points towards their separate ambitions. This would have been around 1958." Paper and pencil games, such as Hangman, Noughts and Crosses, Battleships or Consequences were played and had the advantage of being free. "I folded paper boats and planes but loved to make those little paper things where you could put fingers in the folds and make them open two ways. You lifted flaps and found nice messages underneath (or rude ones!)."

The teddy bear was a universal toy that was given to most children. Another popular cuddly toy was the golliwog, or golly. These black faced, fuzzy-haired, doll-like toys are now regarded as racist parodies of people of African origin and are no longer acceptable. The golliwog was also the logo of the Robinson's Jam company who gave away ceramic golliwog ornaments and enamel badges as a reward for collecting golliwog labels from their products. Almost all girls had one or more dolls. By the 1950s, these tended to be plastic, rather than china-headed or made from Bakelite or Celluloid. These dolls usually had home-made clothes and a girl from a more affluent family might have a pram or cot to accompany her doll. In the 1960s, teenaged dolls such as Sindy and the American equivalent, Barbie, became popular. Sindy was often preferred by parents as being more 'wholesome'. "When I was eleven (1964) I had a Sindy doll, which was then very popular (as were Tressy and Barbie). These were the first teenage dolls and Sindy was the only doll I really remember pestering Mum for. She cost 22s 6d." In the 1960s, trolls became popular. These doll-like figures originated in Denmark, were marketed by the company Dam and came with different coloured hair and in varying sizes.

The 1950s saw plastic toys beginning to replace ones made from lead or wood. Some toys were still home-made and very few required batteries or electricity; exceptions were Hornby train sets and the car racing game Scalextric.[2] "Dad made me wooden toys during quiet spells at work. There was a wooden train, a doll with jointed arms and legs, a dog, a rabbit and a monkey strung between two supports. When these were squeezed the monkey did somersaults. He also made me a base for my many plastic zoo and farm animals. Also home-made was a dolls' house, it even had battery-powered lights. Some of the furniture was home-made too, for example mum made the three-piece suites and dad made the dustbin and coal bin."

The range of toys was much more restricted than it is in the twenty-first century, so many volunteers mentioned the same products. Popular 'small world' toys included soldiers, farm animals, dolls' houses or cowboys and Indians. Model cars were made by Dinkie, Corgi and Matchbox. Britain's 'floral garden' was one of several products that was made from in lead in the first half of the twentieth century but was produced in plastic in the 1960s. Plain, wooden building blocks were still in use but more complex construction and model making toys were Meccano and Bayko. The latter was a fore-runner of Lego[3] and involved sliding bricks between metal rods that would be a health and safety nightmare today. Many boys enjoyed constructing plastic Airfix models. These were primarily aircraft and their assembly involved patience and dexterity, as well as an affinity with glue and a fine paint brush that many of today's children would find alien. Jigsaws continued to be popular as did 'educational' toys, such as chemistry sets. 'Fuzzy Felts' began to find their way into many households in the 1950s. These cut felt shapes, some of which depicted animals, vehicles or body parts, could be arranged and rearranged on 'fuzzy' boards to make patterns and pictures.

Until the late 1960s, toys that were spin-offs from books or television pro-grammes were rare. Early examples of this sort of toy were based on characters such as Mickey Mouse, Rupert Bear, Noddy or Sooty and Sweep. "I recall owning a Muffin the Mule puppet. It was made out of metal, was quite heavy and painted cream and black with some red on it. It came out of the TV series of the same name, where Annette Mills was the front-person for Muffin and she sang, accompanying herself on piano."

Crafts featured as part of children's leisure activities, with crayons, chalks and at end of this period, felt pens being popular. Several participants recalled 'magic' painting books, where painting what appeared to be blank pages with a water-laden brush revealed rather runny colours. In a similar vein, there were blank books that could be scribbled on with pencils to expose a picture. Plasticine was a modelling material that came in packets of different coloured strips. These needed a considerable amount of work with warm hands in order to become malleable enough to shape and the colours soon blended into each other; it also had a distinctive smell that soon transferred to hands. "My Aunty Dora bought me a knitting set with rainbow coloured wool and knitting needles. I also had a creative weaving kit with a loom and loved making purses and other things with it." "I was also quite keen on crafts and particularly remember making 'French Knitting'[4] on a cotton reel with four nails hammered in the top. We also made pom-poms using cardboard milk bottle tops. Milk bottles had wider necks in those days and the tops were just the right size and also had a hole in the middle. Two of these back to back were just right for the job. Wool was wound round until the hole was full, then cut at the edges and tied off between the two tops."

"There were also 'Sticky Shapes', small pre-cut adhesive shapes in bright colours. These came in small boxes and could be licked and stuck down in order to create patterns. You could also get six inch coloured squares, which could be used to cut out shapes of your own." Many children owned John Bull printing sets, tiny rubber letters that could be 'type-set' into wooden or, later, red plastic frames and inked with rather messy ink pads to produce three or four very short lines of type. Spirograph was one of the very first cult toys and in 1966 was on most children's Christmas list. It consisted of a series of plastic cogs, with holes into which ball-point pens were inserted, before turning the cogs in order to create geometric patterns. Etch-a-Sketch was a deeply unsatisfactory toy, which required knobs to be turned in order to create a picture on a board. As lines could only be horizontal and vertical, the results were rarely artistic.

Most children had collections of various kinds and the swapping of duplicates was a feature of acquiring most of these items. Stamps, coins and tea-cards,[5] which were replacing the earlier cigarette cards, were avidly hoarded. "I also learned a lot from cards which came in the tea, I think it was PG Tips. Every box had a card and you got a little book, about A5 size and stuck them in the relevant numbered space. I learned a lot about freshwater fish and wild flowers from those cards." Beads, marbles and autographs were other common subjects for childhood collections.

Books were part of most children's lives, although they were frequently borrowed from the library rather than owned. Popular paperbacks were those produced by 'Armada', which retailed at 2s 6d each and included most of Enid Blyton's output for primary aged children. She remained the most popular children's author throughout this period, although she was often censured as not being a 'good' author and was not stocked by some libraries, or approved of by schools. She wrote for all ages, her 'Noddy' books being the most well known series for younger children. Adventure books, such as those featuring the 'Famous Five' and the 'Secret Seven', were aimed at seven to eleven year olds and were favourites for both boys and girls. Her school stories were also remembered fondly, as were those by Angela Brazil and Elinor M Brent-Dyer's 'Chalet School' series. Other well-read Armada books were pony books by Ruby Ferguson and the Pullen-Thompson sisters, Monica Dickens' 'Punchbowl Farm' series, Malcolm Saville's adventure stories, and W E Johns' books about the airman Biggles.

Children's paperbacks published by Puffin, the junior version of Penguin books, were considered 'better' than those that appeared under the Armada imprint and were slightly more expensive, perhaps 3s or 3s 6d each. These included classics such as *Alice in Wonderland*, *The Secret Garden* and *The Railway Children*; also popular were *Little Women*, *Gulliver's Travels* and *Treasure Island*. Children graduated to adult books at quite a young age and might well be reading Jane Austen or Charles Dickens by the time they got to secondary school.

Ladybird books were small, hard-backed books at prices that might allow one to be purchased with a week's pocket money. Their pages alternated between text and iconic pictures, whose style now epitomises this era. On the whole, they depicted white, middle-class families, with pipe smoking fathers and smiling mothers. In 1964, Ladybird produced 'Peter and Jane' books, which were a learn to read series but Ladybird were most famous for non-fiction books, across a wide range of subjects. "I-Spy books were great fun, small, themed books inviting children to spot and record such things as dogs, cars, trees or street furniture. There was also an I-Spy Club, headed by Big-Chief I-Spy, which was run in conjunction with this series of books. Membership wallets were available and a column in the *Daily Mail* newspaper supported this."

Many children had comics, either weekly, or as a special treat. Young children might have *Chick's Own*, or Enid Blyton's *Sunny Stories*. Older children's comics were aimed at a particular gender. For boys there was *Eagle, Marvel, Dandy* and *Beano*. Girls had *Judy, Girl, Bunty, June and School Friend* and *Diana*. The 1960s saw magazines, such as *Jackie*, being aimed specifically at teenaged girls. In 1965, the first issue of *Jackie* cost 6d. There were also 'educational' comics, such as *Look and Learn*. "For comics I had Enid Blyton's *Sunny Stories* magazine when I was very small; the first issue was in 1959 and I had these from that year. I particularly remember the rebus in each edition 'Reading is fun with Amanda the Panda'. Later I had *Bunty, Judy* and *June and School Friend*, which were printed on newspaper. It was always very exciting when an issue had a free gift, such as a metal ring or a bangle. The best part of *Bunty* was the cut-out doll on the back page of each issue. For ages the doll always looked the same, with her looped up plaits, so the clothes were the same shape and interchangeable. Later she became more modern and was a different shape and with a different blonde hair style each week. I often stuck the clothes and dolls on the back of a cornflake packet to make them more durable. There were also 'Nora and Tilly' cut out dolls who came in Mum's *Woman and Home* magazine."

Many comics produced slightly thicker 'summer specials', designed to take on holiday, or to be read during the school holidays. There were also 'annuals' to tie in with most comic titles; these were issued at Christmas and were popular presents. By the 1960s, annuals were also produced to accompany television programmes, such as *Blue Peter* (1958),[6] or to promote pop groups.

Most houses had a wireless, as the radio was often called and this was something to which the family sat and listened carefully. The concept of a radio that was perpetually turned on to provide a background accompaniment did not arise until the late 1960s. "One thing we did listen to regularly was *Children's Hour* (1922), which was a national institution. It included programmes such as *Toy Town* (1929), *Norman and Henry Bones* adventure stories (1943) and *Nature Parliament* (1954). Uncle Mac (Derek McCullough) was one of the best known presenters. He always used to end his programmes or recordings with the words, 'Goodnight children … (pause) everywhere'." *Listen with Mother* (1950) was a favourite, as were the adventures of *Dick Barton* (1946), secret agent. In the 1960s, teenagers listened avidly to 'pirate' radio stations such as Radio Caroline and Radio London. These music stations took their style from Radio Luxembourg, that broadcast in English on frequency 208.[7]

As television arrived in more households during the 1950s, it began to replace radio. Again, watching the television was a special part of the day and required full concentration. *Watch with Mother* (1953) developed from the radio equivalent and specific programmes, aimed at pre-school children, were aired on certain days of the week. "Daily *Watch with Mother* was a must. *Picture Book* (1955) was on a Monday, *Andy Pandy* (1952) on Tuesday, *Bill and Ben the Flowerpot Men* (1953) on Wednesday, *Rag, Tag and Bobtail* (1953) to be replaced by *Tales from the Riverbank* (1960) on Thursday and my favourite *The Woodentops* (1955) on Friday. This featured Sam who helped Daddy Woodentop, Mrs Scrubbit who helped Mummy Woodentop and the 'biggest spotty dog you ever did see'." "Other children's programmes that have stuck in the mind are the story telling *Jackanory* (1965) programme, *Animal Magic* (1962) with Johnny Morris and *Blue Peter* (1958) hosted, in my era, by Valerie Singleton and Christopher Trace. Each edition included a craft demonstration, which was impossible to replicate and which required copious use of sticky-backed plastic and discarded washing-up bottles. Later, this gave rise to the phrase, 'Here's one I made earlier'. My favourite was *Crackerjack* (1955). Peter Glaze and Leslie Crowther were the hosts, together with Eamonn Andrews. 'It's Friday, it's five to five, it's *Crackerjack*'. Amongst other items was the Double or Drop game in which children won prizes for correctly answering general knowledge questions. You could carry on answering questions as long as you could hold all your winnings. To make things more difficult a wrong answer meant that you were awarded a cabbage that you also had to hold. You were eliminated if you dropped anything or gained a third cabbage. *Twizzle* (1957) was another programme for young children, it was about a boy whose arms and legs could extend. Then there were the adventures of *Lassie* (1954) the collie."

Cinema going was a regular activity for town dwellers and most cinemas ran

Saturday morning sessions especially for children. "I used to go to the Saturday morning cinema when I was around ten or eleven in the mid-late 1950s. It was only a few pence and had films like *Flash Gordon*, *The Three Stooges* and 'Loony Tunes' Cartoons. I have no idea how the staff kept order with a cinema full of unaccompanied children but they did. I think the fear of being turfed out kept us under control. There were singsongs on stage, 'We are the Ovalteenies, happy girls and boys' and prizes if it was your birthday." The cinema was also a popular activity for teenagers; in 1965 a visit cost 4s 6d. "We did not go to the cinema very often but when we did, the showings were on a continuous loop, so one could go in half way through if one wished and then wait for the beginning to come round again. At the end of the complete programme, everybody stood for *The National Anthem*, except for a reprobate few who would make a dash for the exit." Disney films were firm favourites, as were those featuring pop stars such as Cliff Richard, The Beatles and Elvis Presley.

Music formed an integral part of the teenage culture of the 1950s and 1960s. New groups and styles came to prominence. Adults rarely approved of the latest trends. "I was fortunate to be in my mid to late teens when Elvis, Cliff, The Stones, The Hollies and many more singers and groups burst onto the air-waves. Many hours were spent trying to tune into Radio Luxembourg and then Radios Caroline and London, mostly late at night after 'lights out' and usually trying to hear the songs through the appalling crackly interference. Our favourite pastime on a Saturday was to take the bus into Petersfield and spend hours in the record shop with our heads inside the plastic hoods in rows on the wall, listening to the latest releases and deciding which 45 record to buy with our pocket money." "My first ever 45rpm records were *Please Please Me* and *Twist and Shout* by the Beatles, bought for me at Christmas 1963 (age 7) but at the same time, school friends were also being bought records by Cliff Richard.

Organised activities that required special clothing, equipment or lessons, such as playing an instrument, dancing, riding or tennis, were the preserve of the more affluent families. The cost of the uniforms for groups such as Brownies or Guides was also prohibitive for some. Girls who did join the Guides found that it widened their experience and gave them an excellent grounding in many fields that were not covered by the school curriculum. "I really enjoyed Girl Guides; it was structured but fun, I learnt a lot of crafts and earned lots of badges which I displayed down the arms of my uniforms. Looking back, they were mainly geared to making us suitable housewives with badges given for making a sandwich and an egg salad and hospital corner bed-making but also semaphore (easy as my dad was an ex-naval signaller!), plus first aid and lots of outdoor exercise."

Other youth groups, which were frequently attached to a church or chapel, were less inaccessible. Town dwellers might have the option of visiting a bowling alley or ice rink. Even rural teenagers might go to dances but theatre and concerts visits were predominantly for the rich, until pop concerts became popular in the late

1960s; in 1965, a concert might cost 7s 6d. Pop festivals, inspired by the USA's Woodstock, were not well-established until after this period.

Youth Culture

'The key of the door', a symbol of adulthood, was granted at the age of twenty-one. Despite this, as soon as a young person left school and started work they were treated as an adult in many ways and would be expected to make a financial contribution to the household. Paradoxically, these young workers were not considered independent. They would almost certainly still be living at home and subject to parental discipline, until such time as they married and set up homes of their own. "Even up until the time I married I wasn't allowed to stay out beyond 10.30 and I certainly didn't have my own front-door key, so I regularly arrived home to wait for my parents to return from a night out before I could get in!" "When I was about nineteen, working in a solicitors' office as a secretary and had bought my own car, I told my parents I wanted to get a flat. My mother hit the roof. Her main concern was not how would I manage financially or domestically but what would the neighbours think. They would think my parents weren't looking after me properly if I wanted to leave home."

Marriage was a path to independence but a new escape route was opening up. For the first time, significant numbers of young people, from a range of backgrounds, were going to university or undergoing post-school training and this helped to create a sub-set of the population who were neither child nor adult. "In the fifties a child left school and morphed into a miniature adult in adult-style clothes with no transition period."

By the 1960s, being a student meant more than studying. Increasingly, students saw themselves as a force for change. An element of this was a pacifist reaction to the aftermath of the second world war and the belief that their parents' generation had failed in many ways. The protest movement was emerging; The Campaign for Nuclear Disarmament (CND) and peace marches were associated with student culture. "It was the sixties; it was a time of student protest, there were 'sit-ins' but I was generally too busy with working for my degree! I joined in the Oxford protest march about the death of Jan Palach. I did a sponsored walk in aid of Biafra, as there was terrible suffering there because of the Biafran War."

It wasn't just students who were becoming a group with a distinctive identity and culture of their own. The post-war period saw the rise of a new phenomenon, the teenager; a term allegedly first coined by Bill Hailey during his 1957 tour but a concept that evolved a decade earlier. Many young people aligned themselves with one of the teenage groups that developed. This usually involved adopting the required dress style, taste in music and sometimes mode of transport. Employment was easy to come by, giving young people the disposable income to indulge in the fashions and music of their choice and to provide themselves with transport. To some extent, all these groups were anti-establishment, or at least alien to the adult world. Those who belonged to one group often entertained a rivalry with those who identified themselves with a different faction. This reached a climax with the notorious clashes between the mods and rockers that took place in the seaside towns of the south of England on the bank holidays of 1964. The press fuelled fears of a youth sub-culture, which, in all its facets, was painted as being undesirable in some way. For some however particularly those in rural areas, or those who did not continue with education or training beyond school, youth culture passed them by. "Dad huffed indignantly about long-haired layabouts dropping out and living on the dole but I don't think we actually knew any, our lives were quite conventional. My only knowledge of the hippie lifestyle came from watching TV."

There was some overlap between the 1950s beatniks and students. "In the mid-1950s, I remember reading about beatniks, a movement that had started in the USA and when I left home to go to college in 1959, I came across some in the coffee bars and pubs in London, though by this time I think the movement was on its way out. They were serious 'intellectual' long-haired students who wore black turtle neck sweaters and berets and other dark clothes, who listened to and discussed poetry and jazz and drank. The girls used long cigarette holders, I was a little in awe of them as a newcomer up from the 'sticks' but they were probably not very different from me, just 'putting on the style' (in the words of a Lonnie Donegan song). My parents had thought them a bit weird, but harmless!" "Aged about fifteen or so my friend and I were into the 'beatnik' look, or our modified version of it. We had befriended a group of 'beats', young men who were seen by older people as a younger version of tramps or today's beggars on the streets but who were on the whole well-educated young men who had, probably temporarily, dropped out of conventional living and were travelling around and living rough."

The coffee bar culture, that arrived from the America, gave young people, who were too young for pubs but nonetheless saw themselves as adults, a place to congregate. Juke boxes and the advent of the 45rpm 'single' record, allowed café patrons to engage in their music style of preference. 'Ton-up boys' or 'café racers', with their motor bikes and love of rock and roll music, patronised the cafés. "By now the rock 'n' roll era had started and we dressed the part. The boys wore drape coats, boot-lace ties and crepe soled shoes, with DA haircuts and sideburns. The girls wore very full skirts with stilettos and winkle pickers and our hair back combed into beehives and ponytails. We loved all the new modern music and went dancing whenever we could." The American rock and roll influences of the 1950s gave way to the style of the 'mods', who copied what they perceived to be the latest 'modern' European styles. "There were Teddy boys and later mods and rockers. The Teddy boys were the best dancers, around the juke box in the local coffee bar, the mods weren't that interested in the girls, just their image and their scooters. The rockers were just a bit too dangerous for me."

"Then came the mods and rockers, mods on Lambrettas or Vespas and rockers on motorbikes. The mods wore parkas with fur trim and the rockers cycling leathers. Some became Hells Angels but on the whole there wasn't as much trouble as was reported." "Mods had distinctive haircuts mirrored by the pop group The Small Faces. Rockers dressed in leathers, had long hair and appeared quite intimidating. The two groups disliked each other and it often seemed as though war was on the horizon. On many weekends it became noisy and busy in the town centre as these youngsters got together ready to make their way down to Brighton. It was the mid-sixties and many people were hearing in the media all sorts of stories about the young becoming uncontrolled and uncontrollable and we were given the impression that if we had anything to do with people like this we would end up breaking the law. We were told they were a thoroughly bad lot, taking drugs, shouting and swearing, carrying knives and we learnt to keep well away. In truth, many were quite probably innocent young lads who liked biking and scooters and just wanted a good time and some adventure. The trend towards large musical raves was just beginning too. Pop Festivals were being set up as most young people bought the latest records from the pop groups like the Beatles and Stones. The Mersey Beat was strong as was the American black music. Again we picked up all the media attention given to Flower Power, LSD and the general trend towards alcohol and smoking amongst the very young. It must have been a real concern for parents of young daughters at this time as this newfound assertion of adolescents was becoming quite widespread."

By the end of our period, mods disappeared, to be replaced by skinheads. The skinheads, or 'skins' were so called because the boys shaved their heads. Those with particularly closely shaved heads were called 'suedeheads. Despite the fact that early skinheads were influenced by West Indian culture and their music of choice was Tamla Motown or reggae, whose artists were predominantly black, some skinheads adopted a neo-Nazi stance, with gangs of skinheads passing their time attacking those from ethnic minorities. This meant that all skinheads were, probably unfairly, associated with racism and football hooliganism. Rockers morphed into 'greasers', with their Harley Davidson motorbikes, leathers and liking of heavy rock music. Overlaying these groups were the peace-loving hippies, who had evolved from the beatniks. They were identified by their long hair, floral clothes and joss sticks. Here the stereotype was that all hippies were sexually promiscuous and takers of illegal drugs. "There seemed to be two main groups in the area, and I ultimately gravitated towards the 'hippie' element; the 'opposition' was the 'skinheads', unattractive boys in Ben Sherman shirts, above-the-ankle jeans and braces and girls in tonic suits with short haircuts, or a form of the 'mullet', which existed even then. The thing about them that I found most off-putting though, was the attitude that went with the group. I didn't like reggae either; I was into Led Zeppelin. There were plenty of rows at home about clothes, I had exclusively worn mini skirts up until then, now I wanted maxi skirts and fringed jackets as an alternative."

Summary

Childhood in the late 1960s was very different from that experienced two decades earlier. Most families had become more child-centred; young people's opinions were sought and their emotional needs were considered, instead of just focussing on their physical well-being. In a reaction to the privation of the war years, an era of conspicuous consumerism, fuelled by television advertising, was beginning. More emphasis was being put on material possessions and the child of the 1960s would almost certainly have far more toys than their 1940s' counterpart. In addition, they were more likely to have access to an adult who had sufficient leisure time to participate in play and the willingness to do so.

During this period, young people had developed identities of their own as 'teenagers' and were no longer content to be carbon copies of their parents. They had the will, the confidence and the opportunity to challenge the established order and their parents' authority. The road to a new independence for young people was opened up by an education system that facilitated university attendance for those who would previously have been debarred by their social class. Teenagers in work now had the spending power to indulge their life-style preferences, which were often very different from those of their parents. Although there was still a long way to go, young people's horizons were no rigidly longer defined and confined by their class, sex and educational opportunities. A new era was beginning.

The Brief

Write about pregnancy and childbirth, how they were dealt with, the role of the father and where births took place.

Describe child rearing practices. Mention attitudes to breast feeding, as opposed to bottle feeding; where was it acceptable to breastfeed? Did fathers help with feeding or changing nappies? Were babies subjected to a strict routine of feeding/sleeping times? Were they played with or left to their own devices?

What were child-parent relationships like? How much adult attention did children receive? Did mothers and/or fathers play with children? How regularly? What about the role of other family members in child care?

What was considered unacceptable behaviour for children? What were the sanctions and punishments for particular offences?

Were opportunities for play/leisure restricted by chores or homework?

Were toys minimal, treasured items or were there many toys in the family?

What were your favourite toys and what did you long for but never have? Was there any sense of peer pressure to have a particular item? Are you aware of advertising influencing toy purchases or requests?

Were toys primarily shop bought or home-made? What games were played? Include things like board games as well as games with no props, such as hide and seek. Was play a solitary or collective activity?

Describe your reading habits. Were you an avid or reluctant reader? What were your favourite books? Were books bought or borrowed from the library? Did you re-read books?

Did you have comics occasionally or on a regular basis? What titles can you remember?

How did teenagers spend their leisure time? Include information about youth clubs and uniformed organisations. Mention things like the cinema, dance and concert going and parties with friends.

How were teenagers treated? At what age were they considered to be adults? Mention youth culture and attitudes towards groups such as mods, rockers, teddy boys, skinheads, hippies and greasers.

Chapter 8 footnotes

1   A male action figure (never referred to as a doll) who came with various outfits and accessories that mostly represented branches of the armed forces.
2   Hornby did produce clockwork train sets and the original car-racing Scalextric was also clockwork but it was the electric versions that were prized.
3   Plastic Lego clip-together bricks were patented in 1958.
4   This created long woollen cords. It was also possible to purchase a wooden, doll-shaped 'Knitting Nancy', which was a more sophisticated version of the cotton reel.
5   These small cards were given away with packets of cigarettes and later with packets of tea, to create sets on themes such as sports people, trees, cars or African wildlife. The reverse of the cards usually contained text and books could be purchased in which to stick the cards.
6   The dates following various radio and television programmes in Chapters 8 and 9 are the years in which the programme was first broadcast.
7   These stations were unlicensed and broadcast illegally.

47

48

49

50

51

52

53

54

55

56

57

58

59

60
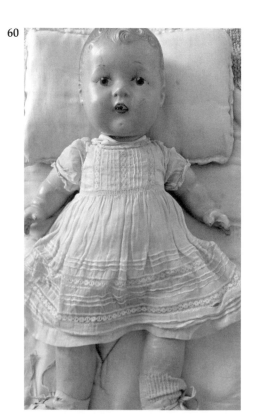

61

62

63

64

65

66   67

68

69

70

71

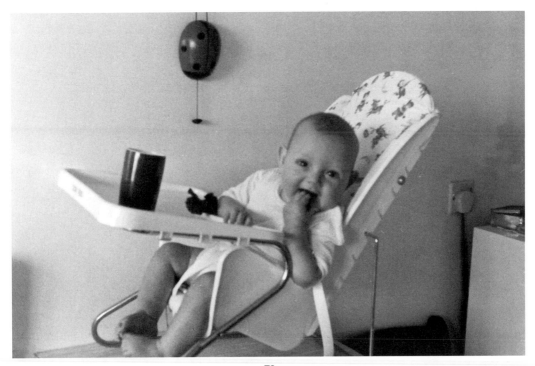

72

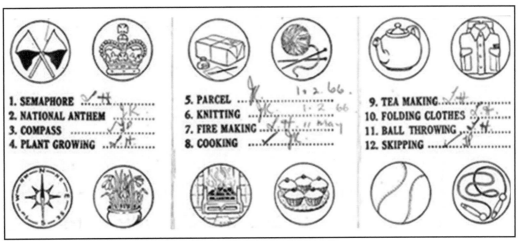

73

WORLD'S POP STARS IN COLOUR COLOUR COLOUR

Australia 1/6 · New Zealand 1/3 · South Africa 15 cents
Rhodesia 1/9 · East Africa 1.60 cents · West Africa 1/6
Sverige Skr. 1 ; 25 inkl. oms. · Norge Kr. 1.50

1'-

11th JULY 1964

Fabulous
Rolling with the Stones
& their mates Gene. P. Hollies Beatles

74

Julie Félix

IN CONCERT WITH

The Settlers • Davy Graham

THURSDAY 25th NOVEMBEF

Tickets now available:

10/6   8/6   6/6   4/-

from Colston Hall, Tel. No. 21768;

Chas. H. Lockier Ltd.,
29-31 Queens Rd. Tel. No. 23885;

Lewis' Travel Bureau

COLSTON HALL

General Manager: F. K. COWLEY, M.I.M. Ent.

BRISTOL

ONE PERFORMANCE ONLY 7.30 p.m.
Presented by THE ENTERTAINMENTS COMMITTEE

Call (Monday—Saturday, 9.30 a.m. - 8.0 p.m.) or return the form below with stamped addresse
envelope and full remittance to COLSTON HALL BOX OFFICE.

Please send these tickets for the JULIE FELIX CONCERT

_____ at 10/6   _____ at 6/6

_____ at 8/6   2. at 4/-

To (Name) Miss S.H. Boyce.

(Address) 36, Parkside Ave.

Winterbourne, Bristol.

I enclose a stamped addressed envelope and ~~Cheque~~/P.O. for £   : 8 s. – d.

75

77

78

79

80

81

82

83

84

85

86

87

88

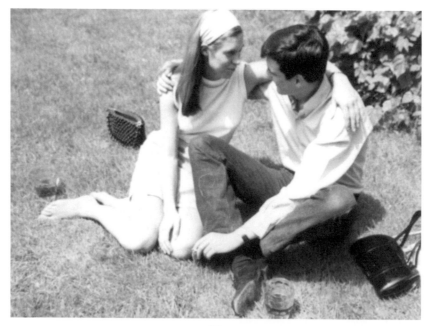

89

90

91

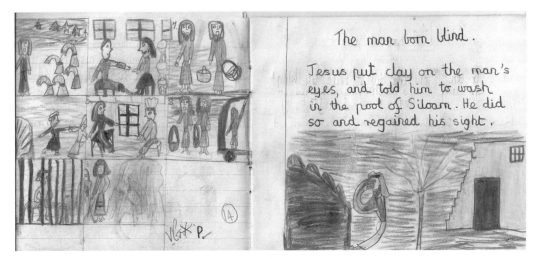

92

There's Just
One You

For
kindness
and for thoughtfulness—
For understanding ways—
For doing pleasant
little things
That brighten
passing days—

CHAPTER 9

It's my Party: leisure and celebrations

Adults' Leisure Activities

Is seems that once they had families, opportunities for adults to engage in hobbies or other leisure pursuits were minimal. "I don't ever remember my parents going out in the evening and leaving me in the care of anybody else." Time that was not spent at work, or in the woman's case doing housework, was often taken up with activities that bordered on being tasks and there was a blurred line between these and hobbies. Many women seemed to spend their 'leisure' time knitting and sewing. Often this was in order to produce clothing and soft-furnishings for the household, rather than a purely pleasurable activity. "My mum's hobbies were also for the benefit of the rest of us, she knitted and sewed and the magazines that she read reflected this. *Woman* and *Woman's Own* were swapped amongst the mothers of the close we lived in, also knitting patterns etc.." "My mother always seemed to be busy with something to do with running the house but I think this included things she really enjoyed doing, such as crochet, dressmaking and knitting."

Although many parents seemed never to leave their children in order to engage in activities of their own, there were leisure pursuits that could be done within the home and jigsaws, crosswords, stamp collecting and family board games were all mentioned. Gardening and DIY come into this category and might be seen as hobbies but were also part of providing for the household. "The garden was both a pleasure and a necessity. Most of the back garden was used for growing vegetables and some fruit, mainly bush fruit like gooseberries and currants and some raspberries. The front garden was made into a small lawn surrounded by perennials and shrubs a hedge of lonicera at the front and under the front windows a hedge of lavender bordered by London pride."

Some women found ways of spending time away from the family or workplace by going to Bingo, or running a Sunday school or Brownie pack. Other activities offered the housewife the chance to earn pin money as well as an opportunity to socialise. "A woman might run a catalogue and visit her neighbours to make sales. In the 1960s, Tupperware parties became common and housewives would hold these at home, trying to earn commission by persuading their friends to buy plastic storage containers of varying kinds." "Another 'hobby' that my mother had was as an agent for National Savings Stamps, which meant that she visited the houses of the people in her group once a week. This was also a social outing, sometimes one of us children would go, sometimes she would go on her own."

The ultimate responsibility for childcare rested with the women; this meant that there were more leisure opportunities for men, who often relaxed by visiting the pub. "The pub might provide a hub for social activity outside the home but seemed to be the preserve of the working classes." "The community was divided between those who went to the pub and those who did not." Other male dominated hobbies were often sport related: watching football or cricket or going fishing. Often men's activities excluded the rest of the family. "My father went out every night either to a men's club or a public house, often after a visit to one or other of the two cinemas in the town. On a Sunday Mother took the three youngest children, including me, in the early evening to the cinema, picking up our sweet ration on the way, after which we joined my father at the pub, which was also a hotel. We sat on the stairs leading up to the bedrooms and crisps and lemonade were sent out to us." Although women might accompany their men folk to the pub, it was generally unacceptable for a group of women to go drinking alone. Gambling was another pastime that was primarily for men. "In the fifties particularly, the football pools were prolific and Littlewoods and Vernon's were the two main operators." "We children all grew up understanding betting on horses or greyhounds. Trips to the racecourse were a favourite day out as most of them had funfairs also so we children were kept amused between races. We went to Epsom, Sandown, Goodwood, Plumpton for horses and Catford and Wimbledon for evening greyhound meetings." Pigeon racing was another popular hobby, stereotypically for working class men from the north of Britain.

The radio was the main source of relaxation for many adults. "Sometimes tuning into a radio station would take some time, you would have to change band i.e. medium wave and long wave and then tune in the frequency on the dial, you quite often got howls, pops and crackles before a clear sound came through and sometimes you missed the program completely." "The radio was called the wireless and we were able to listen to the home and light programmes. The news programmes were important and my mother enjoyed listening to *Mrs. Dale's Diary* (1948) every day. I liked *Children's Hour* (1922). *Palm Court* (1959) and its light classical music could be heard on Sundays but the music of *Family Favourites* (1945) was more to my parents' taste. Radio comedy like *ITMA* (1939), *Round the Horne* (1965) and *The Goon Show* (1951) were favourites and we enjoyed *The Archers* (1951), *Paul Temple* (1938) and *Dick Barton* (1946).

I remember *Beyond our Ken* (1958) and *Have a Go* (1946), which was a quiz. The host was Wilfred Pickles and his wife Mabel; I seem to think that some of the prizes were food, which was probably from the time when so much was on ration. I think catch phrases were, 'Have a Go Joe' and also, 'What's on the table Mabel'?" "We did not have a record player but my mother like to listen to the radio. She liked music programmes, *Sing Something Simple* (1959) and *Billy Cotton's Band Show* (1949), comedy programmes like *Down Your Way* (1946), *Take it from Here* (1948), *Life with the Lyons* (1950), *Ray's a Laugh* (1949), *Educating Archie* (1950); I can smell the Sunday roast just thinking about them." "The radio had to be rationed because it used electricity and my parents were careful to use it as sparingly as possible." In 1967, BBC Radios 1-4 replaced the former Light Programme, Home Service and Third Programme.

"The TV was rented from Radio Rentals and you paid a monthly fee but if it went wrong the company would mend or replace it for no charge." "We never had the television on for background. It would be turned on in order to watch something specific, having consulted the *Radio Times* for BBC programmes and the *TV Times* for programmes on ITV and then it was turned off when the particular programme ended." The only channel was BBC until 1955 when ITV arrived; BBC2 was added in 1964. There were very few children's programmes and there were no all-day transmissions. When there were no programmes you would see the 'test card'; from 1967 this depicted a girl with a blackboard and a clown. "We might watch a quiz such as *Ask the Family* (1967) with Robert Robinson. Other popular quizzes were *Call my Bluff* (1965), *Take your Pick* (1955) and *What's my Line* (1951), where contestants had to guess a person's occupation from a mime. The only soaps, although we didn't call them that, at this time were *Coronation Street* (1960) and *Crossroads* (1964). Comedies included *On the Buses* (1969), *The Likely Lads* (1964) and *The Liver Birds* (1969). Then came the cult 'modern' comedy, *Monty Python's Flying Circus* (1969). A long standing favourite was the game show *It's a Knockout* (1966) and its international equivalent *Jeux Sans Frontier* (1965). We didn't watch much sport, although *Wimbledon* and *Horse of the Year Show* were musts, as was any Olympic coverage. Entertainment shows included *Come Dancing* (1949), now reinvented with an added celebrity element as *Strictly Come Dancing*, *The Billy Cotton Band Show* (1956), with its opening cry of 'Wakey, wakey' and *The Black and White Minstrels* (1958)."

"My father seemed to have control over much that was shown on television, with sport and westerns taking priority. *Rawhide* (1959) and *Bonanza* (1959) he loved but I can remember seeing *The Man From Uncle* (1964) and *Doctor Who* (1963). *The Forsyte Saga* (1967) was one which went on for a very long time. I saw several episodes of *Z-Cars* (1962) and *No Hiding Place* (1959), both police dramas and I came to love watching thrillers when I had my own home, following *The Prisoner* (1967) and *The Fugitive* (1963)." "There was also a spate of American programmes, such as *The Virginian* (1962), which was on Saturday evenings." Other popular programmes were, "*Emergency Ward 10* (1957), *In Town Tonight*, *The Larkins* (1958) with Peggy Mount, *Sunday Night at the London Palladium* (1955), *Panorama* (1953) and *Dixon of Dock Green* (1955)."

Some homes had pianos but access to music was predominantly via the radio or a record player, perhaps a portable Dansette, which was particularly popular with teenagers. Young people usually favoured the pop music of the day but adults had other tastes. "Records played were mostly classical or the dance band music of Glenn Miller and the Dorsey brothers." Although many adults forfeited the opportunity to go dancing once they had children, others did not. "My parents' great love was dancing, which they did regularly. They would go to the Miner's Welfare Hall, the Working Men's Club and Wortley Hall." "Mother also went dancing to the Ladies' Tea Dance every Thursday afternoon when they danced to Victor Sylvester's records from 2.00pm until 5.00pm, breaking for refreshments at 3.30pm (tea, sandwiches and a bun or cake.). This coincided usefully with the end of the local junior school day!"

Reading was something else that seemed to be abandoned by busy parents, even if they had been readers in their single lives. Men read the newspaper, or trade magazines. Women had magazines in order to access knitting patterns or recipes. The series of romantic novels published in huge numbers by Mills and Boon were also popular with women. Some adults did take evening classes, often run by the Workers' Educational Association. At this date, these were more likely to provide an opportunity for acquiring additional work-related skills, or to supplement a formal education that had been curtailed, rather than being the 'hobby' classes that were to become more popular in later years.

"Visits to the cinema comprised the main entertainment for adults unless they were drinkers and then they spent any leisure time in the pub." Young adults, in particular, did go to the cinema, providing there was one that was geographically accessible. "It was about this time that programming at the cinemas changed. Whereas before there was continuous showing from the time the cinema opened at about 2pm until it closed after the last main feature, at about 10.30pm, there were now two programmes; afternoon and evening. This may have been because of the number of epic films now being made. In the forties and fifties, most main feature films were about ninety minutes long and were presented with supporting features of a shorter B film, a newsreel and maybe a cartoon or documentary and trailers for future productions. As well as going into the cinema at the beginning of the programme, it was possible to go into the middle of the programme and sit through, leaving at the point when you went in!" "The cinema was popular, musicals and cowboy films were plentiful. My mother's favourite film star was Gary Cooper. I think one of the first films to which she took me was *Singing in the Rain* starring Gene Kelly. Cinema was a form of escapism from the tedium of life and seats were relatively inexpensive, 1s 9d."

In general, the presence of small children curtailed leisure activities, especially for working class families. Adults in more affluent families might go to concerts, the theatre, dinner-dances or whist drives; sports and other clubs were also mentioned. "I belonged to a club called Ladies' Circle which was the ladies' counter club to Round Table, to which my husband belonged. These clubs did some community service, some fund-raising for Charity and also had social functions.

Ladies' Circle had a monthly dinner meeting at a local hotel with speakers and between our dinner meetings we had coffee evenings in members' homes." Other organisations might be associated with the local church, such as the Young Wives or Mothers' Union. Some ladies belonged the Townswomen's Guild or the Women's Institute. For men there were Workingmen's Clubs, or for the middle classes, Rotary or Freemasons. "My father joined the Civil Defence Corps[1] in the early 1960s. I am not altogether sure what this involved but I remember him teaching me the phonetic alphabet 'alpha, beta, charlie, delta', that seem to have been part of his training. Events organised by Friendly Societies, such as the Oddfellows or Buffaloes (Buffs), also gave adults an opportunity to socialise.

Children's Parties

Children's parties were not universal and were outside the experience of some. Any birthday celebrations for children were much lower-key than those of today and did not normally involve significant financial outlay, hiring large halls, mass outings or competitive catering. "Parties were always held in the house. About five or six friends were usually invited and were expected to bring only a small present, for example a colouring book, crayons, a paint box or ball and they did not take a 'swag bag' home as is now expected, though they did take home a slice of birthday cake if they wished" and perhaps a balloon. "There were also small prizes for games, such as Pass the Parcel." "Little girls wore fancy, flouncy dresses and little boys wore short trousers and maybe a miniature bow tie." "Guests would be expected to dress up in their best frocks with a clean, white, lace-edged hanky in the knicker pocket and bring a small present, usually soap or a handkerchief, for the birthday girl."

Food took the form of a traditional birthday tea. "The table was laid with bowls of blancmange, jellies, trifles, and home-made cakes, Shippam's paste sandwiches (usually left!) and sometimes sausages on sticks or a hedgehog made from cheese cubes on sticks stuck into a grapefruit." "We all sat round the family table and ate sandwiches (generally potted meat and jam but not together!) and jelly and ice-cream. Sometimes the jellies were made in a mould to produce a shape, often of a rabbit and the boys delighted in volunteering to eat the different parts. I remember, when we tried making one at home, being rather disappointed when the ears remained inside the mould." "Jellies were usually served in scalloped-edged, waxed paper bowls that could be thrown away afterwards." "The same eight children who lived nearby always attended each of the parties, with no other attendees. We ate sandwiches with meat paste or egg and buns, iced or butterfly, jelly, custard, blancmange and a home-made birthday cake with the appropriate number of candles." "Candles were lit and *Happy Birthday* was sung and a wish made after the candles were blown out. As we grew older the words of *Happy Birthday* were modified: 'Happy Birthday to you, Squashed tomatoes and stew, Bread and butter in the gutter, Happy Birthday to you!' Or 'Happy Birthday to you,

You should be in a zoo. You look like a monkey. And you smell like one too!'"
"Candle-blowing might be followed by 'the bumps'. Children grabbed the wrists
and ankles of the hapless birthday child so that they were held parallel to the floor.
They were then 'bumped' up and down, so their bottoms touched the floor once
for each year of their age."

Party games seemed to be the same, wherever the parties were held. Hunt the
Thimble (or slipper), Postman's Knock, Squeak Piggy Squeak, Musical Chairs, Pass
the Parcel, Pin the Tail on the Donkey, Musical Statues, Musical Bumps, Blind Man's
Bluff, Simon Says and Kim's Game. Particularly for younger children, action songs
such as *Ring a Ring a Roses, Farmer's in his Den, In and out the Dusty Bluebells* (or
windows) or *Oranges & Lemons* might form part of the party fun. The party-going
experience might be blighted by the need to 'perform'. "The entertainment was
heavily dominated by each child being expected to perform 'a party piece', a small
piece of poetry or a song which the poor child in question would have learned by
heart and be ready to recite whenever adults demanded. I used to recite *I had a Little
Shadow that went in and out with Me.* Games were played and some adult would be
roped in to play any necessary piano accompaniment." "Sleepovers were unheard
of, at least in our circles but around the early 1960s, fancy-dress parties started to
become popular."

Party giving rarely extended beyond primary school age. "Once I got to
grammar school, I was too old for parties, so I was allowed to choose one friend to
accompany me for a treat instead. One year it was a trip to the cinema followed by
burger, chips and Knickerbocker Glory in the Wimpy Bar opposite, the next year a
trip to the circus, the year after was a visit to a funfair and the year after, a meal out
at a 'real' Chinese restaurant in the King's Road Chelsea." "In the 1960s, when we
were in our teens, my parents used to spend the evening in the kitchen, with the
television temporarily set up in there, while we had the record player on loudly in
the front room and played Murder and Postman's Knock. There was a phase, I think
when we were in the fourth form at secondary school, when parties involved
inviting the whole class, many of whom would come. And we really did play
Postman's Knock and go outside the room to kiss a person of the opposite sex.
Which did provide some useful kissing practice. Of course, this phase didn't last
long, because as soon as people began to pair off as boyfriends and girlfriends, they
didn't want to play any more. Then the parties changed a bit. Music on the record-
player as before but couples sat on the sofa or in armchairs or on the floor, the lights
were turned off and kissing (called snogging) ensued. To be fair, sometimes we
danced and we ate and drank as well."

Special Occasions

Special occasions usually marked a religious festival, or a right of passage.
Birthday celebrations were normally confined to children, with many adults barely
acknowledging their own birthdays. If adults did receive presents, they were likely

to be useful items and this might extend to gifts for teenagers. "Generally, presents were far less grand and consisted of books, writing paper and matching envelopes, bath oil or hand cream, perfume (4711, Lily of the Valley, Ashes of Roses) or embroidered handkerchief sets, sometimes with my initials in the corner. In my teens I occasionally got a record token or book token, much appreciated but presents were mostly clothing, a new jumper or skirt, money for a special pair of shoes, scarves or stockings." "Postal orders were popular with aunts and uncles, 2s 6d or, if we were very lucky, 5s." "The twenty-first birthday present was usually a significant one from the family such as a gold watch or silver cigarette case, or another piece of jewellery." "For my twenty-first birthday I received exactly £21 from my parents, an enormous sum to me in 1966."

"As we grew older, we would have a joint birthday celebration, like all going out for a special meal. As far as I remember, the most special meal out in those days was steak; it wasn't the commonplace meal it is today. I also remember that when we were older and if we went to a licensed restaurant, Dad would order a bottle of wine. Again, that was something special, people didn't drink wine with meals at home."

"Weddings in the 1940s and 1950s were far from the lavish occasions that they are nowadays. During the years of austerity and clothes rationing, brides either borrowed a wedding dress or wore a coloured dress or two piece costume, which could be worn afterwards. Some lucky ones were able to have a dress made for them from parachute silk; grooms wore uniform if they were in the forces. The wedding party was also smaller, with the number of bridesmaids limited to one or two." "Because of food rationing, sometimes family members clubbed together to provide a cake and it was known for a false cake, made of cardboard or plaster, to be used." It was rare to mark wedding anniversaries, except perhaps silver (twenty-five years) or gold (fifty years). Christenings and confirmations were important occasions but usually consisted of just the religious service, with perhaps the giving of a Christening mug, a bracelet, or a prayer book.

Some families celebrated Easter. "I remember my Mother colouring hens' eggs by adding vegetables to the water they were cooked in and leaving them to go cold: beetroot for pink, onion skins yellow/brown, spinach green etc.. Later we decorated them with crayons and sticky coloured paper. This probably began while sweets were still on ration; chocolate eggs did not come till later." "We had red eggs and hot cross buns on Good Friday, a decorated cake and chocolate egg on Easter Day. We went to Holy Communion even if we hadn't been for the rest of the year."

Halloween had little significance; we had not yet imported the 'trick or treat' culture from America but Guy Fawkes' Night was often marked. "Our family didn't go in for parties but I do remember having a couple of friends to a bonfire night tea, when Mum had made Swiss rolls into Catherine wheels and sherbet fountains into rockets. There were jacket potatoes in the bonfire and Dad carefully let off all the fireworks, which were much gentler than today's horribly noisy explosives.

Even so, we were sent to ask permission from neighbours on both sides before they started." "We loved making patterns with our sparklers and letting off a few Roman candles, rockets or Catherine wheels in the garden." "Although fireworks were hard to come by in the forties, we had large fires at a number of sites. October half term saw armies of children dragging old furniture, mattresses, car tyres and tree trunks to their sites. Rival gangs burnt fires down only for them to be rebuilt again and again. Older boys camped out all night guarding the fire ready to defend it." "On November 5th local charity fund raising group Ryde Buccaneers organised a Guy Fawkes competition for local children, followed by a torchlight procession led by their own giant Guy, to the Cornwall Slipway. Here they had built a large bonfire, which was lit by some of the torches, after all the Guys had been deposited on it. This was followed by a firework display, which was doubly spectacular with the fireworks reflected in the water. There were toffee apples for sale. Locals brought their own fireworks as well; we had sparklers but some of the bigger boys brought different kinds of 'bangers' to scare the girls by throwing them towards them. Besides thunderclaps, which just made a big bang, there were squibs which shot along the ground, shooting sparks before they exploded."

Others celebrated New Year's Eve. "In South Yorkshire there was a strong tradition of first footing, where for a piece of coal you could get yourself invited into the home of any neighbour, or they would come to us." "We often had friends round to see the new year in on New Year's Eve. We would watch Andy Stewart and Moira Anderson in *White Heather Club* (1958) on the television."

Local carnivals were events that were mostly confined to seaside areas. Families would dress up and ride in themed floats, drawn by a tractor, or open lorries would be used (see figure 2). Girls vied to be the carnival queen for the day. Others would walk in fancy dress as part of the parade. The visit of a fair or circus was another opportunity for an exciting outing. Street parties to celebrate the Coronation were community affairs, with union jacks flying, bunting and trestle tables laden with sandwiches, cake and jelly (see figure 9).

The Festival of Britain in 1951 also got a mention. "I remember seeing the Skylon, a shiny needle-shaped sculpture and then we visited the 'Dome of Discovery' where I saw television for the first time, on a TV set with a screen about nine inches across; the picture was in black and white and seemed to be tinged with green to me. In an adjacent stand they were 'filming' live what was on the screen so we could go from one to the other to see it was the same! My other memory of the Dome of Discovery was a machine in which you could put your hand to experience the cold wind that Scott of the Antarctic faced at the South Pole!" "It's a shame that the whole thing was dismantled after a short time, so much of what was displayed there then would be equally fascinating now! Only the Festival Hall remains." "After that we went to the Festival Pleasure Gardens where there was a 'tree walk' above ground on boards through the branches of the trees, where you could look down on the crowds and some of the exhibits such as the miniature railway and the Guinness Festival Clock, which was my favourite. It gave a mechanical show every fifteen minutes, with doors that opened and toucans that danced, a man catching fish and other characters from Guinness advertisements."

Christmas

Almost all volunteers described Christmas as the main family celebration of the year and even those for whom budgets were limited made efforts to make the occasion special. "Nothing quite compared to Christmas in our lives as a day of celebration." The preparations and anticipation were often as important as the day itself. "Christmas did not start so far ahead of the actual event in those days. Some families did not put up their Christmas trees until Christmas Eve. The build up to Christmas was accompanied by the opening of the cardboard doors of an advent calendar. These were the sort with pictures behind; it was long before chocolate advent calendars were made. I would get a new one most years but still kept and opened the old ones." "In the run-up to Christmas I would write a letter to Santa and Dad would carefully fold it and place it on a small shelf at the back of the fire where it wouldn't burn. Next day the fairies had always collected it and taken it safely to Father Christmas." "I would be taken to my father's firm's Christmas party. I just remember a huge unfamiliar hall and lots of unknown children, all the offspring of employees of Murphy Radio where my father worked. There must have been food and entertainment and a present to go home with." "The 'works" children's party seems to be a thing of the past now but I think it was very normal in large companies or factories back then. We would do the usual things, play games such as Musical Chairs and we had tea at huge long trestle tables and wore party hats. I don't think these came out of crackers because I seem to remember them being quite stiff, with elastic that went under the chin. We always had paper dishes with jelly in and I seem to remember it being quite noisy. I think the adults would sit around the walls and chat while we all sat at these long tables down the middle of the room. The culmination would be the visit of Father Christmas."

"In the fifties every department store had its own Father Christmas Grotto and I was certainly taken to the one in our local department store. A corner of the store would be transformed into a magical setting such as a winter wonderland or an elves' workshop. Excited or nervous children would queue for the chance to meet Father Christmas, to assure him that they had been well-behaved all year and to confide what they really wanted for Christmas. In those more innocent times they might even sit on his lap and have their photograph taken. On leaving they were given a small present, suitable for a boy or girl as appropriate." "On Christmas Eve, we left a tray in the hearth with a mince pie, a glass of sherry for Father Christmas and a carrot for Rudolph."

The food marked out the day as being different and might have been prepared over several weeks. "Months of preparation went on in the kitchen, making a pudding, a cake, chutneys and mince pies. Then at Christmas, the killing of the chicken, plucking, stuffing and cooking it." "While making the cake Mum would ask us each to stir it while she mixed it. Some sort of alcohol was put into the cake. Nearer Christmas she gave it a brush with one of her home-made jams and covered it with home-made marzipan. This was much better than any shop bought marzipan I've tasted. Then came the royal icing which was roughed up before she placed figures of Christmas trees, snowmen and the like on the top. A ribbon was tied around the cake." "She wrapped a sixpence in grease proof paper and put it inside the Christmas pudding before steaming it. This was done by placing the full pudding bowl wrapped in a cloth and tied with string, into a pan of boiling water. It steamed for a long time. On Christmas day one lucky family member would find the sixpence in their bowlful of pudding!" "We had the same sweets always, a tin of Quality Street, a box of figs, some trays of dates, those orange and lemon crystallised slices, Jellied Fruits and Turkish Delight. Every Christmas we bought my Father a large tray of various slabs of toffee which came with its own little hammer to break it up."

Alcohol assumed less of an importance than it seems to today but Christmas might be the one occasion in the calendar when alcohol was consumed at home. "Dad bought some alcoholic drinks (the only time in the year that we had alcohol in the house) and arranged them on the sideboard in the dining-room." "Just at Christmas we had beer, port and whisky in the house. Wine with meals was only introduced in the sixties when Tony and I returned home for Christmas bearing a suitable bottle. Christmas tea with ham, cold turkey, salad, cake and trifle was often shared with the larger family of aunts, uncles and cousins. This depended on being able to walk to their houses or on the family car if petrol was available, there being neither bus nor tram on Christmas day." The Christmas meal was frequently followed by listening to the 3.00pm Queen's speech on the radio or, later, television.

Decorations were often home-made and treasured from year to year. The pièce de resistance was invariably the Christmas tree. "A real Christmas tree was proudly brought in by Dad and put up in a corner for us to decorate. The same decorations were used each year. The ones I remember were the real candles and their clip-on holders. Great care had to be taken not to burn the tree or catch the furnishings alight. We used cotton wool to put on the branches to look like snow and this was also put around the base of the tree on the soil in the pot. Red crepe paper was wound around the tree pot. The lights lasted from year to year. They were the type that screwed in the holders and if one was a dud, none of the lights worked." "Christmas lights were just introduced but they were a nightmare! They never seemed to work from year to year and my father had to spend ages going through each screw-in coloured bulb to see which one had blown." "Of course we always had a Christmas tree and originally it was a real one, until Mum got too fed up with the mess it made and ordered an artificial one from Lewis', the big department store in Birmingham. It must have been one of the early artificial trees, in the very early 1960s. It was 7ft 7ins tall (it said so on the box it was packed away in each year) and the branches were all like dark green bottle brushes, not very realistic!" "Most years Mum would buy something new for the tree. I still have one or two of the 'new' decorations which got put away in their original packing from Woolworth's with their 1s 3d price labels on; actually I remember those were deemed expensive!"

"Our tree decorations included a rather scary looking choir boy. He was actually a cake decoration, which is why he had to be garrotted by wire in order to be hung on the tree. There were plastic angels, plastic birds and a set of stars and snow flakes that consisted of two halves enabling them to be slotted together to form a three-dimensional ornament. There were also glass baubles including ones that were shaped like houses. Then there was the set of decorations whose stomachs consisted of concertinaed paper and similar large balls and bells. We always made our own paper chains but there were commercial paper garlands that also worked on a concertina principle. Balloon blowing was always a hazardous activity. We had cylindrical, cardboard balloon pumps but the process made an awful noise and there was always the danger of them popping. I used to hide under my bed with the dog. I still have 'angel chimes' which revolve and make an irritating noise when the candles under them are lit and the heat causes them to move." "Many of our decorations were hand-made and we spent hours cutting coloured paper into strips and gluing them into chains. We also bought home Chinese paper lanterns made at school and made crepe paper streamers to decorate the ceilings. In later years, I made Christmas bells out of Teacher's whisky bottle tops, painting them white and dipping the bottom edges in silver or gold glitter, then drilling a hole in the top to hang a bead clapper and a loop to put them on the tree."

Card giving might be confined to far-flung family and friends. "Sometimes we were also given Christmas cards with pre-printed pictures to colour, which could be sent to family and one or two friends." Present giving was also not on the prolific scale of the twenty-first century. Stockings, socks or pillow cases would contain a few small items. "The stocking-fillers were traditional, always including an orange in the toe and a bar of Cadbury's milk chocolate. The remaining gifts would have been inexpensive and wrapped in the flimsy, garishly printed paper which was standard at the time." "In the foot of the stocking there would be a pink or white sugar mouse, a couple of Brazil nuts and maybe almonds or hazelnuts, a clementine or an orange." "Chocolate coins, covered in gold foil and encased in a red net, were a common stocking-filler and by the 1960s, there might also be foil-wrapped chocolate items on the tree. We abandoned the latter after the year when the dog ate them."

Children might expect one 'main' present from their parents and perhaps a 'selection box', containing a variety of chocolate bars or an 'annual', a hardback book full of stories from a favourite comic. "We didn't have masses, usually a main present from Mum and Dad, which would be something we really wanted and might be quite large, like a dolls' pram or a doll for me, *Jane's Fighting Ships* for Steve. Then there might be a new board game and we always had a Cadbury's selection box each. Grandad would give me a foreign doll and Steve something for his train set. Other presents from our relatives and Godparents would be relatively small."

Adults often did not give each other presents and children's presents to adult family members might be home-made. "When we were young, we always tried to give my parents a hand-made gift, made and wrapped in great secrecy. I remember string pot cloths, drawn-thread tray cloths, embroidered hankies, frilled aprons, home produced bath salts in decorated bottles, knitted tea cosies, gloves and ties." "I can recall making presents for close relatives. I have vague memories of spill holders and felt glasses' cases."

After Christmas, thank-you letters would be written and decorations put away. Often wrapping paper would be saved for re-use. "The paper was always smoothed out and saved for another year, cutting off any sellotape round the edges, so the papers got smaller and smaller each year." For some, notably town-dwellers, the aftermath of Christmas might involve a pantomime. "We always went to the pantomime shortly after Christmas, at the Ashcroft Theatre in Croydon. These normally starred Cyril Fletcher and Dame Peggy Ashcroft and included a Harlequinade, which was superfluous to the plot. We usually had good seats at the front on the left as you faced the stage. I have no idea how early mum had to book, or how much she had to pay, to get these premium seats. Being at the front was very important as, at some point, children would be invited to go up on stage and it was whoever could get there quickest. I don't remember being disappointed. The lucky children would then help with the audience participation song and I think, were given a small gift."

Holidays and Outings

For most of this period, those for whom a holiday was a financial possibility would be likely to travel by train to a UK seaside town for what is now referred to as a traditional 'bucket and spade' holiday. To avoid struggling with luggage on public transport, this was frequently sent on in advance. "In the early days we did not have a car so would travel by train. Our luggage went on ahead as 'passenger luggage in advance' and the trunk would be waiting for us when we arrived." Many people only had two weeks' paid holiday a year, so sometimes the breadwinner was not able to be present for the whole of the holiday; some women and children went alone, being joined by their men folk at the weekend. The timing of the holiday season might be enforced by a factory shut-down. "In the 1950s and early 1960s we had what was locally known as 'Wakes Weeks'; factories and mills would close as would smaller shops and the towns would be virtually ghost towns, as everyone headed to the coastal resorts for their annual holiday."

Seaside accommodation was likely to be in a guest house, which might provide bed and breakfast or 'full board' and the latter may well include lunch. A 1950s' holiday guide for Swanage in Dorset suggests some of the features that a holidaymaker might find desirable. "'Attractive picnic lunches; television in smoke room for guests' entertainment; food that is good, appetising and liberally served; sunny house in nice garden; comfort, cleanliness, civility and good food; bedside lights; separate tables; Yorkshire fare (this is in Dorset); two bathrooms and preference given to Methodists during heavy booking periods'." "Guest houses in Swanage at this time were charging five and a half guineas[2] 'with children sharing family rooms at reduced rates according to age'. The main thing all the hotels seem to advertise is hot and cold running water (what other sort of water is there?!) in all rooms and interior sprung mattresses, so this was obviously what was looked for at the time and all you could desire."

"At a Yorkshire hotel in the late 1960s the tariff was as follows: 'Room and Breakfast £1 17s 6d. Inclusive terms cover Apartments, Baths, Towels, Breakfast, Luncheon, Afternoon Tea and Dinner. For a stay of 3, 4, 5 or 6 days: per day £2 15s. For stays of a week or longer: per week 17 guineas. Ground floor twin-bedded room, with private bathroom, extra 7s 6d per day for each guest. Picnic lunches are provided on request. Early Morning Tea is supplied on request, 2s 6d. Service Charge 10%. Adequate safe parking for residents' cars free of charge. Covered accommodation for four cars, 1s per night. Lock-up garage, 2s 6d per night'." "A lovely holiday at a farmhouse in Berrynarbour (Ilfracombe) was where we enjoyed bed, breakfast and evening meal for £7 per head for the week in 1968."

For most people, the holiday centred round sitting on the beach, usually on striped, canvas deck-chairs that could be hired on arrival (see figure 79). The more adventurous might rent a beach hut, basically a wooden shed, occasionally with shared facilities where cups of tea could be made, or a kettle could be boiled on a primus stove. This provided a place to store beach paraphernalia and shelter from inclement weather. "As soon as we got to the beach, wherever it was, Dad would go and get a beach tray. A big tray of tea with a china teapot, china cups and saucers, milk jug and sugar bowl. Mum would have made sandwiches and we usually got pasties in the town before we went to the bus station." "I would rush along to the 'Ocean Bay', where one could buy useful things like flags for sandcastles. It was all we wanted, sea and sand and sunshine." There might be a visit to the show on the pier, a donkey ride or a Punch and Judy show to watch. Candyfloss, rock and ice creams would be special treats. "Ice-cream filled Lyons Maid Mivvi lollies were 8d, the Walls equivalent was the Split. Lurid coloured Zooms, which were meant to look like a rocket and chocolate-topped Treble Hit lollies cost 6d." "Holiday budgets included the cost of hiring where we stayed, the petrol for our car, the treat of a daily ice cream for my brother and an Orange lollipop for me and once a week, treats of a visit to the cinema, tea and buns in a teashop and take away fish and chips." "Holidaymakers, then as now, sent post cards to family and friends and the 1950s were the heyday of the 'saucy' postcard, by Donald McGill and his ilk, with their double entendre cartoons. We learned a lot and had some giggles from those postcards displayed outside the many gift shops! Those were more innocent times though and there was nothing obscene or that could be really offensive."

Owning a car, or even a motorbike and sidecar, opened up the opportunity for camping or caravanning holidays, which were a more economical option than guest houses. "In 1959 my parents bought a caravan and from that time our annual holiday would involve going to Wales with the caravan being pulled by first the Triumph and later the Wolseley. In 1963 they decided the weather in Wales was not suitable for caravan holidays and we would go abroad. Again my father planned the whole thing and we took the caravan over to Holland crossing from Harwich where the caravan had to be lifted onto the ferry by a crane. From Holland we went to Germany and stayed at caravan sites in the Black Forest, then we presumably came home the same way." Those who were Guides or Scouts also had opportunities to camp. "The annual camp with the Guides was for me a wonderful experience. Camping was basic: sleeping in old army bell tents, collecting wood and cooking on a wood fire, food kept warm in a hay box and collecting water in buckets from a farm tap. Meals were eaten sitting on groundsheets. Sleeping was directly on a groundsheet on the ground. We travelled to camp in a lorry. We would sing songs all the way, waving at everyone as we peered out of the back of the lorry. Once on the camp site our only means of transport was a bicycle for emergencies."

Holiday camps were at their most popular and slightly primitive accommodation, that was nonetheless catered, together with plenty of on-site leisure opportunities, appealed. "The chalets were pretty basic in those days, with no indoor plumbing. They were all on one level and all they were really, was a series of little one-roomed boxes. Ours had a small double bed and a set of bunk beds, with a washbasin in one corner. In the centre of each row, there was a shower and toilet block and there was a tannoy system right outside our window, which woke us up each morning for breakfast and to let everyone know when it was time for your particular sitting for lunch or dinner. This was also used for announcements to inform you of any activities taking place, such as the knobbly knees contest, or glamorous granny, or bathing beauties. However, this all seemed magical to an eleven year old girl on her first 'proper' holiday away from home." "I can still remember the enormous indoor swimming pool with the artificial vines and flowers intertwined in the beams in the ceiling, which was always hot and steamy, with an overpowering smell of chlorine coming from the water. The outside pool was huge too but due to the unpredictable English weather, I don't remember using that as often as the indoor pool. I was also amazed that you could go on any of the fairground rides, without having to pay any extra to do so and I also used to enjoy all the Redcoats'[3] evening shows." "We had our own chalet and every morning the loudspeaker in the chalet would blast out Zip-a-dee Do-dah so you didn't miss breakfast, each part of the camp having set meal times. By the end of the week we were ready to take a pair of nail scissors to the wires." "Mum booked a week at Butlin's, she spent most of her time trying to track down her fourteen and sixteen year old daughters who had found themselves surrounded by hundreds of testosterone charged young lads; teenage heaven! Evenings were spent in the ballroom where we danced to the latest releases, including Bobby Darrin's *Mack the Knife* and daytimes we spent in or around the pool, trying to escape the sound of the tannoy chivvying us from one place to another."

Gradually, tastes became more sophisticated. "My sister and I clubbed together to have a holiday in Jersey, flying for the first time ever and sharing a twin room in a good hotel with an outdoor swimming pool, just off the town centre. The total cost for the two of us was £51 2s, £16 4s for the two return flights and £34 13s for the twin room and that was for full board!" The 1960s brought the era of the package holiday and foreign travel was an option that was now available to a wider section of society. "In 1964 we had a holiday in Spain by coach, after a short flight across the Channel, driving through France and to Spain. I think the seventeen day holiday cost us £36 each with full board. Although there were two drivers one drove the whole way and there was no legislation then. One night we drove into the mountains where the driver drank the wine and liqueurs with rest of us before driving back down the mountain."

Holidays might have been beyond the budget of some families but day trips were more attainable. These often took the form of a coach or 'charbanc' tour organised by a local employer, Sunday school or social club. "We had a number of excuses for a charabanc outing: Sunday school, pub, works, anything." "The Sunday school outing was an important village event. Most of the village families would come; I think we needed two coaches. We went to Bristol Zoo once. I remember my sister getting stung by a wasp. We rode on the elephant. It must have taken a long time to get there, in a coach, long before the motorways. Everybody would sing on the way home. There would be an organised tea in a café, before we embarked on the return journey."

Families with cars had more scope for days out but many day-trips took place by bus or train. 'Rover' or 'run-about' tickets could be purchased that allowed unlimited travel for a day. "When I was about eleven, a friend and I would by a 'joint rover' ticket, which meant we could travel on any red bus or the underground for the day. We used to like trying to get to the end of the Northern line, which was about as far from home as we could go. I can't imagine children of this age being allowed or encouraged to do this today." Outings were often family, or community, affairs. "Our parents took us on the bus to big public parks in Rotherham or Barnsley. Occasionally we would have a day trip to the east coast if the local firm was advertising an excursion. Mother was very enterprising; if she fancied going somewhere in particular, she would book a coach and get the passengers. This would be after she returned to work in 1962 and had many colleagues interested in a day to York, Ascot or Haworth. The only other transport was dad's motorbike." Coach travel was popular and coach companies advertised trips to places of interest, shopping trips, chances to go to the theatre or 'mystery' tours.

The Brief

Write about how adults spent non-working time. Please note how much time was available for leisure activities. Think about hobbies, sports, music (both listened to and performed), books or magazines read, favourite films, television and radio programmes.

How were birthdays celebrated for children and adults? Consider presents, their quantity and cost, parties and special treats. Describe children's parties and party games. Was party giving expected? Recall memorable birthdays, presents and celebrations.

How was Christmas spent? Who played host to whom? Who gave and received presents, how many and at what cost? What food was eaten? What were the special family rituals and traditions? Describe Christmas decorations, were these bought or home-made?

Mention other festivals and celebrations, such as Easter, Halloween, Guy Fawkes Day, Jubilees and Sunday school outings.

Write about memorable day trips. How often might these take place? How did you travel? What was the budget for such outings?

Describe holidays, did your family go away? Consider destinations, accommodation, modes of travel, cost and activities once on holiday.

Chapter 9 fottnotes

[1] The Civil Defence Corps was a peace time organisation, formed as a result of the Civil Defence Act of 1948, which placed the responsibility for training volunteers on local authorities. Its role was not dissimilar to that of the Home Guard.

[2] This is likely to have been per person, not per room and equated to £5 15s 6d. See Chapter 5 for an explanation of the currency of the time.

[3] The Redcoats were the entertainments' team, who wore red jackets and led the various activities on offer. Butlin's main rival, Pontin's, dressed their staff in blue jackets.

CHAPTER 10

The Times they are a-Changin': relationships and attitudes

Family and Friends[1]

In general, parent-child relationships were functional rather than emotional and many volunteers mentioned the absence of physical demonstrativeness. "With hindsight, I realise that there was very little physical show of affection towards me as a child, although I'm certain that my parents loved me in their own way. Touching, cuddling and hugging were not commonplace amongst either my family or our friends that I remember; more emphasis was directed toward behaving 'properly', doing as we were told and good manners at all times." "Displays of emotion were strongly discouraged in our family and emotional responses, feelings etc. were never discussed. This made the negotiation of relationships quite complex." "When I had nightmares for a while I took to creeping in with my mother, a stop was soon put to that and I was more or less told to snap out of it. Snapping out of things was often the advice, rather than talking things over. We never went in for self indulgence." "Although I am sure my parents and siblings loved me, there was very little show of affection between us, including our parents, nor was there any emotion. Hugs never happened, a brother and I were the only ones to even kiss my mother on leaving the house. I can hardly remember a single conversation with my father, the longest I had was on the day before he died, how sad." "According to my grandmother's and paternal aunt's generation, children should be seen and not heard. We were always on our best behaviour with them around and I was never sure if they liked us or not."

"We were certainly well looked after as children and given a good education and so on but I felt there was a definite lack of warmth. I remember feeling quite lonely as a teenager and I certainly would not have confided in my parents if anything bothered me." "Looking back, the impression was really that most of the time we operated as three separate units within one family. I played with my friends all day and later, went to school and gradually widened my horizons. My mother ran the house and saw her own friends; my father went to work and connected with his friends by writing long letters. There wasn't much significant communication or discussion in our family. My mother and father didn't talk to each other in any meaningful way beyond the everyday practicalities and they certainly didn't involve me in discussion of anything of significance which might be going on in the adult world." "My parents did not discuss private feelings or ideas very much at all, whether these were social, political or philosophical."

"I became a teenager in 1961 when the Swinging Sixties and all that they entailed were just beginning. My poor parents were in effect Edwardians, born in the first decade of the twentieth century, so they found it hard to come to terms with the huge social changes in attitude, manners and dress. I wasn't a wild teenager. I didn't drink too much, or take drugs and only smoked the odd cigarette. But I did want to go out and about to concerts and parties and to come home late and to wear fashionable outfits." "There was a much greater social distance between all adults and children, which included parents and children, than nowadays. For example, a child never called an adult by their first names. If they didn't give them a title, Mr or Mrs, then it was 'auntie' or 'uncle'." "We were taught to respect those in authority such as the local policeman, the doctor, the priest, neighbours and of course, our teachers."

The older generation may not have shared the family home but there were still perceived responsibilities where elderly relatives were concerned. There was no longer the expectation that the last and often the youngest, unmarried daughter would remain at home to look after their parents but their care was not a duty to be delegated to outsiders. "There certainly was the expectation that elderly relatives would be looked after and when my grandmother died, my grandfather lived alternately with us and at my uncle's house. It was not an ideal arrangement but at least he was cared for." "Support for elderly relatives was practical I think rather than emotional. Around 1955 my great grandmother came to live in a residential home near us, I don't remember there was ever a possibility she would have lived with us or with her daughter, my grandmother. My grandfather became ill around 1960 with a muscle wasting disease and my grandparents moved to live in a flat about three miles from us." These arrangements were not universally successful and inevitably families fell out. "For a while Nana used to go and stay with Auntie Clara, her sister-in-law, with whom she'd always been great friends. That was until the year they fell out over the gravy, apparently one made it with flour and the other used cornflour. That was the end of that. Sadly, they never spoke to one another ever again."

Pets could become important family members and were often substitute siblings for only children. "My cat, Smokey, was a big part of my life from when I was five up until she died when I was fourteen. She was given to me on my fifth birthday. As usual, I had to do a 'close-eyes', as we called it. I closed my eyes and held out my palms and mum placed this tiny black kitten into them. I was so surprised and so delighted and I loved her from that day onwards." "I hated being an only child and had hordes of imaginary brothers and sisters to create a biologically impossible family for myself. The nearest I had to a sibling was my dog, whom I loved unreservedly."

When it came to friendships outside the family there was not always a free choice. "Most parents expected you to mix with 'decent' people, i.e. those of 'good moral character'!" "My early friendships, when I was at primary school, were mostly with the children of my parents' friends." "Inevitably, one's first friends were those who lived nearby and then one's contemporaries at school. They came from families similar to mine both in class and financial resources." "When I was a schoolgirl, friendships were influenced by where you lived as there was no internal (town) bus and some children, of course, lived on outlying farms. Then again, it also depended a great deal on what happened at 'the great divide', the eleven plus. It was quite difficult to keep in touch with your previous classmates when they went to a different school, all had to make new friends and things in common were less."

Parents also put limitations on boy-girl relationships. "My mother didn't like my boyfriend, this was someone who lived nearby but his mother was a widow and not well off. I remember very clearly my mother bemoaning to me one day 'why can't you go out with someone whose mother I can invite for tea?' Looking back now I really think she was more worried about what others might think and how that would reflect on her, than about my welfare." "My parents did not show their feelings for one another openly though I always felt that they were very fond of one another and I do not think that shows of affection between my boyfriend and I would have been acceptable at home. I remember feeling somewhat embarrassed when my friend and her boyfriend were openly kissing and cuddling at her parent's home in front of her parents. This would never have occurred in my own home. I remember on one occasion my mother saying to me that I shouldn't do that, when I leant across my boyfriend to reach a book, so cuddling would have been shocking." It was not just parents who created barriers to relationships, there were peer pressures too. "When I started going out with friends to discos etc. it was a given that, as a Bideford girl, you didn't go out with a boy from Barnstaple, I don't why this was but that was definitely how it was then."

Sexual Relationships

The general expectation was that young people would grow up to have a relationship with a 'suitable' person of the opposite sex, that this relationship would result in marriage and that sexual intercourse would not occur until after that marriage. "It seemed to me that not getting married was a terrible fate and one to be avoided. I had also enjoyed being a bridesmaid at my cousin Valerie's wedding and dreamed of being just like her when I got older." The anticipation was that there would be "an engagement and then a very conventional wedding, white, church, bridesmaids young and old, big reception, going away car with tin cans on the back, etc.. Marriage (for women) was still being seen as one of the great objectives of life." "As for 'living in sin' it was just that, a SIN! There was one lady in the village who had a child and no husband as far as we knew and everyone talked in hushed tones about her and her situation." "It was almost unheard of for anyone to leave home or live together before they were married. Couples generally lived at home while they saved up to get married."

There was often a mystique about the opposite sex; this was worse for those who were not at co-educational schools. "Because I was educated with boys at both primary and secondary level and also was one of the few girls in the science sixth form, I have never had any particular anxieties in relationships with the opposite sex. This was not the case with my friends who were educated at single sex schools; they were very self-conscious and awkward in the presence of the other sex. Even when they were adults this showed itself in what I regarded as unnecessary flirtatiousness in the women and embarrassment and a sense of superiority in the men." An additional difficultly was the reluctance to discuss relationships and the paucity of sex education.[2]

Fear of pregnancy was a limiting influence on sexual relationships for much of this period. "I was married in 1942 at the age of nineteen and had received no formal sex education, just things I was told by my older sisters. I didn't have sex until after I was married, I would have been far too scared. We didn't use any birth control but I tried not to have sex too much; I didn't really enjoy it, just thought it was my duty to my husband." "Later on in life I spoke to my mother about a daughter of a friend of hers who had recently married but couldn't consummate the marriage as she was scared, poor girl. My mother told her friend to tell her daughter to lie back and think of England, just get on with it like the rest of us. Much later on I found out from an aunt that my mother hated sex and had never enjoyed it." "There was much heavy petting but we never had full intercourse, I think because we were both terrified of me getting pregnant." "Relationships with the opposite sex were never discussed but there was a general feeling that it was best not to have them!"

"I had boyfriends from the age of twelve. Our behaviour was very innocent and very gauche. We held hands in darkened rooms at parties and at the cinema an arm across the shoulder was the height of daring." "Pre-marital sex in the fifties and sixties was definitely happening but still disapproved of." "There were occasions when I had a boyfriend staying at our house and we would contrive to have sex; I think by then my mother had probably decided that she didn't want to know! It would not have been acceptable, in our family anyway, to have shared a bed openly, so there had to be creeping about on the landing and creeping back at dawn, it was just the same when I was staying at my boyfriend's house." "Promiscuity was unacceptable but some 'necking' (kissing) and then 'petting' was alright if you were 'going steady'. There seemed to be a scale to stages of petting and there was banter around the classroom amongst the boys about how far they had gone with a girl (I have a feeling that much of this was made up, out of bravado!)." "Promiscuity was acceptable for men but not for women. A man would be called 'Jack the Lad' but a woman a 'slut' or 'good time girl'. So there was a double standard weighed in the favour of men." "The prevailing attitude in the fifties and sixties was that 'nice girls didn't have sex before marriage'. But throughout history unmarried girls had become pregnant, rarely through choice but often by accident or as a result of ignorance, coercion or even rape. Terms such as 'she's got herself into trouble' put the blame squarely on the female, regardless of the fact that it takes two to make a baby and it was invariably the girl's responsibility to deal with the aftermath."

The consequence of pre-marital sexual encounters might be unwanted pregnancy. "Pregnancy outside of marriage was scandalous, especially teenage pregnancy which was kept very quiet. I remember being quite shocked when one of the older girls was expelled from school for being pregnant. Interestingly, it was usually the girl who got the blame, in phrases like 'she's gone and got herself pregnant.'" "In 1963 my older sister got pregnant at the age of sixteen. Mum was totally shocked and unsympathetic and dad was a little more caring but any decisions were out of his hands. It was decided very early on that the baby would be adopted. In the home her pregnancy was never discussed and we younger children knew nothing about it. When it was time to go into hospital we were told that she was in hospital to lose weight. I was eight and my brother was four. I remember sitting in the waiting room at the hospital while Mum and Dad went in to see her and reading some notices on the wall that used the word 'maternity'. I cottoned on then to what the situation was and explained it to my brother (not that he probably understood) and told him never to mention it. The baby was placed for adoption from the hospital and there was no contact ever again."

Marriage, even if it was not the required nine months before the birth, was the preferred option. "I had a cousin who was quite a bit older than I was and he 'had to get married'. I don't think we went to the wedding but I seem to remember some sort of reception and the bride wearing a suit, rather than a wedding dress. It was almost as if there was a rush to make it all OK." "There were two occurrences of local teenagers getting pregnant, who were obliged to get married quickly and quietly. At least one of these ceremonies was held at 8am (the earliest time it could be held legally), so that no-one would be around to see."

For the young in the 1960s sex before marriage was becoming less hazardous due to the greater availability of contraception. To an extent, it was also less unacceptable. "Pre-marital sex must have been accepted among the circle I was in, we certainly made sure we knew how to get contraception which was sensible and I can remember that David Steel's Abortion bill became law in 1967 and we all thought that was a great advancement, quite liberating to think a woman would not have to proceed with an unwanted pregnancy."

Predatory sexual encounters were often glossed over. "In the fifties and sixties it was my experience that if a man, married or otherwise, got fresh, you just asked him about his wife and children or just plain slapped his face. I had resorted to both when accosted in the stationery cupboard or in the office. It was almost accepted that there would be some who would try it on but it was easy to deal with it." "We had two paedophiles in the village but the word was not known to us. One of them was the local butcher, a Methodist who sang in the choir. If a young girl went to the shop on her own he would try to get her behind the counter and touch her inappropriately. We always got friends to go with us but did not explain this to our parents. It was as if parents and children lived in a parallel universe. The other one was a bachelor who gave the boys tuppence to let him put his hand up their trouser leg. We were soon stopped from playing in his garden when my brother was asked why he was given tuppence."

"Divorce was not an option unless you were well off so most people soldiered on even if they were in unhappy marriages. The majority of people got married in church and took the vows seriously, with the intention of staying together." "Divorce was generally regarded as being rather improper and dangerously modern." "Divorces were generally what film stars had!" "My parents' generation looked on divorce as failure, you stuck together through thick and thin. When I married in 1969 my brother was courting a divorced lady with two children. When my mother heard that he wanted to bring her to the wedding she flew into a rage saying, 'She can't go into church, she is divorced!'. I was astounded and angry at her attitude, especially as she never went to church, not even at Christmas."

Same sex relationships were seldom discussed and homosexuality was, of course, illegal for most of this period. "My recollection of attitudes towards homosexuality comes not from my peer group or from home (where it did not seem to arise as a subject for discussion) but from the media. There were appalling stereotypes, particularly of homosexual men e.g. *Round the Horne* (1965). I don't think female homosexuality was acknowledged at all." "Most homosexuals must have kept quiet about their sexuality and some would not admit to it, even marrying to allay suspicion (I feel that this may have been the case with one member of our extended family). They were referred to as 'queers', 'fairies' or 'pansies' but usually without any rancour. In the Fifties, the radio programme *Round the Horne* (1965) had a regular segment featuring 'Julian and my friend Sandy', who were obviously homosexual, though it was never stated and no one seemed to object." "I remember reading in the news about people who were homosexual e.g. Brian Epstein, the Beatles' manager who very sadly committed suicide and also Stephen Ward, who gained notoriety in the Christine Keeler affair and was also someone who took his own life. So it was seen as something to be ashamed of admitting and something decent society disapproved of so it had to be kept quiet about. I recall derogatory terminology used to describe homosexual men, such as 'perverts' 'poofters', 'queers', 'faggots' or 'queens'; the word 'gay' had not yet been adopted in this context. Lesbian women mainly escaped derision though." "Much has been written about children in same sex boarding schools forming homosexual relationships but I was never aware of this happening at our school. When in the younger years we perhaps had infatuations for certain senior girls, those who were attractive and/or excelled at sport but these were never reciprocated so could not be called relationships. Almost all the staff were single females and some did share living accommodation but I don't remember thinking this was unusual (perhaps I was naïve) but with hindsight I now see many were in lesbian relationships."

Feminism[3]

The women's suffrage movement had been particularly active in the latter years of the nineteenth century and in the period up to the equalisation of the franchise in 1928. Perhaps in part due to the Depression, the second world war and its aftermath, the middle years of the twentieth century saw a lull in feminist campaigns. The 1960s however brought what is often referred to as 'the second wave of feminism', newly termed 'women's lib'.[4] The availability of the contraceptive pill in 1961, the Abortion Act of 1967 and revisions to the Married Women's Property Act in 1964, which gave women more financial independence, all contributed to provide an opportunity for new freedom for women. Women were being given greater educational opportunities and were starting to take more prominent roles in society, providing inspirational role-models. For example, Barbara Castle who became the first and only, female First Secretary of State in 1968 was just one women who was making inroads into a traditionally male arena.

Although the seeds of change were beginning to germinate by the 1960s, this was still an era when women were undoubtedly second class citizens. There was no legal obligation to treat women equally in the workplace and many people, women included, would not have regarded this as being unacceptable. Gender stereotypes also ruled most households, with clearly defined roles for males and females that largely went unchallenged. "Men still expected to be the main breadwinner, some even not allowing wives to work outside the home. Neither did they take much part in child rearing except in terms of discipline." "If a woman went to work it was suggested that the man wasn't up to the job of providing for his family and so was looked down on." "In 1946, roles were clearly defined into what jobs or duties were expected of each gender but war-time had allowed women to do work previously allocated to men and attitudes changed. It came as a surprise to many that women had sexual appetites too, rather than being just the objects of male desire!"

"In our family women were definitely inferior, as was common for that time. I remember being incensed by my parents' and elder sister's views that it was so good of my husband to let me study and go to university! I was working at the time, running the household and fitting in study when the children were asleep! As another example, I had an uncle who would not purchase two comfortable armchairs and his hard-working wife always sat on a wooden kitchen chair!" "I began to appreciate just how far behind women were in society. Whether it was equality in the workplace or in the home, there were differences. These became more apparent as I was living up North and some of the women had come from homes where the men folk were quite domineering and had less respect for wives and daughters, keeping them in their place. I could not go up to a bar in those days and order a drink, indeed I was not socially comfortable doing that anyway. It was regarded as unladylike."

Those who did fight for women's rights were frequently see as eccentric by society as a whole. "Feminists were often made fun of and labelled as 'bra-burners', after supposed incidents where women protested against being seen as sex objects. They were sometimes accused of being man-hating lesbians or attempting to emasculate men and of having hairy armpits. Greer's *The Female Eunuch* wasn't actually published until 1970 but there was certainly a build up to it during the sixties. 'Women's lib' was the term often applied to this second wave feminist movement and many deemed it a derogatory term for a concept which threatened to undermine the patriarchal society we were used to and that had served so many so well for so long."

Race and Religion

This was by no stretch of the imagination a time of political correctness. What would now be considered to be blatantly racist views were widely held and applauded. "The term 'foreigners' came to be used quite widely to represent anyone who came into our country from elsewhere and they were all regarded as a group one did not know, understand or wish to be connected with." For some, 'foreigners' lurked closer to home. "As well as a negative attitude to all things perceived to be foreign, the same attitude prevailed for those at the other end of the village." Certain racial groups were vilified at particular times, often because they were regarded as being some sort of threat, or because they engendered a sense of unease as they were in some way 'not like us.' Immediately after the war, anti-German feeling was at a height. "Although I had no German family con-nections, our west-country surname sounded Germanic to our south London neighbours. This caused a certain amount of hostility as late as the 1960s." "It was also thought to be acceptable to malign the Irish, who were widely regarded as being stupid. Comedians and television programmes reflected xenophobic attitudes without censure. *Til Death Us Do Part*, which aired on BBC television from 1965, featured a character, Alf Garnett, whose right-wing, racist views have become notorious but which were seen at the time as being both acceptable and amusing." The influx of waves of Commonwealth immigrants meant that town dwellers were confronted by those whose 'different from us' ethnicity was immediately apparent. As ever, diversity aroused suspicion. "It must be remembered that when I was a child the British Empire had not long begun to disintegrate and the Commonwealth had only been formed in 1949, the year I was born. Schools still taught using maps and atlases with vast swathes coloured pink as in the days of the Great British Empire when Britain really did rule much of the world and there was a prevailing confidence in Britain as still being a great and independent nation. As I recall it, white people and mainly white men at that, were still viewed as the dominant form of human being and black people as inferior, uneducated, almost savage and animal-like in comparison."

"We moved into a large town which had a significant African and Caribbean population, even as far back as the 1950s. I quickly grew aware of how things were in society at the time. I was taught to keep well clear and not to socialise as if these folk were not the same as us." "Redditch, in the mid-1950s, received a massive influx of Afro-Carribean people and my mother was closely acquainted with many of them as she worked in a GP surgery. Her attitude was a fairly traditional antipathy, despising their easy access to health and other benefits and their acceptance of poor living standards. This mistrust of foreigners was widespread in my experience, not only among my own family. I can recall opinions and comments from many acquaintances, that I would be ashamed to repeat and which would receive total condemnation today. In particular, black people were regarded as almost subhuman, a different species."

"All black people were referred to in my childhood by the now unacceptable 'N'[5] word. I don't think people thought of themselves as racist, it was just how it was." "Other widespread expressions used to describe those of African, Asian or West Indian origin were 'darkies' or 'coloureds'; you might see an advert for a room to let that said 'no coloureds' and that was legal and acceptable." "Possibly the most commonly used derogatory term for black people in Bristol was 'WOG' and its use was often justified by saying it was an acronym for 'Western Oriental Gentleman' and therefore actually a complimentary term. But it wasn't." "The presence of a black household was deemed to 'lower the tone' of a neighbourhood." Despite the prevailing attitudes to people of colour, "most of our summer weekends were spend at the outside pool in South Chingford, where all us white people tried to go brown, strange world!"

For many, there was little or no contact with those from different racial backgrounds. "At all the schools I went to, there was not one child who was of a different ethnicity. Everybody in our village was white and 99% born in Yorkshire." "My world, as I saw it as a child in the 1950s, was made up of white British people. I had no concept of anyone with skin that was any colour other than my own and very little concept of people from other countries." "I can only remember one occasion when a black man came to the village to sell goods. All the children were ushered in and the poor man was left to look through the windows. He was a talking point for days." "When I was about nine or ten I got to know an American family, the father worked for the USAF at the nearby base. I remember bringing the boy, who was around my age, home to play at my house. I was completely amazed at my mother's reaction. She was visibly shocked and unwelcoming to the little boy who was black. It had never occurred to me that he was of a different colour, we were just friends and his family had welcomed me into their home. It was my first exposure to racial prejudice and I had not seen it coming."

Post-war Britain was markedly Christian and most people would declare themselves as belonging to the Church of England, even if they rarely attended. If fact, in 1951, about fifteen percent of the population went to church on a weekly basis.[6] Even those who did not go to church regularly would be likely to consider church-going as admirable. "There was a general consensus that respectable and decent people went to church. Most people, well everyone I knew at least, married in a church and had a funeral service in a church and all children in my circle of family and friends routinely and dutifully had their children christened in a church." "Church attendance was expected in the village; how else would people get to know each other? Some of them would have gone down the pub, of course but that was a bit different! The church was at the centre of village life in a way it is not today." "Nearly everyone sent their children to Sunday school; I'm not sure to what extent this was to give adults a small amount of child-free time! Far fewer adults were regular attendees." "By the time I was the age for Sunday school my parents no longer attended services themselves, yet still saw it as the 'done thing' to send me along to Sunday school. It was accepted as providing a good, moral start in life for children and of course schools still had religious assemblies every morning before lessons started, so religion was definitely a big part of a fifties' child's life. Songs I remember singing include *Jesus wants me for a Sunbeam* and *Jesus bids us Shine*."

"The Sabbath, to Nana, was sacrosanct and the one day of the week that the sanctuary of the front parlour could be entered. Here, the heavy net curtains concealed the splendour that could be seen but rarely touched. The majestic aspidistra graced the polished oak table in the window bay, sombre, moralising paintings dominated the dull green walls, as stern warning to the daughters of the house to behave in a manner expected of a 'good' family. During my own childhood the Sunday afternoon tea ritual persisted; the silver tea-trolley was wheeled in ceremoniously as the family sat meekly perched on the edge of the straight-backed chairs and bone-china cups of tea would be handed round, together with a two-tiered glass cake-stand of tinned salmon and cucumber sandwiches and Nana's home-made fruit cake. Sometimes the piano lid would be raised, music books taken from their secret hideaway under the padded top of the piano-stool and we would all sit in reverence as Grandpa recited on the ivory keys. More often than not the patriotic strains of *Jerusalem* or *Land of Hope and Glory* would regale us, reminding us, lest we forget, of the glorious and victorious empire that was Great Britain!"

"Religion was something that was not discussed at home and church attendance was not expected by my parents but it was woven into the fabric of life generally and therefore inescapable. By 'it' I mean the mainstream Anglican church. It was there at primary school (Church of England controlled), with visits from the vicar and some obligatory church services, at Brownies (church parade) and it oozed from the radio via a range of programmes, many of which took a high moral tone. At grammar school it was there in every assembly and in Religious Education, which was essentially a study of the New Testament. There was no discussion of the validity of the Christian (Protestant) faith (i.e. how much evidence) and people of other beliefs (Roman Catholic, Jewish) were thought rather 'odd', although it is difficult to pin down where exactly this view came from. Atheism or indeed Humanism were never on the agenda and it was difficult for young people who came to doubt what was effectively religious indoctrination, to know how to raise it. The Church of England, a male dominated institution, was very much part of the established order and not to be questioned."

'Hellfire and Damnation' in worship was largely a thing of the past. "The God that I learnt about was a forgiving and generous God, not a punishing one and neither of my parents ever used religion as a weapon or to strike fear or superstition in my heart." The gender divide extended to religious practices. "Congregations comprised mostly women and children but all vicars/ministers were male as were churchwardens, sides-men, etc." Women taught in Sunday schools, arranged flowers, made teas and occasionally played the organ. Religion was regarded as a private matter. "Although they had a very strong faith and were very involved in church life they never discussed religious ideas. My mother, in particular, was very interested in different ideas, such as the possibility of reincarnation and other more esoteric subjects but although she might write to a newspaper or join local groups, she never really discussed these with us."

Religious differences were further grounds for divisiveness and prejudice. "In my world of the 1950s and 1960s, the varying branches of the Anglican church regarded each other with distain. Jews and Catholics, whom you might come across, were viewed across an unfathomable divide. Knowledge of faiths beyond these was very limited and you certainly didn't expect to encounter their adherents in your daily lives." "Village people and my family were narrow-minded. There were divisions as to whether you were Church of England (C of E), Methodist, Wesleyan or Primitive Chapel. There was much friction when two chapels amalgamated." "Particularly in rural areas, religions other than Christianity were never encountered but there was prejudice against those of different denominations; a church-chapel divide and as for Roman Catholics!" "We knew little of Islam, Buddhism or other non-Christian denominations." "Differences between various denominations and even within denominations, were felt very strongly. For instance, my parents did not like their local parish church at first and every Sunday we took the train (we didn't have a car at the time) to a nearby town where the style of worship was more to their taste. People did not often change from one denomination to another. My mother's move from Methodism to

Anglicanism was quite unusual." "There was a substantial Jewish community and they too had their own school. As a child I remember thinking they were some sort of alien beings as they wore skull caps and they were always referred to in a slightly derogatory way, as if inferior to us."

"I certainly don't remember being particularly aware that there were any religions other than Christianity in its British form and had no concept whatsoever of Islam, Hinduism, Sikhism, Buddhism or any other religion that other people in the world might be part of. I just assumed that everyone in the UK was a Christian, at least nominally. I would probably have heard of 'atheists' but not really grasped what they did or didn't believe in." "I do not think there were any Roman Catholics, known as 'popists' in the village. The only Roman Catholics known would be the Irish labourers, who came every year for the potato and sugar beet harvests. We were certainly not allowed to mix with them. I do not know if anyone had heard of Sikhs and Muslims."

"By the 1960s, the dawning of a more secular society, perhaps, in part, a product of post-war cynicism, was apparent." "We weren't strongly religious, in fact as time went on, we became more an atheist family. But it was important to mother that we were seen to attend." "I didn't know anyone who took religion very seriously, it seemed to be just a space to fill in on official forms. At the end of the 1960s, when I was admitted to hospital, I decided this was a silly charade, so when asked my religion I said, 'None'. The nurse looked thoughtfully at the form, then said, 'I'll put C. of E., shall I?' Atheism was obviously not accepted at that time!"

Politics and Class

Like sex and religion, politics was anther topic that was not widely discussed. Wives and children might be expected to vote along the same lines as the man of the house. "My father, who was in business, voted Conservative as, *of course*, did my mother." "My parents were not keen on me being so 'red' and criticised my views. They thought I would grow out of it." "Voting was seen as a civic responsibility and the turnouts were much higher than they are nowadays."[7] Many constituencies tended to re-elect the same party for generations and links between the Labour Party and the trade unions were strong. The era began and ended with a Labour government, sandwiching fourteen years of Conservative rule. The Prime Ministers and their parties were:

    1946-1951 Clement Attlee Labour
    1951-1955 Winston Churchill Conservative
    1955-1957 Anthony Eden Conservative
    1957-1963 Harold MacMillan Conservative
    1963-1964 Alec Douglas-Hume Conservative
    1964-1970 Harold Wilson Labour

"In those days there was a much clearer divide between the parties and really only two featured (Conservative and Labour), the minority parties such as the Liberals held very few seats in Parliament or locally. Voting was also pretty much on class lines with working class people more likely to vote Labour and middle and upper class people to vote Conservative." "My dad voted Labour because it was 'the working man's party'. He read *The Daily Mirror*. They didn't talk politics and I don't know how much they really thought about it although my dad obviously thought that the Labour Party represented him which, in those days, it probably did." "Newspapers, then as now, had political bias which served to reinforce people's own political leanings as they tended to read only those they agreed with and believed only what they read. The news reported was not actually untrue but incomplete, slanted to give an impression of the point of view they required, by omission of facts. The power of the press is quite frightening but at that time was not generally recognised."

Those who lived through this era were very class aware. In 1946, there was little expectation that one would belong to anything other than the class of one's parents and indeed it might be audacious to consider that movement between classes was possible. "There were the upper classes, aristocracy and the like, middle class professionals, 'white collar' workers who did not get their hands dirty and 'blue collar' workers who were employed in factories or at labouring jobs." "What was important was not to 'get above yourself'." "There was an attitude of knowing your place and respecting your betters." This did begin to change with the advent of the eleven plus, which provided, in theory, the possibility of better educational opportunities for all classes. "The rigid divisions of class became more flexible after the war. Education allowed more to aspire to university and thus opened routes into the professions, so that the children of working class people moved into the professional and middle classes, blurring the distinctions. Thus arose an inverted snobbery where some proudly claimed to be working class but had never worked with their hands in industry or agriculture." "Class was much in evidence in the 1950s and we would have looked down on the rag and bone man, beggars, criminals, all those who were different, whether on grounds of colour, race, creed. Sometimes prejudice extended to those who lived on local council housing estates."

Class dictated who you might associate with. "There was certainly class distinction. The family of the local manor house, the vicarage and the GP never spoke to the rest of us. We were somewhere in the middle with teachers, railway workers, publicans and shop-keepers. We were not allowed to play with the children of labourers." "Friendships were not allowed with children from the other end of the village, which was considered rough." "I had the uncomfortable situation of being on the wrong end of prejudice as an eleven year old. I had started my secondary school and had made a new friend called Vera, we got on well and I was invited to her house, which was very large and 'posh', after school one day. I met her mother and she asked where I lived, I told her my address (this was on a council estate), she looked like I had shot her and left the room. I was never allowed in the house again, and Vera wasn't allowed to come to mine, I was totally confused and embarrassed by this."

"I grew up in a village where society was stratified by social class. For the first ten or so years of my life I only mixed with 'people like us'. In other words, I spent all my time with 'nice' middle-class families. ('Nice' was my mother's favourite adjective, meaning approved or accepted). The indicators for people of the right sort for us were manners and accent. There were conventions of behaviour and anyone who didn't conform to them was looked upon with at best, doubt and at worst, suspicion." "Speech, mannerisms, conduct, the way we lived our lives in general was supposedly so different that we were taught to look the other way, to ignore and our prejudice became apparent." "I think there was definitely a sense of judgement around the way we spoke in the fifties and sixties. Upper class people and those on BBC television spoke with 'received pronunciation' and this was aspired to by those who sent their children to elocution classes. Certainly if you had a Northern or West-country accent you might well be considered inferior socially, as a stereotype. Sixties Britain was definitely London-centric." "People with received pronunciation were often perceived as being better than those who used a regional accent." "Northern accents were looked down on but my father said an accent was acceptable if the grammar was correct." "I grew up with a great deal of attention paid to class. Certain behaviours dictated how well you had been brought up. Speech was important, accent, the kind of words used, behaviour patterns, how you dressed, all these things could pinpoint pretty accurately where you fitted in in society."

"In courtship there would be much said by respective families. Farmer's sons were expected to marry farmer's daughters. Girls from the High School would not dream of being seen out with anyone from the labouring classes." Sometimes the divide was crossed. "My father as a farmer's son was a little higher in social class than my mother who was a farm labourer's daughter and this was reflected in where they went to church. My grandparent's on my father's side attended the Church of England, whereas my mother was a Methodist." "My mother, whose father was an accountant, 'married beneath her' in 1947; my paternal grandfather was a railway porter. The ten year age gap between my parents and post-war upheavals helped to gloss over this but it was seen as unusual." "The 1950s saw the end of the 'debutantes' season'. The season was a way of introducing aristocratic young ladies to eligible bachelors and launching them into adult society ('coming out'). It was for seventeen year olds, lasted a summer long and included attendances at numerous parties, balls and social events, such as Ascot and the Dublin Horse Show, culminating in presentation at Court to the Queen. A great deal of money was spent on the correct clothes and styling and giving parties or balls by the families involved. It was little more than a glorified marriage market, as it was expected that the girls should become engaged by the end of the season.

By the time of the last 'coming out' in 1958 however, there were many more girls from 'new money' families than from the old 'county' or aristocratic families."

Celebrities

Twenty-first century celebrity culture was something that would be unrecognisable to the post-war generation. The royal family were the closest thing to celebrities in the 1940s and 1950s. "During and immediately after the war we were very patriotic in our attitude. The royal family held our admiration for their support by refusing to leave London during the Blitz. The Queen Mother is reported as saying that she could not leave when the people of the East End had to stay after the terrible bombings. We sang songs at school like *Rule Britannia*, *Hearts of Oak* and *Land of Hope and Glory* almost every day. *The National Anthem* was played at the theatres and sports venues and we all sang the words. It wasn't until later years that people snuck out of the cinema as soon as the anthem was played. We followed the progress of any foreign visits by the royal family especially their Commonwealth tour in the 1950s. When King George VI died, we were heartbroken and only the magnificent coronation of Elizabeth gave us a view of a new future." "The Queen in our family was a bit like the Church of England, just a part of it which was there and which was respected." "The royal family were almost universally respected. The Union Jack was flown on public buildings on their birthdays and *The National Anthem* was played on the radio. I don't think people resented the fact that they lived such a privileged life, it was seen as their birthright." "We had a royal scrap-book and pasted in newspaper and magazine cuttings about the royal family. There was great excitement when the Queen's children were born." "Royalty came right at the top of the ladder and seemed highly respected. Both my grandparents and parents would sit down to watch the Queen's speech at three o'clock on Christmas Day and we tried hard to watch official engagements which were televised once we had a TV. Royal weddings and trooping of the colour were de rigueur!"

Then, as now, the media had an impact on the celebrities of the day. Particularly in the 1940s and 1950s, there was respect for war heroes and those who accomplished feats of daring, such as Edmund Hillary. Sporting events from the 1948 Olympics, held at White City in London, to the 1966 world cup victory all provided people to worship from afar. This was aided by the increased access to these proceedings via television. Particularly amongst the young, there was a gradual moving towards idols who might be seen, by some, to be less worthy of adulation. The cinema and magazines provided fuel for this particular fire. By the 1960s, film stars were being replaced on their pedestals by pop stars and those who appeared on television.

Language

Without doubt, language evokes an era; cult slang is incomprehensible to the generations that come before and after. Expletives, attitudes to swearing and indeed what is considered to be bad language also change. "Swearing was less common then than it is now. Men usually refrained from swearing in front of women or children and it certainly wasn't acceptable for us children to swear." "In our family, language was so indicative of being well brought-up and well-educated that we never experienced swearing." "It was ok for parents to say the odd 'damn' and 'blast' and even, when desperate, 'bloody'. I do remember that 'sod' and 'sodding hell' were common swear words about this time outside the house. I used to check any new words I heard in the family dictionary but it wasn't always useful." "The main swear words I was aware of as a child were simply 'bloody' and 'bugger' and I'd heard 'fuck' at school very occasionally but was not aware of any others really. People sometimes said 'Jesus Christ', 'Christ almighty', or at a push 'Good Lord' or 'My God', mainly religious words like that. But more often innocent words were used, such as 'crikey', 'crumbs', 'gosh', 'my giddy aunt', 'lummy', 'lummy Charlie' and my mother's favourite exclamation, 'Good garden peas'!"

There were a large number of dialect words that were in regular use in particular parts of the country but there appear to have been two main influences on the more widely used slang words of this period. Firstly, Americanisms, a hang-over from the presence of American servicemen during the war and bolstered by the availability of American films. Secondly, the language of the hippies in the 'flower power' era at the end of the 1960s. "It is strange how many slang words described something good. Believe it or not, in the 1950s, we were still using expressions like 'smashing', 'wizard', or even 'spiffing', 'top-hole' or 'the tops'. All these have undertones of the middle classes of the pre-war period but they appeared in books, such as school stories and therefore found their way into everyday conversation." "'Having a ball' meant that you were having a good time. Anyone who was 'fab' was considered attractive. When invited to a party if you did not join in people would call you 'a party pooper'. When asked if you have 'got the dosh' or if you have 'the readies' this was a reference to having the money. I often heard boys refer to their father as their 'old man' and to their mother as their 'old lady.'" "Relatives were 'the folks'." "If someone was thought of as strange they were called an 'odd ball'." "I heard my brothers talking about 'spivs' and 'wide boys' after they came back from London, a 'spiv' it seems was a man who was a flashy dresser and a 'wide boy' did not do regular work but lived off his wits." "A 'bloke' was a man, usually youngish, whereas a girl was a 'bird'." "A girlfriend might be a 'doll' or a 'babe'." "Your vehicle was your 'wheels.'"

"Most of the words I recall come from the hippy era and were used by the young. Any one who was up-to-date was 'with-it', 'groovy' or 'cool', the opposite was to be 'square'. 'Swinging', 'outa sight,' 'far out' and 'way out' were other ways of describing something favourable, whereas 'dodgy' was the reverse. If you liked something you would be said to 'dig it', or it would be 'your bag'. Having a 'blast' was having a good time, 'a gas' was something fun and 'a drag' was not. Phrases often ended with the word 'man', so 'cool man' or 'far out man', even if you were talking to a female." "'The scene' was the fashionable or acceptable environment. A 'bash' or a 'happening' was a gathering or party, which would take place at someone's 'pad' (or home). To 'crash' was to spend the night at someone's house and to 'chill out' was to relax." "'Freaking out' might mean getting cross or scared but it was also used to refer to a style of 'head-banging' dancing to heavy rock music of the end of the sixties, which usually involved much nodding of the head."

"There were also words specifically associated with drug culture. Drugs were 'dope' or 'gear' (although gear also meant good); to 'score' or to get 'high' or 'stoned' was to take drugs. The drugs themselves had names such as 'acid', 'speed', 'pot' or 'weed'. A 'joint' or 'reefer' was a drug filled cigarette. These were always easy to spot as they were fat roll-ups. Ordinary roll-up cigarettes were seen as being the preserve of slightly disreputable old men." "Cigarettes were 'fags' and to get drunk was to be 'pissed'." To be 'zonked' was to be exhausted but might also refer to being under the influence of drugs or alcohol."

Conflict

Attitudes to personal violence were different. Physical punishment for children, at home and at school, was normal. Young boys would be encouraged to 'stand up for themselves' and use physical force against playground bullies. Physical domestic abuse between adults occasioned mild disapproval but was considered to be a private matter between the couple concerned. The idea that the woman in the relationship could be the abuser was totally alien. "Although it seemed to be common knowledge in the area it seems none of the neighbours felt able to report it. I think their attitudes were that they could not intervene between husband and wife and what was happening was their own business." The concept of emotional abuse was not considered.

Young men had to do National Service from 1949, when all healthy eighteen year olds, who were not in exempted occupations, were required to serve for eighteen months. This term of service was extended to two years in 1950. It was possible, in theory, to conscientiously object but this was frowned upon. Immediately after the war, the atmosphere was one of fierce patriotism and the general perception, amongst the older generation at least, was that Britain could do no wrong. There was a pervading resentment towards those who had been conscientious objectors or 'conchies'. "My father was in the Air Training Corps but as a farmer's son he had an exempted profession and so was not called up to fight during the war. This was seen as acceptable but not fighting due to pacifism was considered cowardly and almost sneered at, continuing for many years after the war, 'He was a pacifist you know……..'" The post-war generation began to see things rather differently. "I think those who had been through the recent war saw pacifists as cop-outs, weak and cowardly, whereas the younger generation wanted no more wars, were idealistic and adopted an attitude of 'make love not war', probably influenced by the recent Vietnam and Korean wars that lost so many US lives and didn't really have successful outcomes. Also there had was the ongoing Cold War between the West and the USSR and the threat posed on both sides by nuclear weapons. I remember the Bay of Pigs and the Cuban missile crisis; I was at school when this happened and was aware of something potentially world-threatening happening." "We were all 'pacifists' in that we did not want war but people who avoided military duty on the grounds of conscience were not respected. The possibility of nuclear war sharpened efforts to avoid conflict and actually kept the peace." As National Service came to an end[4] there was increasing support for movements such as The Campaign for Nuclear Disarmament (CND) and many students took part in the peace marches of the 1960s.

Summary

Our lives are shaped by our relationships with the people around us. Volunteers described 1950s' family dynamics that were more formal and interaction that was more restrained than the twenty-first century experience. Pre-marital sexual encounters were inhibited by social mores and by the fear of an unwanted pregnancy; gender stereotypes prevailed. If relationships shape a person, then it might be said that attitudes shape an era and opinions and attitudes are threaded throughout this book. It is clear that attitudes are influenced by those around us, initially our families, "For the first eleven or twelve years of my life my attitudes were absorbed from my parents" and then from our peers or through the media. "The attitudes and behaviour patterns amongst your role models in the community and social group in which you are nurtured are extremely strong, whether good or bad, right or wrong and they often leave a lasting legacy which may be difficult to erase."

By the 1960s, horizons were widening beyond all imagination. Those who grew up in this period often had an education that was broader than that of their parents. The television opened up new worlds and more people had the wherewithal to travel further and return with new ideas. The establishment of a youth culture impacted on fashion, on music and on identity. Near full employment and increasing disposable incomes meant that desires could be indulged and the age of conspicuous consumerism had arrived. In a reaction to post-war austerity, homes looked different, fashions changed and lives were different.

Most participants agreed that the years between 1946 and 1969 brought huge cultural shifts in many aspects of their lives. By the end of the era, the way in which family members interacted with each other was beginning to change. Parenting was more child-centred and gender stereotypes were being eroded. Women were no longer content to be second class citizens and young people were finding their identity in a way that had never been known before; our elders were not always right. The sexual revolution was just part of the dawning of this new age. Whilst we look back and 'Remember Then', it was undoubtedly true that this was a watershed and the times they were indeed a-changing'.

The Brief

Write about friendships and friends. Were there any constraints on who would be considered 'suitable' as a friend? Were 'friendships' imposed by your parents?

Write about relationships within the family. How did family members interact, what signs of affection were acceptable or expected? How often did you see extended family members and what was the relationship like when you did?

Comment on the role of physical violence in relationships. How was corporal punishment for children viewed? What were the attitudes towards domestic abuse?

Include looking after elderly relatives and support (emotional, financial and practical) for family members who did not share your home. Was there an expectation that support would be given?

Describe relationships with the opposite sex. What were the expected courtship rituals? How did this differ from reality? How much influence did parents, friends and society have when choosing a partner?

Write about family pets, if any. Did pets play and important part in the life of your household?

What follows is about attitudes, not just your own but the prevailing attitudes of the time.

Write about attitudes towards religion, church and Sunday school attendance. Include feelings towards those of different faiths, or different branches of the same faith. Include attitudes towards atheism. Was church attendance expected?

What were common attitudes towards and participation in, politics? Was it expected that you would support a particular party? Would political leanings have been discussed?

Describe attitudes towards foreigners, ethic minorities and immigrants. Was racism apparent, accepted or abhorred? 'Foreigners', could include those from the next village if applicable.

How were issues such as premarital sex, illegitimacy, divorce and promiscuity viewed? Include attitudes towards homosexuality.

To what degree was there an awareness of social class? How were those from different classes perceived?

How common was swearing? Were certain words taboo? What was the reaction to regional accents?

List common slang or 'cult' words of the era.

What was the attitude towards warfare? How were pacifists viewed?

Describe how women were treated. What was the reaction to feminism?

Who were the celebrities of the day. How were the royal family perceived?

Do you think that attitudes were different for those from different geographical, religious or social backgrounds?

Chapter 10 footnotes

[1] See also Chapter 8 for memories of parent-child relationships. Relationships with neighbours are discussed in Chapter 1.

[2] See Chapter 7.

[3] Comments have already been made about the role of women in the home and the workplace; see, in particular, Chapters 2 and 5.

[4] Short for 'women's liberation', the term was first used in print by Juliet Mitchell in 'Women: the longest revolution' in New Left Review 1966 Nov-December 11–37 but is believed to have been first coined two years earlier. Sarachild, Kathie 'Consciousness-Raising: a radical weapon' in Sarachild, K, Hanisch, C., Levine, F., Leon, B., Price, C. (eds), Feminist Revolution (Random House 1978) pp. 144-50.

[5] I fully appreciate my contributor's reluctance to use this word but in the interests of not sanitising history and whilst abhorring its use, I feel I must say that the word was 'nigger'. Janet Few

[6] Gorer, Geoffrey Exploring English Character (Criterion Books 1955) p. 451, quoted in Brown, Callum G, Religion and the Demographic Revolution: women and secularisation in Canada, Ireland, UK and USA since the 1960s (Boydell Press 2012) p. 83. In the 2011 census, 59% of the population claimed to be Christian and a further 24% aligned themselves with another religion 2011 Census (KS209EW) Religion, local authorities in England and Wales". ons.gov.uk. Regular Church of England attendance in 2011 however was just over a million https://www.churchofengland.org/media-centre/news/2013/05/church-annual-statistics-for-2011.aspx.

[6] During this period, general election turnouts ranged from 75% to 83%. In the twenty-first century turnouts have been between 59% and 66% http://www.ukpolitical.info/Turnout45.htm.

[7] The last call ups were in 1960 and all conscripts were demobilised by 1963.

Timeline 1946-1969

1946 First session of the United Nations' General Assembly

1946 Terence Rattigan's *The Winslow Boy* is published

1946 Alistair Cooke's radio series *Letter from America* is first broadcast

1946 Film *The Best Years of our Lives* is released

1946 Popular songs include *Zip-a-dee-do-dah*

1946 The bikini is launched

1946 Dr Spock's childcare manual is published

1946 The publication of children's book *Thomas the Tank Engine* by Revd. Awdry

1946 The Jitterbug becomes a popular dance

1946 Free milk is provided in schools

1946 Television licences are introduced

1946 First Pontin's holiday camp opens

1946 The Family Allowance benefit is first paid

1946 33 die in a disaster at Bolton Wanderers' football stadium

1946-7 Severe winter weather

1947 School leaving age is raised from 14 to 15

1947 The National Service Act is passed, this was amended in 1948 and came into force in 1949

1947 First Edinburgh Festival

1947 Nationalisation of the coal industry

1947 Polio epidemic

1947 The Co-op opens the first ten self-service supermarkets, marketed as 'Q-less shopping'.

1947 Princess Elizabeth marries Philip Mountbatten

1947 Women are allowed to become full time students at Cambridge University

1948 London Olympics

1948 First waves of immigration from the Commonwealth on *HMS Windrush*

1948 The introduction of the National Health Service

1948 Gandhi assassinated

1948 Radio series *Mrs Dale's Diary* first broadcast

1948 Film *The Red Shoes* released

1948 Popular sings include *All I want for Christmas is my Two Front Teeth*

1948 Nationalisation of the railways

1948 Bread is no longer rationed

1948 The 33rpm long playing record is introduced

1948 Introduction of 'The New Look' fashion style

1948 Polo mints come on the market

1948 Arab-Israeli War

1949 45rpm single records became available

1949 The first self-service launderette is opened

1949 George Orwell's *Nineteen Eight Four* is published

1949 Popular songs include *Some Enchanted Evening* and *Rudolph the Red-nosed Reindeer*

1949 Clothes rationing comes to an end

1949 The Commonwealth is created, evolving from the British Empire

1949 Nationalisation of the gas industry

1950 London dock strike

1950 The radio programme *Listen with Mother* is broadcast for the first time

1950 Korean War begins

1950 The Kenwood Chef food mixer goes on the market

1950 The term of National Service is extended to two years

1950 Post-war petrol rationing ends

1950 A pilot of the radio series *The Archers* is broadcast

1951 Films *A Streetcar named Desire, The African Queen* and *Strangers on a Train* are released

1951 Musical *The King and I* opens in New York

1951 Festival of Britain

1951 *The Goon Show* is first broadcast on the radio

1951 The first Miss World beauty pageant is staged

1951 Zebra crossings are introduced

1951 The first National Parks are designated

1951 School certificate is abolished in favour of GCE examinations

1951 First episode of the radio serial *The Archers*

1952 Death of George VI and accession of Elizabeth II

1952 First screening of *The Sooty Show* on television

1952 First British atomic weapon is tested

1952 A prescription charge of 1/- is introduced

1952 Agatha Christie's play *The Mousetrap* begins its record-breaking run

1952 The end of the utility furniture scheme

1952 Children's TV series *Watch with Mother* is first screened, although some of the individual programmes had been screened earlier

1953 Coronation of Elizabeth II

1953 Arthur Miller's *The Crucible* is published

1953 133 die in the sinking of the car ferry *MV Princess Victoria*

1953 The structure of DNA is revealed by Crick and Watson

1953 Tetley introduce tea-bags

1953 Edmund Hillary and Sherpa Tenzing became the first men to climb
     Mount Everest

1953 Laura Ashley begins selling printed fabrics

1954 All rationing ends

1954 The first Wimpy Bar, owned by Lyons Corner House, opens

1954 Tolkien's *Lord of the Rings*, William Golding's *Lord of the Flies* and
     Dylan Thomas' *Under Milk Wood* are published

1954 Roger Bannister runs a mile in under four minutes

1954 Elvis Presley records released include *I Love You Because* and *Blue Moon*

1955 Warsaw Pact

1955 First Berni Inn opens

1955 Polio vaccination is introduced

1955 The National Childbirth Trust is formed as The Natural Childbirth Trust

1955 Vietnam War breaks out

1955 Airfix start to sell scale model kits

1955 Very hot summer and accompanying drought

1955 Fatal rail crashes at Milton and Barnes kill 11 and 13 respectively

1955 Ruth Ellis is the last woman to be hanged in the UK

1955 ITV begins broadcasting

1955 First fish fingers, produced by Birdseye, go on sale

1956 Death of actor James Dean

1956 The bank interest rate is 5·5%, the highest for more than twenty years

1956 Suez Crisis

1956 Collared doves breed in the UK for the first time

1956 Double yellow lines are introduced

1956 Premium bonds are introduced

1956 The world's first nuclear power station is opened at Calder Hall

1957 90 people are killed in the Lewisham train crash

1957 The drug Thalidomide was prescribed for anxiety and severe morning
     sickness, leading to babies being born with limb malformations.

1957 Britain tests an H bomb

1957 *Panorama* broadcasts the Spaghetti Tree 1st April hoax

1957 Wolfenden Report recommend that homosexuality is decriminalised

1957 The white £5 note is replaced

1958 First episode of the children's TV programme *Blue Peter*

1958 First parking meters are introduced

1958 Cliff Richard's first single *Move It* is released

1958 First Cod War with Iceland

1958 The final debutante season, where aristocratic girls 'came out' into society
     and were presented to the monarch

1958 Lego bricks are patented

1958 Race riots in Notting Hill, London

1958 Formation of the Campaign for Nuclear Disarmament (CND)

1958 The motorway system opens

1958 Vivian Fuchs leads the first overland expedition across Antarctica

1958 21 die in the Munich Air Crash, including 7 members of the Manchester United football team

1959 First Barbie doll

1959 BBC screen *Juke Box Jury* for the first time

1959 Regional postcodes are introduced in some areas

1959 The first Mini car is sold

1959 Xerox's 914 'easy to use' photocopier goes on sale

1960 First kidney transplant in the UK

1960 Last National Service call-ups for compulsory military service

1960 First traffic wardens in London

1960 Harold Macmillan's 'Wind of Change' speech, signalling an era of decolonisation

1960 The BBC televise Princess Margaret's marriage to Anthony Armstrong-Jones

1960 The farthing (worth ¼ of a penny) is withdrawn

1960 First episode of the soap opera *Coronation Street*

1960 60,000 demonstrate against nuclear weapons in London

1960 D H Lawrence's *Lady Chatterley's Lover* becomes a best seller following the lifting of the ban on its publication

1961 The Beatles' first performance at *The Cavern Club*

1961 First *Mothercare* shops open

1961 Betting shops are legalised

1961 Russian astronaut Yuri Gagarin becomes the first man in space

1961 BBC's *Songs of Praise* first broadcast

1961 The Initial Teaching Alphabet (ITA) is introduced as a method of teaching reading

1961 The contraceptive pill becomes available on the National Health Service

1961 The construction of the Berlin wall, dividing East and West Germany, begins

1962 LEAs are obliged to provide students with grants for living expenses and tuition fees

1962 Panda crossings are introduced

1962 The first coloured Sunday supplement is issued by *The Sunday Times*

1962 The first James Bond film *Dr No* is shown

1962 London trolley buses are discontinued

1962 First regular hovercraft service from Wallasey to Rhyl

1962 Cuban Missile Crisis

1962 Elizabeth Lane appointed as the first female County Court judge

1962 The Beatles first single *Love Me Do* is released

1962 Golden Wonder produce flavoured crisps

1962 Several deaths from smog in London

1962-3 Severe winter weather

1963 Assassination of US President J F Kennedy

1963 The first episode of the sci-fi TV series *Doctor Who* is screened

1963 Dr Beeching institutes major cuts to the railway network

1963 London to Aldermaston marches against nuclear weapons

1963 The Great Train Robbery

1963 Sindy, the 12 inch, teenaged doll is launched as a rival to the American Barbie

1963 The Profumo affair, a political scandal following an affair between
     John Profumo, secretary of state for war and model Christine Keeler

1963 Mary Whitehouse launches a campaign to 'clean up' television

1963 The lava lamp is marketed

1964 *Jackie* magazine for teenaged girls is launched

1964 BBC2 begins broadcasting

1964 Brook Advisory Centres open, giving information about contraception
     and sexual health

1964 The term 'women's liberation' is first used

1964 Ladybird produce 'Peter and Jane' learn to read books

1964 Forth Road Bridge opens

1964 *Play School* is screened for the first time

1964 *Top of the Pops* is broadcast for the first time

1964 Resale price maintenance, which allowed manufacturers to dictate the price
     at which shops sold their products, is abolished

1965 The comprehensive school system begins to be rolled out

1965 Death of Winston Churchill

1965 The gangsters the Kray twins are arrested

1965 Mary Quant sells mini skirts in her King's Road shop

1965 The first Asda supermarket opens

1965 Certificates of Secondary Education (CSEs) are introduced

1965 Goldie, a golden eagle, escapes from London zoo and is recaptured after
     13 days

1965 The first episode of the children's TV puppet series *Thunderbirds* is screened

1965 Sir Stanley Matthews retires from playing first division football

1965 The Beatles' film *Help* is released

1965 The word fuck is used for the first time on British television

1965 'Moors Murderers' Ian Brady and Myra Hindley are arrested

1966 Polytechnics are established

1966 The first cross channel hovercraft service begins

1966 Aberfan disaster 144 people, 116 of them children, are killed when a coal
     spoil-heap collapses

1966 Leslie Thomas' *The Virgin Soldiers* is published

1966 England's football team win the World Cup

1966 All figure telephone numbers are introduced

1966 The first credit card is issued by Barclay's bank

1967 Arab-Israeli Six Day War

1967 Homosexuality between consenting adults over the age of 21 is legalised

1967 Breathalysers are introduced

1967 The Whitsun Bank Holiday is replaced by the Spring Bank Holiday, which is fixed for the last Monday in May

1967 Milton Keynes is designated as a new town

1967 Nationalisation of the steel industry

1967 Sir Francis Chichester completes a single-handed circumnavigation in his yacht *Gypsy Moth IV*

1967 The Beatles release the LP *Sgt Pepper's Lonely Hearts Club Band*

1967 Abortion becomes more easily available

1967 Sandie Shaw, performing barefoot, wins the Eurovision Song Contest for the UK with *Puppet on a String*

1967 First heart transplant

1967 The tanker the *Torrey Canyon* runs aground off Land's End causing a serious oil spill

1967 Donald Campbell is killed attempting to beat the water speed record on Coniston Water

1967 Civil War in Biafra

1967 First colour television broadcasts, regular broadcasts were to begin in 1969

1967 The liner the QE2 is launched

1967 The world's first cash machine is opened by Barclay's Bank in Enfield, Middlesex

1967 Foot and mouth outbreak

1967 Britain's Ann Haydon-Jones is runner up to Billie-Jean King in the Wimbledon tennis championship

1967 BBC Radios 1-4 replace the Light Programme, the Home Service and the Third Programme

1968 First episode of the TV sit-com *Dad's Army*

1968 New coins are issued prior to decimalisation in 1971

1968 The Beatles' film *Yellow Submarine* is released

1968 The last steam engine runs on a main-line passenger route

1968 The first performance of Andrew Lloyd-Webber and Tim Rice's *Joseph and the Amazing Technicolour Dreamcoat*

1968 'I'm Backing Britain' campaign is launched to boost the British economy

1968 'Rivers of Blood' speech on immigration by Enoch Powell

1968 The first Isle of Wight pop festival

1968 Robert F Kennedy is assassinated

1968 The Irish 'Troubles' begin

1968 The Race Relations Act outlaws discrimination on the grounds of ethnicity

1968 The introduction of a two-tier postal system with first and second class stamps. A standard letter (weighing up to 2oz.) cost 4d to send second class and 5d first class.

1968 Prescription charges are re-introduced

1968 American Civil Rights campaigner Martin Luther King is assassinated

1969 The age of majority is reduced from 21 to 18

1969 Prince Charles is invested as Prince of Wales

1969 Protests and a 'sit-in' by students at the London School of Economics

1969 Woodstock rock festival in US

1969 The first B & Q DIY store opens

1969 First man lands on the moon

1969 The halfpenny (ha'penny) is withdrawn

1969 Death penalty is abolished in the UK

1969 The maiden flight of the Concorde aircraft

1969 The first episode of the cult TV series *Monty Python's Flying Circus* is shown

The Brief

Write about national and local events that had an impact on your life, or which you particularly remember from this period. This can be a list of 'headlines'. Cover things such as 'firsts', extreme weather events, items from the world of entertainment and the arts, notable inventions and scientific developments, political events and foreign affairs.

Describe any life defining moments.

Who influenced your life in a significant way? Include public figures, celebrities, teachers, friends and family members.

As you have written your memories thematically, you may also like to compile a personal chronology of key events in your life. This can include anything from the birth of a child, moving house or starting a new job, to going on holiday or attending a pop concert.

Roots

I am from the terraced, three bed-roomed house behind the cinema.
I am from the comfort of the familiar and the smell of a paraffin heater.
I am from the open fire grate in my bedroom, the violets by my bed side, the hot
   toddy made with home-made elderberry wine, when I felt poorly.

I'm from the lavender at the front door, the rambling rose entwined on the front
   fence and the lilac; I remember their scent. The long, thin garden at the back
   with chickens at the bottom.

I'm from the 40s & 50s and post-war recovery. From Mum, Dad and two brothers.
From Aunts and Uncles….Aunty Paula from Vienna, teaching me whist and other
   card games.
I'm from sitting round the table in the "kitchen" listening to the Goons on Tuesday
   nights over the speaker from Radio Rentals.

I'm from eating fish on Fridays and from bathing once a week.
From washing myself at the kitchen sink and sometimes using newspaper for toilet
   paper.
I'm from having to wear too big clumpy boots to infant's school on the first day of
   term because "that's all I could get."
From the copper in the "scullery" for boiling laundry, the mangle and the meat safe
   in the back yard. The Anderson Shelter we used for a bike shed.

I'm from "children should be seen and not heard" and "eat everything on your
   plate, there are starving children who would be glad of it"
I'm from putting food and drink out for Father Christmas and finding a sixpence
   in the Christmas pudding.

I'm from Gosport by Portsmouth Harbour and the Tyrol in Austria.
From the smell of the sea and watching boats.
From trips on the Harbour Ferry.
From roast meat, apple pie and custard, bread pudding and macaroni pudding.
I'm from Tyrolean music, yodelling, snitzel, strudel, goulash and frankfurters.

I'm from the stony beach where my younger brother had his mouth stung by a
wasp when it landed on his ice-lolly.
I'm from Mum's ornate mirror in the middle room, and the button box in the
cupboard, the big dictionary on the high shelf.
From the piano, in the front room, cold as ice.

Sue Armstrong

List of Participants

Sarah Akhtar née Bynoe
Sue Armstrong née Peirce
Gail Barber
Hazel Barnard née Horn
Hazel Beckett née Cumpsty
Pam Blackaby née Burns
Enid Booth née Bingham
Doreen Braund née Bray
Janet Braund now Few
Heather Bright now Anderton
Violet Bright née Smith
Lynne Brock
Vera Burrell
Joyce Chapman
Irene Clucas née Nancollis
Thelma Crane
Margaret Ely
Elaine Evenden
Gail Everett
Stephanie Fox
Shirley Francom
Linda Garnett née Anstey
Gillian Gatehouse
Rita Gerrard
Christine Gibbins née Hatley
Sue Giddy née Marshall
Sue Gotley
Yvonne Hasler
Paula Heard
Janet Henwood
Rosemary Hood
Mary Ibbotson
Janet Jakes
Angela Jesson née Briant
Lyn Layton

Ann Long née Johnstone
Lesley Moreland
Lesley Halls Newman
Sue Nickels née Boyce
Penny O'Conner
Pamela Palgrave
Wendy Pedlar née Wisden
Yvonne Penrose
Jeanne Perrett
Tessa Phillips
Jennifer Poole
Janet Rainer now Wiggins
Marina Reed
Lynne Ridler Wall
Loretta Rivett
Monica Roberts
Sheila Sharman née Smith
Shirley Stallard née Lacey
Susan Stanley
Rosemary Stewart née Fry
Rachel Taylor née Atack
Christine Temlett née Pulleyblank
Vivian Thomas
Marion Turner née Moulton
    previously Pettitt
Linda J. (Carlton) Hauley née Vodden
Barbara Ellen Watts née Ball
Jackie Weaver
Gill Willett
June Wilmore
Margaret Wilson
Sandra Windeatt

Other ladies who wished to remain
    anonymous

Picture Credits

1   1950 Primrose Cottage, Midsomer Norton 1950 Sheila Sharman née Smith
2   Carnival Shirley Stallard née Lacey
3   Interior Pamela Palgrave
4   Interior Rosemary Stewart née Fry
5   Chalet Bungalow Marina Reed
6   Coronation Fancy dress 1953 Yvonne Penrose
7   Interior 1951 Janet Braund now Few
8   Interior 1951 Janet Braund now Few
9   Coronation Party 1953 June Wilmore
10 Eastville Park Lake c.1957 Sue Nickels née Boyce
11 Interior Angela Jesson née Briant
12 Car Christine Temlett née Pulleyblank
13 Interior Violet Bright née Smith
14 Telegram Sue Nickels née Boyce
15 Waring and Gillows' advertisement 1959 Linda Garnett née Anstey
16 Homevac Electrics' advertisement 1963 Sue Nickels née Boyce
17 Osokool advertisement
18 Housing Estate Letter 1947 Gill Willett
19 Bill for kitchen alterations 1964 Sue Nickels née Boyce
20 G.E.C. advertisement *Good Housekeeping* Magazine 1955 Jeanne Perrett
21 Granville Builders' advertisement Linda Garnett née Anstey
22 O'cedar *Good Housekeeping* Magazine 1955 Jeanne Perrett
23 Mother and daughter Sandra Windeatt
24 Mini-dresss 1962 Hazel Barnard née Horn
25 Swimming costume Enid Booth née Bingham
26 Children's coats 1954 Susan Stanley
27 2 girls 1962 Barbara Ellen Watts née Ball
28 Couple 1948 Sue Nickels née Boyce
29 Wedding dress made from a parachute 1947 Janet Braund now Few
30 Child's swimming costume Sue Giddy née Marshall
31 Gor-ray advertisement *Good Housekeeping* Magazine 1955 Jeanne Perrett
32 Earrings Sue Nickels née Boyce
33 Youthlines Girdle advertisement *Good Housekeeping* Magazine 1955 Jeanne Perrett
34 Clarks Shoes' advertisement 1953 Margaret Ely
35 Debenhams' Advertisement

79   Relaxing on the beach 1955 Sarah Akhtar née Bynoe
80   Seaside outing Christine Temlett née Pulleyblank
81   Birthday card Sue Nickels née Boyce
82   Birthday card Sue Nickels née Boyce
83   Whist drive in a private garden 1949 Rosemary Stewart née Fry
84   Cricket match Sarah Akhtar née Bynoe
85   A picnic by car Christine Gibbins née Hatley
86   Birthday party Sarah Akhtar née Bynoe
87   London Hazel Barnard née Horn
88   Coach tours advertisement 1961 Sue Nickels née Boyce
89   Couple 1968 Sarah Akhtar née Bynoe
90   *Good Housekeeping* Magazine 1955 Jeanne Perrett
91   Valentine's card Sue Nickels née Boyce
92   Sunday school exercise Jeanne Perrett
93   Valentine's card Sue Nickels née Boyce

Front cover, clockwise from the top left
Barbara Watts née Ball
Janet Braund now Few
Hazel Barnard née Horn
Sheila Sharman née Smith
Lesley Moreland
Sue Nickels née Boyce
Linda Garnett née Anstey
Rita Gerrard
Christine Temlett née Pulleyblank
Monica Roberts
Sandra Windeatt
Marion Turner née Moulton previously Pettitt

Back cover from the left
Sue Armstrong née Peirce
Irene Clucas née Nancollis
Shirley Stallard née Lacey
Heather Bright now Anderton
Rosemary Stewart née Fry

Index